Crossplane Mastery
A Definitive Guide to Cloud-Native Multi-Cloud Infrastructure Management with Kubernetes

Nova Trex

© 2024 by Wang Press. All rights reserved.

No part of this publication may be reproduced, distributed, or transmitted in any form or by any means, including photocopying, recording, or other electronic or mechanical methods, without the prior written permission of the publisher, except in the case of brief quotations embodied in critical reviews and certain other noncommercial uses permitted by copyright law.

Published by Wang Press

For permissions and other inquiries, write to:
P.O. Box 3132, Framingham, MA 01701, USA

Contents

1 Introduction to Cloud-Native Infrastructure — 11
   1.1 Understanding Cloud-Native Architectures 12
   1.2 Benefits of Cloud-Native Infrastructure 16
   1.3 Key Components of Cloud-Native Ecosystem 21
   1.4 Challenges in Adopting Cloud-Native Solutions 25
   1.5 Current Trends in Cloud-Native Technologies 29

2 Understanding Kubernetes: The Backbone of Cloud-Native — 33
   2.1 Kubernetes Fundamentals 34
   2.2 Kubernetes Architecture Overview 36
   2.3 Deployment and Scaling of Applications 40
   2.4 Service Discovery and Load Balancing 44
   2.5 Storage Options in Kubernetes 49
   2.6 Networking in Kubernetes Clusters 53
   2.7 Kubernetes Security Essentials 57

3 Getting Started with Crossplane — 63
   3.1 What is Crossplane? 64
   3.2 Installation and Setup 67

	3.3 Crossplane Providers	72
	3.4 Configuring Crossplane Workloads	76
	3.5 Declarative Infrastructure Management	80
	3.6 Crossplane API and Extensibility	85
	3.7 Troubleshooting Common Issues	91

4 Provisioning Cloud Resources with Crossplane — 97

- 4.1 Setting Up Cloud Credentials 98
- 4.2 Understanding Crossplane Compositions 103
- 4.3 Managing Compute Resources 108
- 4.4 Provisioning and Managing Databases 113
- 4.5 Networking and Security Resources 118
- 4.6 Leveraging Crossplane Packages 124
- 4.7 Automating Resource Management 129

5 Managing Multi-Cloud Environments — 135

- 5.1 The Concept of Multi-Cloud Strategies 136
- 5.2 Crossplane's Role in Multi-Cloud Management 139
- 5.3 Defining and Managing Multi-Cloud Applications . . . 143
- 5.4 Data Consistency and Integration Across Clouds 147
- 5.5 Ensuring Reliability and Availability 152
- 5.6 Cost Management and Optimization 156
- 5.7 Security Considerations in Multi-Cloud 160

6 Integrating Crossplane with DevOps Pipelines — 165

- 6.1 DevOps and Infrastructure as Code 166
- 6.2 Crossplane in CI/CD Workflows 169
- 6.3 Automating Resource Deployments 173
- 6.4 Version Control for Infrastructure Configurations . . . 176

6.5 Ensuring Consistency Across Environments 180
6.6 Monitoring and Feedback Loops 184
6.7 Case Studies of Crossplane in DevOps 188

7 Security and Compliance in Cloud-Native Infrastructure 193
7.1 Understanding Cloud-Native Security Challenges . . . 194
7.2 Implementing Identity and Access Management 198
7.3 Securing Containerized Environments 202
7.4 Compliance in Multi-Cloud Deployments 207
7.5 Best Practices for Data Protection 211
7.6 Automating Security with DevSecOps 215
7.7 Incident Response and Remediation 219

8 Monitoring and Observability for Crossplane Managed Environments 225
8.1 Principles of Observability in Cloud-Native Systems . . 226
8.2 Integrating Crossplane with Monitoring Tools 229
8.3 Building Dashboards for Cloud Resource Visibility . . . 233
8.4 Setting up Alerts and Notifications 238
8.5 Analyzing Logs and Traces 242
8.6 Capacity Planning and Optimization 246
8.7 Feedback Loop for Continuous Improvement 251

9 Scaling and Optimizing Cloud-Native Infrastructure 257
9.1 Understanding Scalability in Cloud-Native Systems . . 258
9.2 Auto-Scaling Strategies and Implementations 261
9.3 Optimizing Resource Utilization 265
9.4 Performance Tuning for Cloud Applications 269

9.5	Cost Optimization in Cloud Environments	273
9.6	Ensuring High Availability and Resilience	278
9.7	Using Crossplane for Dynamic Scaling	282

10 Case Studies and Best Practices · 287

10.1	Real-World Crossplane Implementation	287
10.2	Multi-Cloud Deployment Scenarios	291
10.3	Scaling Cloud Resources with Crossplane	295
10.4	Security and Compliance Best Practices	299
10.5	Optimizing Costs Across Cloud Providers	302
10.6	DevOps Integration Success Stories	306
10.7	Lessons Learned and Future Trends	309

Introduction

The Multi-Cloud Imperative

In an era defined by digital transformation and pervasive technology, businesses across the globe face the imperative to be fast, flexible, and resilient. Central to this evolution is the adoption of cloud-native architectures, which have redefined the potential of IT infrastructure. At the forefront of this architectural shift are advancements that facilitate powerful, distributed systems, enabling organizations to operate and innovate with remarkable agility. With the growing complexity and variety of applications, the shift towards a multi-cloud strategy has become not just advantageous, but essential.

Crossplane: A Game Changer

This book, "Crossplane Mastery: A Definitive Guide to Cloud-Native Multi-Cloud Infrastructure Management with Kubernetes," dives deeply into how Crossplane revolutionizes the management of cloud-native infrastructure. Crossplane introduces a paradigm shift by empowering Kubernetes to extend beyond just container management, offering a unified method to provision, manage, and orchestrate resources across multiple cloud services.

As organizations seek to leverage the best capabilities of each cloud provider, Crossplane emerges as a vital tool. It enables developers and operations teams to define and manage a variety of cloud resources with Kubernetes Custom Resource Definitions (CRDs), promoting a true multi-cloud approach. This book will guide you through adopting Crossplane, illustrating how it streamlines the orchestration of diverse cloud services under the powerful umbrella of Kubernetes.

Structure of the Book

Foundational Concepts

We begin our journey with foundational concepts, laying the groundwork for understanding the principles that fuel cloud-native systems. This includes an exploration of Kubernetes, which serves as the backbone of cloud-native application orchestration, explaining how it fosters agility and resilience in deploying applications at scale.

Crossplane Architecture and Integration

Subsequent chapters delve into Crossplane's architecture and its seamless integration with Kubernetes. We will unpack the core components of Crossplane, such as the control plane, providers, and managed resources, and demonstrate how these components transform Kubernetes into a powerful tool for infrastructure as code (IaC).

Practical Implementation

Our practical sections offer insights into deploying and managing cloud resources using Crossplane. Through step-by-step configurations and real-world scenarios, we explore how to provision services across multiple clouds, ensuring dynamic scalability and bursting capabilities.

Managing Multi-Cloud Environments

Managing multi-cloud environments presents challenges in interoperability, security, and compliance. We provide strategies and techniques to address these challenges effectively, explaining how Crossplane can harmonize disparate cloud services, safeguarding your operations with robust security practices and regulatory adherence.

Integration with DevOps Pipelines

The book emphasizes the synergy between Crossplane and DevOps methodologies, illustrating how Crossplane can be embedded within CI/CD pipelines. This integration enhances automation, reduces operational overhead, and drives efficiencies across development and operations teams.

Monitoring, Observability, Scaling, and Optimization

Insight into monitoring and observability is vital for maintaining the health of your infrastructure. We cover best practices in these areas, along with approaches to scaling and optimizing resource utilization, ensuring your applications deliver optimal performance.

Real-World Application and Best Practices

The book concludes with a compelling analysis of real-world case studies showcasing successful Crossplane implementations. These case studies, along with distilled best practices, provide you with the tactical insights necessary to adapt and thrive in contemporary IT environments.

Empowering Cloud-Native Infrastructure Management

Crossplane is more than a tool; it is a catalyst for change in how we envision and execute multi-cloud strategies. As you progress through this book, you will gain the knowledge and skills necessary to master the intricacies of cloud-native infrastructure management. Designed for engineers, architects, and IT leaders, the insights here will fortify your capabilities to design, scale, and optimize infrastructure that meets today's dynamic demands with precision and efficacy. Embark on this comprehensive journey to harness the full potential of Crossplane and transform your organization's cloud-native future.

Chapter 1

Introduction to Cloud-Native Infrastructure

Cloud-native infrastructure represents a shift towards building and running applications that fully leverage the benefits of the cloud computing delivery model. It is defined by a set of principles and practices that enable organizations to build scalable, resilient, and manageable applications in dynamic environments. Emphasizing modularity, scalability, and resilience, cloud-native approaches use technologies like containers, microservices, and orchestration tools such as Kubernetes. Organizations adopting cloud-native strategies can achieve significant efficiency improvements, enter new markets more quickly, and scale operations seamlessly. Understanding these components and their interplay is essential for effectively transitioning to and harnessing the power of cloud-native infrastructure.

1.1 Understanding Cloud-Native Architectures

The term "cloud-native" defines an approach characterized by a set of principles and practices distinct from traditional infrastructure models. This paradigm shift influences how software is designed, built, and deployed, emphasizing operational excellence, agility, and architectural modularity. At its core, cloud-native computing leverages continuous integration and continuous deployment (CI/CD), containerization, microservices architecture, and dynamic orchestration to deliver applications optimized for cloud environments.

- **Core Principles**: Cloud-native architectures are underpinned by several essential principles, including scalability, resilience, flexibility, and observability. These principles guide the development and deployment process, enabling developers to create robust applications that can scale horizontally to handle varying loads seamlessly.

- **Scalability** is central to cloud-native architecture, which often utilizes stateless processes and horizontal scaling. Statelessness refers to the ability of a system to treat each request independently, without relying on previous interactions. This allows for easier replication of processes across multiple nodes, making it straightforward to increase or decrease resources dynamically.

- **Resilience** involves designing systems that gracefully handle failures and continue to function. This is achieved through techniques like circuit breakers, bulkheads, and load balancing, which ensure that failures in one part of the system do not cascade. Cloud-native systems often incorporate redundancy and rollbacks to further enhance resilience.

- **Flexibility** in cloud-native systems supports rapid adaptation to changes, whether they are in user demand, new features, or unforeseen failures. The architecture facilitates frequent code deployments through automated pipelines that verify and integrate changes efficiently, minimizing manual intervention and errors.

- **Observability** extends beyond traditional monitoring by providing insights into the system behavior not just in terms of uptime but by delivering metrics, logs, and traces. Observability tools allow developers to debug issues and optimize system performances proactively.

- **Architectural Characteristics**: To embody these principles, cloud-native architectures incorporate particular characteristics distinct from traditional monolithic approaches. Primary among them is the adoption of a **microservices architecture**, which breaks applications into series of small, independent, and loosely coupled services. Each service represents a specific business capability and can be developed, deployed, and scaled independently. This contrasts with monolithic designs, where scaling typically involves scaling the entire application regardless of demand in one particular area.

  The deployment unit of choice in cloud-native applications is often the **container**. Containers encapsulate applications and their dependencies, promoting environment consistency across the development lifecycle and simplifying deployment workflows. This containerization is frequently managed by tools such as Docker, while orchestration systems like Kubernetes plan and schedule container execution across clusters.

  Another characteristic is the adoption of **polyglot programming**. Because services are decoupled, they can be implemented in different programming languages that best fit the task, enabling developers to select optimal tools and frameworks without being restricted to a specific stack.

- **Differences from Traditional Infrastructure**: Traditional infrastructure models typically rely on scaling single, monolithic applications vertically—through adding more resources to existing servers or by enhancing the capabilities of a single large node. In contrast, cloud-native architecture advocates for distributed systems where components are loosely coupled and exhibited across a cluster, enabling horizontal scaling. This change also affects how failure is perceived and managed.

  Cloud-native systems tend to employ a paradigm of

event-driven architectures, relying on events to trigger asynchronous processing across microservices. This is a distinct shift from synchronous communication used in monolithic models, which can become bottlenecks under high volume workloads.

The implementation of **declarative management models** forms another stark contrast. In cloud-native ecosystems, infrastructure is defined as code, using templates or scripts to manage deployment configurations, resources and system states consistently. The Infrastructure as Code (IaC) approach ensures repeatable infrastructure changes while providing an audit trail.

- **Programming Example**: Consider a simple example illustrating a transformation from monolithic-based development to a cloud-native microservice using containerization:

```
# Monolithic Flask Example
from flask import Flask

app = Flask(__name__)

@app.route('/processingA')
def process_A():
    # Trigger some processing
    return 'Processing Function A'

@app.route('/processingB')
def process_B():
    # Trigger another processing
    return 'Processing Function B'

if __name__ == '__main__':
    app.run(debug=True)
```

In a monolithic design, all processing functionalities are retained within a single application, limiting scalability. Refactoring to a cloud-native approach, the microservices architecture separates these services:

```
# Processing A Microservice
from flask import Flask

app_A = Flask(__name__)

@app_A.route('/processingA')
def process_A():
    # Processing functionality
```

1.1. UNDERSTANDING CLOUD-NATIVE ARCHITECTURES

```
    return 'Processing Function A'
if __name__ == '__main__':
    app_A.run(debug=True)
```

```
# Dockerfile for Processing A Service
FROM python:3.8-slim

WORKDIR /usr/src/app

COPY requirements.txt ./
RUN pip install --no-cache-dir -r requirements.txt

COPY . .

CMD [ "python", "./serviceA.py" ]
```

Each service, now isolated, can be containerized, allowing independent deployment and scaling. Combined with orchestrators like Kubernetes, these services maintain operational integrity against fluctuating demands.

- **Operational Considerations**: Within cloud-native environments, the operational procedures differ significantly from traditional methods. Incorporating **CI/CD pipelines**, cloud-native architectures ensure code is built, tested, and deployed automatically. This not only increases deployment frequency but also enhances the reliability of the code through automated testing layers.

  Further, **service mesh frameworks**, such as Istio, have become vital for managing communication between microservices. Service meshes offer observability, traffic management, and security, optimizing microservice interactions and mitigating the challenges of polyglot architectures.

- **Security Implications**: Security in cloud-native architectures must pivot to accommodate new runtime, network, and data dynamics. Security measures should be ingrained at every layer, beginning from **image signing** to ensure container images have not been tampered with, to **network policies** enforcing boundary controls among services. Concepts such as **zero-trust security** networks are prevalent, requiring authentication and validation at every request-level interaction.

Emphasizing these early in the design process reduces vulnerabilities that arise from rushed or patchwork solutions, prevalent in monolithic upgrades.

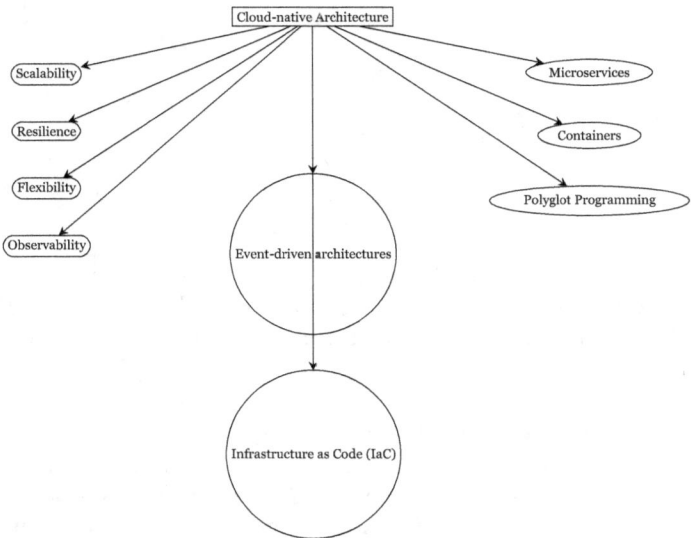

Cloud-native architectures represent a transformative step in software development, emphasizing efficient resource usage, improved application resilience, and consistent operations. Their focus encompasses core principles and efficient design patterns unique to cloud environments, fostering not only a shift in methodology but a paradigm focused on agility and scalability. This foundation provides a framework that, when effectively executed, equips organizations with the tools needed to innovate swiftly in the expanding digital ecosystem.

1.2 Benefits of Cloud-Native Infrastructure

Cloud-native infrastructure redefines the paradigm of application development and deployment by delivering numerous enhancements that refine and augment traditional approaches. This paradigm shift underscores several critical advantages such as flexibility, scalability, resilience, and operational efficiency, enabling organizations to remain competitive in a rapidly evolving technological landscape.

- **Flexibility in Deployment and Development** One of the primary benefits of cloud-native infrastructure is the enhanced flexibility it offers both in development and deployment phases. Architectures built with a cloud-native mindset employ microservices that allow developers to select the optimal language and framework for each service. This freedom facilitates a **polyglot programming environment**, optimizing performance by leveraging the best tool for each specific task.

    Moreover, Continuous Integration and Continuous Deployment (CI/CD) pipelines, an integral component of cloud-native environments, further enhance flexibility. These pipelines automate the testing and delivery of code, reducing bottlenecks in development cycles and enabling rapid iteration. Consequently, organizations can swiftly respond to changes in market demands or customer feedback, deploying updates seamlessly across distributed environments without the traditional delay associated with monolithic deployments.

- **Scalability and Elasticity** Cloud-native infrastructure inherently supports horizontal scalability, which is essential for coping with fluctuating demands. Applications are designed as distributed systems, where stateless microservices can be dynamically scaled to handle increased load. This ability is particularly critical for modern applications experiencing unpredictable demand spikes.

    In practice, scalability in cloud-native environments is achieved using orchestration platforms like Kubernetes. These platforms provide sophisticated **scaling features** such as autoscaling, which adjusts the number of active pods automatically based on defined metrics such as CPU and memory usage. This ensures resource allocation is optimal and cost-effective, providing elasticity that matches current workload requirements.

```
# Example of a Horizontal Pod Autoscaler in Kubernetes
apiVersion: autoscaling/v2beta2
kind: HorizontalPodAutoscaler
metadata:
  name: example-hpa
spec:
  scaleTargetRef:
    apiVersion: apps/v1
    kind: Deployment
    name: example-deployment
  minReplicas: 1
  maxReplicas: 10
  metrics:
  - type: Resource
    resource:
      name: cpu
      target:
        type: Utilization
        averageUtilization: 50
```

The code above configures an autoscaler in Kubernetes that adjusts the number of replicas for an application based on CPU usage, maintaining efficiency both in performance and in cost.

- **Resilience and Reliability** Cloud-native architectures enhance application resilience, guaranteeing higher availability and fault tolerance. Services are designed with failures in mind, employing techniques such as **circuit breakers**, which prevent failures from propagating through the system, and **load balancers** that distribute traffic efficiently, avoiding points of failure.

  Redundancy is another critical factor, achieved by deploying multiple instances of a service across geographically distributed data centers. This approach ensures that if one instance fails, others can maintain service availability without noticeable disruption to end-users.

  Furthermore, cloud-native infrastructure takes advantage of **immutable infrastructure patterns**, where servers are never modified after deployment. Instead, new versions are baked into fresh images and deployed, guaranteeing consistency across environments and minimizing potential discrepancies that accrue over time.

- **Operational Efficiency and Cost Optimization** Cloud-native design patterns are conducive to substantial operational efficiencies and cost optimizations. One significant component is the use of **containerization** for application deployment, achieved through technologies like Docker. Containers are lightweight and provide fast startups, allowing rapid scaling and deployment, conserving computational resources compared to traditional VMs.

```
# Running a Docker container for a Node.js application
docker run -d -p 3000:3000 --name node-service app-image:latest
```

Docker containers encapsulate applications along with necessary dependencies, promoting consistency and reducing deployment time across development, testing, and production environments.

Additionally, the **pay-as-you-go model** prevalent in cloud-native infrastructure translates to cost savings for businesses. This economic model aligns resource costs with actual consumption over fixed-resource models, inherently reducing overhead.

The adoption of cloud-native architectures further benefits from the consolidation of monitoring and logging solutions. Platforms that combine various observability tools into a singular dashboard enhance productivity by offering comprehensive insights into system health, real-time operational data, and analytics, supporting informed decision-making.

- **Enhanced Collaboration and Innovation** By adopting cloud-native approaches, teams benefit from improved collaborative environments. Microservices, as independent units, enable parallel development amongst diverse teams, each focusing on individual components of an application without conflicts common in monolithic setups. This methodology encourages an **agile workflow**, facilitating innovation and the rapid incorporation of new features.

  Furthermore, cloud-native infrastructure supports the integration of **DevOps practices**, where developers and operations teams work symbiotically throughout the product lifecycle, from design and development to production support. This results in a more robust, reliable, and efficient development pipeline and infrastructure management.

- **Security and Compliance** Cloud-native environments inherently adopt security paradigms suited for distributed architectures. The implementation of **service mesh technologies**, facilitate the secure communication between services, adding layers of security such as mutual TLS and traffic encryption.

Additionally, implementing security policies using **security as code** paradigms enhances compliance. This involves defining security configurations within the same IaC templates, ensuring uniform application across deployment environments.

```
# Kubernetes Network Policy Example restricting communication
apiVersion: networking.k8s.io/v1
kind: NetworkPolicy
metadata:
  name: restrict-traffic
spec:
  podSelector:
    matchLabels:
      app: myapp
  policyTypes:
  - Ingress
  ingress:
  - from:
    - podSelector:
        matchLabels:
          app: ingress
```

The above policy restricts ingress traffic to pods labeled as 'myapp', ensuring security constraints align with operational needs.

Adopting cloud-native infrastructure imbues a multitude of strategic advantages—making it an attractive option for modern enterprise development. Its underpinning principles provide organizations with the flexibility to innovate continually, scale efficiently, and operate resiliently across distributed ecosystems. Over time, the integration of cloud-native infrastructure, with its foundation on modular, observable, and scalable components, empowers enterprises to achieve a competitive posture in increasingly interconnected markets.

1.3 Key Components of Cloud-Native Ecosystem

The adoption of cloud-native practices relies on an ecosystem composed of several critical components that collectively enable the development, deployment, and management of highly scalable and efficient applications. These components interoperate to facilitate the principles of agility, scalability, resilience, and operational efficiency integral to cloud-native architecture. Key elements within this ecosystem include containers, microservices, orchestration systems, continuous integration and continuous deployment (CI/CD) pipelines, and infrastructure as code (IaC). Understanding these components and their interactions is paramount for organizations aiming to leverage the full potential of cloud-native infrastructure.

- **Containers:** Containers are fundamental building blocks in the cloud-native paradigm, offering a means to package and deploy applications and their dependencies in a consistent environment. Unlike traditional virtual machines, which include a complete operating system, containers encapsulate just the application and its libraries, while sharing the host OS kernel. This efficiency results in significant improvements in startup time and resource allocation.

- **Docker** is currently one of the most popular containerization technologies, providing developers with tools to create and manage containers. The following example illustrates a Dockerfile, which is used to build a container image for a Python application:

  ```
  FROM python:3.9-slim

  # Set the working directory
  WORKDIR /usr/src/app

  # Install dependencies
  COPY requirements.txt ./
  RUN pip install --no-cache-dir -r requirements.txt

  # Copy application code
  COPY . .

  # Set the command to run the application
  CMD ["python", "app.py"]
  ```

In a Dockerfile, each instruction defines a new layer in the image. This layering enables efficient versioning and control, as changes are isolated and managed across distinct image versions.

- **Microservices:** At the heart of cloud-native architecture is the microservices approach, where applications are decomposed into small, independently deployable services each responsible for a distinct business function. This decomposition enables different teams to work autonomously with limited dependencies, reducing the complexity and risk associated with deploying an entire monolithic system.

  Microservices communicate predominantly through language-agnostic protocols such as HTTP/REST or gRPC, enhancing interoperability across services developed in different programming languages. An example microservice using a Flask API might look like:

  ```
  from flask import Flask, request, jsonify

  app = Flask(__name__)

  @app.route('/service', methods=['GET'])
  def service():
      return jsonify({"status": "Service is operational"})

  if __name__ == '__main__':
      app.run(debug=True)
  ```

  Microservices further benefit from the encapsulation provided by containers, enabling them to include all dependencies within their defined environment, streamlining deployment to different infrastructure.

- **Orchestration Systems:** Cloud-native systems composed of numerous containers and microservices necessitate orchestration for effective management. Orchestration systems automate the deployment, scaling, and operation of application containers, facilitating resource optimization and resiliency. Kubernetes is the de facto standard for container orchestration, providing comprehensive tools for managing containerized applications in a clustered environment.

  Kubernetes manages applications using several core objects, including Pods, Services, and Deployments. A basic deployment configuration in Kubernetes is defined through a YAML file:

```yaml
apiVersion: apps/v1
kind: Deployment
metadata:
  name: sample-app
spec:
  replicas: 3
  selector:
    matchLabels:
      app: sample-app
  template:
    metadata:
      labels:
        app: sample-app
    spec:
      containers:
      - name: app-container
        image: sample-app-image
        ports:
        - containerPort: 80
```

In this deployment, Kubernetes instructs the orchestration system to maintain a state with three replicas of the application, managing their lifecycle, placing containers across nodes, and handling updates in rolling fashions.

- **Continuous Integration and Continuous Deployment (CI/CD):** The CI/CD methodology is crucial in cloud-native environments for sustainably integrating code changes into production environments. Continuous Integration involves automatically building and testing code changes before integration, while Continuous Deployment extends this workflow by automating the release of verified code to production environments.

Tools such as Jenkins, GitLab CI, and CircleCI facilitate CI/CD pipelines with features like automated testing, build artifacts, and triggered deployments upon successful test pass. This results in faster release cycles and reduced human errors.

```json
{
  "stages": [
    {
      "stage": "build",
      "script": "npm install && npm run build",
      "when": "on_success"
    },
    {
      "stage": "test",
```

```
      "script": "npm test",
      "when": "on_success"
    },
    {
      "stage": "deploy",
      "script": "deployment-scripts/deploy.sh",
      "when": "on_success"
    }
  ]
}
```

Such configuration files specify stages, conditions, and commands to execute at each phase of software delivery, enabling automated, reliable deployments.

- **Infrastructure as Code (IaC):** IaC is a pivotal component in the cloud-native ecosystem, allowing developers to provision and manage infrastructure through code rather than manual configurations. This approach provides consistency, repeatability, and transparency in infrastructure configurations, aiding in version control and collaborative enhancements.

Tools like Terraform and AWS CloudFormation provide frameworks to describe and deploy cloud resources in declarative templates. These tools enable the automation of environments that evolve together with application code.

```
provider "aws" {
  region = "us-west-2"
}

resource "aws_instance" "app_server" {
  ami = "ami-12345678"
  instance_type = "t2.micro"

  tags = {
    Name = "MyAppServer"
  }
}
```

Such definitions automate resource creation, enabling infrastructure changes to undergo the same review processes as application code, leading to a more unified operational framework.

The cloud-native ecosystem, comprising containers, microservices, orchestration, CI/CD, and IaC, offers a comprehensive framework that empowers organizations to achieve high scalability, flexibility, and resilience. These components, while operating in synergy, redefine application development and operations, facilitating the creation of robust, distributed systems tailored to dynamic, cloud environments. As organizations adopt these paradigms, they derive benefits including reduced time-to-market, improved resource efficiency, and enhanced reliability—key factors for success in a digital-first economy.

1.4 Challenges in Adopting Cloud-Native Solutions

The transition to cloud-native solutions, while offering substantial benefits in scalability, agility, and operational efficiency, presents a set of unique challenges that organizations must navigate effectively. These challenges are often rooted in the complexity of adopting new technologies, the need for cultural shifts within development and operations teams, and the management of sophisticated distributed systems environments. Understanding and addressing these challenges is crucial for organizations striving to fully leverage the potential of cloud-native architectures.

- **Complexity of Distributed Systems**
  Cloud-native architectures are inherently complex due to their reliance on distributed systems, where applications are decomposed into microservices that communicate over a network. Managing such distributed architectures involves addressing a range of issues related to service discovery, inter-service communication, fault tolerance, and data consistency.

  One specific complexity is achieving **service discovery**, which involves dynamically locating services within a network as they scale in and out. Tools such as Consul or third-party integrations within Kubernetes facilitate this by enabling services to register and discover other services seamlessly. However, configuring and maintaining such tools requires a deep understanding of network topologies and efficient design patterns.

  Handling **inter-service communication** effectively is

another challenge. While HTTP/REST is commonly used, it often brings overhead due to its stateless nature. Protocols like gRPC offer performance improvements, but involve an additional learning curve and the integration of protocol buffers for serialization.

The asynchronous communication model used in cloud-native systems can also lead to **data consistency challenges**. Ensuring eventual consistency across distributed databases can be complex, necessitating the implementation of patterns such as the **saga pattern** to manage long-running, distributed business transactions.

- **Cultural and Organizational Shifts**
  Adopting cloud-native solutions requires significant cultural changes within an organization, impacting both the development and operations teams. Traditional IT cultures often involve silos where development, quality assurance, and operations work in isolated environments. Cloud-native architecture, however, necessitates the integration of **DevOps principles**, where cross-functional teams collaborate throughout the lifecycle of a product.

  Promoting a **DevOps culture** involves integrating practices such as continuous integration and delivery, infrastructure as code, and the adoption of collaborative tools like version control systems (e.g., Git) and collaborative playbooks. DevOps emphasizes shared responsibility, where developers take part in operations, building greater service accountability and reliability.

  Another cultural shift required is a **mindset change** regarding failure. In traditional models, failures are generally seen as detrimental and must be avoided at all costs. Conversely, cloud-native ecosystems embrace failures as learning opportunities, incorporating practices such as **chaos engineering** to prepare systems and teams for inevitable disruptions.

- **Skills Gap and Capacity Building**
  One of the considerable challenges in adopting cloud-native solutions is the skills gap, as organizations often lack expertise in

contemporary cloud-native tools and methodologies. Professionals skilled in container technologies, orchestration platforms like Kubernetes, and modern CI/CD processes are in demand. Bridging this gap necessitates investment in **training and capacity building**, fostering skill development that aligns with the organization's transition goals.

Organizations may consider partnerships with educational platforms or leveraging training programs offered by cloud providers to enhance proficiency in necessary skills. Career development opportunities, including certifications such as Certified Kubernetes Administrator (CKA) and Certified Kubernetes Application Developer (CKAD), can also provide valuable credentials.

This skills transition must be supported by updated documentation and active learning cultures where experimenting with proofs of concept and pilot projects enhances understanding and practical skills.

- **Security Concerns and Compliance**
  Cloud-native environments, while offering advanced technologies, require redefined security strategies. Traditional perimeter-based security approaches are often inadequate due to the dynamic and distributed nature of cloud-native architectures. Instead, the focus shifts towards securing individual components through network policies, authentication, and identity management.

  Threat vectors in cloud-native environments can include known vulnerabilities in container images, insecure APIs, and insufficient network isolation. Utilizing secure images from trusted registries and implementing security scanning tools integrated within CI/CD pipelines help mitigate some of these risks.

  ```
  # Using Trivy to scan a Docker image for vulnerabilities
  trivy image example-image:latest
  ```

  Compliance also becomes more complex, particularly for industries with rigorous data protection laws such as GDPR or HIPAA. Implementing robust **observability solutions** is crucial for ensuring auditing, logging, and real-time monitoring comply with regulatory standards. Tools like Prometheus, Grafana, and Fluentd enable visibility into operations, allowing vigilant tracking and response to security incidents.

- **Resource Management and Cost Control**
  Efficient resource management is another challenge, as cloud-native solutions often involve orchestrating vast numbers of small, transient workloads across distributed environments. Proper resource allocation reduces unnecessary expenditure and can prevent resource contention, which may affect performance and scalability.

  Achieving optimal resource management involves implementing **policies for autoscaling**, using Kubernetes or similar platforms to automatically adjust the number of service instances based on real-time demand. However, improper configuration can lead to underutilization or overspending, making it important for teams to regularly audit consumption metrics and adapt policies accordingly.

  Furthermore, cloud-native solutions demand a shift to **cost attribution and transparency**, where practices such as tagging resources aid in detailed usage tracking and facilitate optimized spending aligned with business objectives.

- **Legacy Integration and Transition**
  Many organizations struggle with the **integration and transition** of legacy applications to a cloud-native model. Legacy systems, often characterized by tight coupling, monolithic architecture, and outdated technologies, complicate migration strategies due to dependencies and lack of standardization.

  Organizations can address this challenge by incrementally decomposing applications into **macroservices** or partially containerizing components that communicate through API gateways. A transitional approach such as this balances operational requirements with innovation, optimizing the migration timeline and reducing associated risks.

  Ultimately, redefining existing systems to fit a distributed, cloud-native architecture requires not just technical capability but **strategic vision**, careful planning, and an openness to adopt phased approaches to overcome associated hurdles.

While adopting cloud-native solutions presents significant challenges including system complexity, cultural shifts, skill deficits, security management, cost control, and legacy transition, organizations ready to navigate these intricacies can reap substantial benefits. Addressing these challenges methodically through a combination of strategic planning, investment in skills, and operational adaptations is pivotal for transforming cloud-natives into catalysts of innovation and growth. The path, while demanding, promises evolutionary progress and enhanced competitive advantage when successfully embraced.

1.5 Current Trends in Cloud-Native Technologies

The landscape of cloud-native technologies is rapidly evolving, driven by a relentless pursuit of innovation, efficiency, and scalability. These advances are reshaping the way applications are developed, deployed, and managed. Understanding the current trends in cloud-native technologies is crucial for organizations seeking to harness the full potential of these modern architectures. Key trends include the proliferation of serverless computing, the rise of service mesh architectures, the increased focus on AI and ML integration, and heightened emphasis on security and observability.

- **The Proliferation of Serverless Computing**
  Serverless computing is gaining traction as an evolution in cloud-native architecture that abstracts server management entirely, enabling developers to focus purely on code and logic. In a serverless model, cloud providers dynamically allocate resources, executing functions on demand without maintaining infrastructure.

  Technologies such as AWS Lambda, Google Cloud Functions, and Azure Functions exemplify serverless computing by offering on-demand execution with a granular billing model. This model eliminates idle server costs, offering greater cost efficiency and scalability. A typical function implemented using AWS Lambda can be defined as follows:

```
def lambda_handler(event, context):
    # Parsing incoming event data
    name = event.get('name', 'World')

    return {
        'statusCode': 200,
        'body': f'Hello, {name}!'
    }
```

In this example, the function is triggered by an external event, with resources provisioned automatically by the cloud provider. This flexibility accelerates development processes, especially in scenarios involving variable loads or event-driven applications.

- **The Rise of Service Mesh Architectures**
  As cloud-native ecosystems increasingly adopt microservices, the complexity of managing service-to-service communication also rises. This is where service mesh solutions like Istio, Linkerd, and Consul come into play, offering a dedicated layer for managing service interactions within a distributed application.

  A service mesh is responsible for handling concerns such as load balancing, service discovery, authentication, and observability, decoupling these aspects from the application logic. By using sidecar proxies injected alongside application pods, service meshes enable enhanced traffic management and policy enforcement without changing application code.

  Service meshes provide critical features, including traffic splitting to enable canary releases, which allows deploying new versions of services gradually to a subset of users:

```
apiVersion: networking.istio.io/v1alpha3
kind: VirtualService
metadata:
  name: canary-rollout
spec:
  hosts:
  - example-service
  http:
  - route:
    - destination:
        host: example-service
        subset: v1
      weight: 90
```

1.5. CURRENT TRENDS IN CLOUD-NATIVE TECHNOLOGIES

```
    - destination:
        host: example-service
        subset: v2
      weight: 10
```

Here, traffic is split between two versions of the service, gradually transitioning to a newer release while monitoring system behavior.

- **Increased Focus on AI and ML Integration**
  The integration of artificial intelligence (AI) and machine learning (ML) into cloud-native architectures represents a trend towards smarter application runtime environments. Cloud service providers are now offering robust platforms and APIs that streamline the development and deployment of AI and ML models.

  Azure Machine Learning, AWS SageMaker, and Google AI Platform enable organizations to train, test, and deploy learning models in a scalable fashion using cloud-native infrastructure. A data scientist can deploy a pre-trained model with AWS SageMaker using an endpoint definition in JSON:

```
{
    "EndpointConfigName": "MyEndpointConfig",
    "ProductionVariants": [
      {
        "VariantName": "AllTraffic",
        "ModelName": "MyModel",
        "InitialInstanceCount": 1,
        "InstanceType": "ml.t2.medium"
      }
    ]
}
```

  These capabilities empower organizations to build intelligent applications with real-time adaptive features, such as recommendation engines or anomaly detection, underpinned by robust cloud-native infrastructure.

- **Heightened Emphasis on Security and Observability**
  Security remains a central concern in the cloud-native ecosystem, evolving continually with trends towards zero-trust architectures and enhanced observability. In response to diverse threat vectors, technologies like Kubernetes have integrated advanced se-

curity features, such as pod security policies and network policies, which practitioners must configure with precision.

An example Kubernetes Network Policy for security purposes might resemble:

```
apiVersion: networking.k8s.io/v1
kind: NetworkPolicy
metadata:
  name: secure-backend
spec:
  podSelector:
    matchLabels:
      role: backend
  policyTypes:
  - Ingress
  ingress:
  - from:
    - podSelector:
        matchLabels:
          role: ingress
```

Complementing security efforts, observability in cloud-native systems is achieved through tools like Prometheus for metrics, and Grafana for visualization, providing comprehensive insights across distributed systems. Observability facilitates rapid diagnosis and remediation of potential issues, transforming reactive management into proactive assurance of performance and reliability.

Current trends in cloud-native technologies illustrate a shift towards even more abstracted, intelligent, and secure architectures, poised to transform application development and delivery profoundly. The strides in serverless computing, service mesh architectures, AI and ML integration, and advanced security and observability indicate a robust trajectory towards resilient, scalable, and efficient cloud-native infrastructure. Embracing these trends allows organizations to position themselves at the forefront of technological innovation, adeptly navigating challenges and capturing emergent opportunities within the cloud paradigm.

Chapter 2

Understanding Kubernetes: The Backbone of Cloud-Native

Kubernetes serves as the cornerstone for modern cloud-native architectures, providing a robust platform to automate the deployment, scaling, and management of containerized applications. Its architecture facilitates seamless orchestration of containers, ensuring efficient resource utilization and application reliability. By abstracting infrastructure complexities, Kubernetes enables developers to focus on building scalable applications while maintaining high availability and fault tolerance. As organizations move towards microservices, Kubernetes offers dynamic service discovery, load balancing, and automated rollback capabilities. Understanding Kubernetes is pivotal for leveraging its capabilities effectively in cloud-native ecosystems, given its role in facilitating agile development and operational efficiencies.

2.1 Kubernetes Fundamentals

The core of Kubernetes lies in its ability to facilitate the management of containerized applications across a cluster of machines. This section delves into the foundational components and terms that form the backbone of Kubernetes, providing an essential understanding of its operational paradigm.

Kubernetes operates on a cluster architecture. A cluster consists of at least one control plane and multiple worker nodes. The control plane is responsible for maintaining the desired state of the cluster, making decisions on behalf of the cluster's intelligence, and managing workloads. Each node represents a single machine within the cluster, which could be either a physical machine or a virtual one in a cloud environment, and they all run containerized applications defined by the user.

At the most basic level, Kubernetes abstracts applications into sets of containers, through primary concepts such as Pods, which are the smallest and simplest Kubernetes object. A Pod encapsulates one or more containers that will always run as a single cohesive unit on the same logical host. This grouping is beneficial for sharing resources between containers, such as network and storage, and facilitating isolation from other containers in separate Pods.

One of the primary purposes of Pods is to act as a unit of deployment and scalability. All containers in a Pod share the network space and can communicate with each other using localhost. This design choice makes Pods exceptionally well-suited for containers that are tightly coupled and need to share resources like storage volumes and file directories.

```
apiVersion: v1
kind: Pod
metadata:
  name: example-pod
spec:
  containers:
  - name: example-container
    image: nginx:latest
    ports:
    - containerPort: 80
```

In the above example, a single container within a Pod uses the nginx:latest image and listens on port 80. This configuration ensures

2.1. KUBERNETES FUNDAMENTALS

that the Pod, and hence, its container, is correctly started within the Kubernetes cluster.

The node is another fundamental component, responsible for providing the Kubernetes runtime environment. Nodes execute the so-called Kubelet, an agent that listens to the API server on the control plane and ensures containers are running in a Pod. Additionally, the node runs a container runtime, typically Docker, CRI-O, or containerd, facilitating the actual management of container operations.

The control plane encompasses a set of components that manages the cluster activities. The *API Server* acts as the front end, exposing the Kubernetes API. The *etcd* component serves as Kubernetes' back-end state store, a highly-available key-value store that maintains the cluster's current status.

The *Scheduler* is another critical control plane component, responsible for distributing workload across available nodes. When you deploy a Pod, the Scheduler assigns it to a specific node in the cluster, balancing load according to resource availability and constraints.

```
apiVersion: v1
kind: Node
metadata:
  name: worker-node-1
spec:
  taints:
  - key: "example-key"
    value: "example-value"
    effect: "NoSchedule"
```

This example showcases how a node is configured within Kubernetes, utilizing taints to influence Pod scheduling decisions. Taints and tolerations ensure that Pods are not scheduled onto inappropriate nodes, establishing rules around which workloads can safely run on a node.

Reinforcing these foundational entities, the concept of controllers in Kubernetes manifests through various constructs such as ReplicaSets, Deployments, and StatefulSets, which manage the lifecycle and orchestration of Pods.

A *ReplicaSet* ensures that a specified number of Pod replicas are consistently running. They are employed in managing stateless applications where the precise identity of each Pod is not necessary.

```
apiVersion: apps/v1
```

```
kind: ReplicaSet
metadata:
  name: example-replicaset
spec:
  replicas: 3
  selector:
    matchLabels:
      app: example
  template:
    metadata:
      labels:
        app: example
    spec:
      containers:
      - name: example-container
        image: nginx:latest
```

Within this configuration, a ReplicaSet maintains three instances of the Pod running the assigned container. Should a Pod fail or terminate, the ReplicaSet automatically creates a new Pod to maintain the desired state.

For greater operational flexibility and rolling updates, Kubernetes employs Deployments, which sit atop ReplicaSets and provide version control and rollback abilities for Pods. Meanwhile, StatefulSets cater to applications requiring unique network identifiers per Pod and stable, persistent storage, making them suitable for databases and other stateful services.

Understanding these foundational terms and their applications facilitates the effective harnessing of Kubernetes' capabilities in a cloud-native ecosystem, paving the way for cloud infrastructure's agility and scalability. The frameworks provided by these core components underlie the sophisticated orchestration mechanisms of Kubernetes, offering a robust foundation for professional development and operations practices.

2.2 Kubernetes Architecture Overview

Kubernetes is engineered as a highly modular and extensible platform that manages containerized applications across distributed environments. Its architecture reflects this modularity, consisting of essential components that contribute to the system's reliability, scalability, and

2.2. KUBERNETES ARCHITECTURE OVERVIEW

flexibility. This section provides a comprehensive insight into the architectural components of a Kubernetes system, focusing on the role of the control plane and worker nodes.

The fundamental principle of Kubernetes architecture is to decouple system-specific configurations and applicative logic, thus providing a unified platform capable of managing diverse applications uniformly. The architecture is primarily divided into two parts: the control plane and the worker nodes. The control plane is the core hub for managing the cluster, handling the orchestration and scheduling of workloads, while the worker nodes execute the containers.

- **Control Plane Components**

The control plane components govern the cluster's lifecycle and manage its state. Among these, the API Server is the pivotal component, serving as the interface for both user and internal communications. It exposes the Kubernetes API, receiving requests from users through kubectl, client libraries, or the web UI and orchestrating internal operations by validating and processing these requests.

```
apiVersion: apiregistration.k8s.io/v1
kind: APIService
metadata:
  name: v1.example.k8s.io
spec:
  service:
    name: example-api
    namespace: default
  group: example.k8s.io
  version: v1
  insecureSkipTLSVerify: true
```

The API Server relies heavily on *etcd*, a distributed key-value store, which serves as Kubernetes' persistent backend to store its entire configuration and state, including node information, Pod specifications, and service definitions. The design of *etcd* enables stringent reliability and consistency guarantees, critical for managing distributed systems.

Alongside the API Server and etcd, the Scheduler plays a fundamental role as the decision-maker for Pod placements on suitable nodes. Its operations depend on a sophisticated scheduling algorithm that evaluates factors such as resource availability, affinity/anti-affinity rules, and data locality to fulfill the desired state described in the deployment configurations efficiently.

The *Controller Manager* is another crucial component. It runs a suite of controller processes that handle routine task automation, ensuring the desired state defined in the API Server manifests in the cluster state. As new resource controllers like ReplicaSets, Deployments, and StatefulSets are defined, the Controller Manager ensures the creation, deletion, and synchronization of Pods.

```
apiVersion: controller-manager.config.k8s.io/v1alpha1
kind: LeaderElectionConfiguration
resourceLock: configmaps
leaderElect: true
leaseDuration: 15s
renewDeadline: 10s
retryPeriod: 2s
```

The configuration above illustrates Leader Election, a critical feature for ensuring high availability of controllers. If a controller fails, another process promptly takes over, maintaining operational continuity.

- **Worker Node Components**

Worker nodes, the runtime environments for workload execution, encapsulate the containerized applications. A worker node runs several vital components, including the container runtime, kubelet, and kube-proxy.

The container runtime (typically Docker, containerd, or CRI-O) is responsible for managing container lifecycle operations, such as image management, container execution, and networking. The container runtime ensures container operations remain separate from the Kubernetes orchestration layer, enabling flexibility in choosing application infrastructure.

The *Kubelet* is an agent running on every node in the cluster. It listens for the instructions issued by the control plane through the API Server and acts by scheduling containers based on the specifications defined in Pod manifests. The Kubelet maintains the desired operational state locally on each node and reports the node's status back to the control plane.

```
kind: KubeletConfiguration
apiVersion: kubelet.config.k8s.io/v1beta1
clusterDNS:
```

2.2. KUBERNETES ARCHITECTURE OVERVIEW

```
- "10.0.0.10"
clusterDomain: "cluster.local"
runtimeRequestTimeout: "10m"
```

This Kubelet configuration file sets parameters that are essential for proper operations, like DNS configuration and runtime request timeouts, ensuring Kubelet's successful integration with the cluster network for service discovery.

Kube-proxy provides vital network functionalities for the Pod's communication by maintaining network rules on each node. It forwards incoming packets to the correct Pods across the different nodes, ensuring the flexibility of network configurations and abstracting internal network complexities from the user. This abstraction allows for seamless resource request handling, thereby optimizing the service discovery process.

Kubernetes integrates seamlessly into various networks using the Container Network Interface (CNI), enabling advanced traffic and request handling capabilities across Pods and services. Layered on this basic infrastructure, Service objects abstract the notion of a logical set of Pods, providing a stable endpoint for other services or traffic from external clients.

The Kubernetes network model embodies the notion of flat networking, which mandates that every Pod can communicate openly with each other without Network Address Translation (NAT). This holistic approach simplifies container communication, aligning well with the microservices architecture by facilitating independent, lightweight service interactions.

Kubernetes also embraces extensibility and customization, offering advanced mechanisms such as CRDs (Custom Resource Definitions) and Operators. These extend the Kubernetes API to oversee custom workloads or operational domains, incorporating them into the Kubernetes management framework. This capacity allows organizations to tailor their architecture tightly to specific implementations, automating complex processes which are dynamic, scalable, and robust.

The architecture of Kubernetes demonstrates a balance between modularity, flexibility, and scalability. Each component and function is built to be decoupled from others, ensuring robustness against failures, facilitating continuous improvement through updates, and scaling seamlessly to accommodate growing workloads.

This deep understanding of Kubernetes architecture equips developers with the necessary knowledge to harness its full potential, organizing complex containerized application systems effectively. By leveraging Kubernetes' architectural strengths, operators can deliver microservice-based applications efficiently, benefiting from enriched developer productivity, reduced operational burdens, and enhanced system reliability.

2.3 Deployment and Scaling of Applications

In the dynamic landscape of cloud-native technologies, Kubernetes stands out for its ability to automate the deployment, scaling, and management of containerized applications. This section delves into how Kubernetes orchestrates these operations, enhancing both efficiency and reliability while ensuring applications meet demand effectively.

Deployments in Kubernetes Deployments are fundamental in Kubernetes, representing a declarative approach to application deployment. A deployment defines the desired state for your Pods, managing the orchestration of ReplicaSets that ensure the application runs consistently as specified. It offers advanced functionalities such as rolling updates and rollbacks, maintaining application availability during updates.

```
apiVersion: apps/v1
kind: Deployment
metadata:
  name: nginx-deployment
spec:
  replicas: 3
  selector:
    matchLabels:
      app: nginx
  template:
    metadata:
      labels:
        app: nginx
    spec:
```

2.3. DEPLOYMENT AND SCALING OF APPLICATIONS

```
containers:
- name: nginx
  image: nginx:1.14.2
  ports:
  - containerPort: 80
```

In this example, the Deployment specification declares an application requiring three replica Pods of an nginx server, facilitating a highly available configuration across the Kubernetes cluster. The deployment controller continuously monitors this state, creating a new ReplicaSet if deviations occur.

Rolling Updates and Rollbacks Rolling updates allow for seamless upgrades of applications without downtime, crucial for maintaining service continuity. The Deployment controller updates instances of the application incrementally, reducing the risk of issues during deployment. Should an update introduce defects or instability, the built-in rollback mechanism can restore the previous stable state.

```
kubectl set image deployment/nginx-deployment nginx=nginx:1.16.0
```

The command above updates the nginx Deployment to a new image version. Kubernetes automatically starts replacing old Pods with new ones while maintaining the specified number of replicas until the update completes.

If a rollback is necessary due to unexpected failures or performance degradation, the kubectl rollout undo command reverts changes:

```
kubectl rollout undo deployment/nginx-deployment
```

The rollback process is just as crucial as rolling updates, minimizing potential disruptions to operations.

Scaling Applications Kubernetes excels in scaling applications to match demand through horizontal scaling, which increases or decreases the number of Pod replicas based on CPU utilization, memory stats, or custom metrics. This automatic scaling adjusts resource allocation to align with real-time demand patterns, optimizing availability and performance.

```
apiVersion: autoscaling/v1
```

```
kind: HorizontalPodAutoscaler
metadata:
  name: nginx-hpa
spec:
  scaleTargetRef:
    apiVersion: apps/v1
    kind: Deployment
    name: nginx-deployment
  minReplicas: 1
  maxReplicas: 10
  targetCPUUtilizationPercentage: 50
```

The HPA configuration above automatically scales the number of nginx Pods between 1 and 10 based on the CPU utilization threshold. Kubernetes aggregates Pod metrics and makes scaling decisions, promoting operational efficiency and service reliability.

Advanced Scaling Techniques Kubernetes supports custom metrics and vertical scaling to address specific scaling scenarios. Custom metrics, defined using the custom metrics API, allow applications to be scaled based on user-defined metrics specific to application logic or business KPIs, enhancing the precision of scalability decisions.

Vertical Pod Autoscaler (VPA) provides another dimension by adjusting the resource requests and limits for containers within a Pod. This is particularly beneficial for resource-intensive applications that experience fluctuating demands, ensuring optimal resource allocation without altering the Pod's replica count.

Deployment Strategies Kubernetes supports multiple deployment strategies that balance rollout speed, resource consumption, and risk management. Understanding these strategies allows for tailoring deployment processes to individual application requirements.

- **Recreate Strategy**: This simple strategy terminates old Pods before creating new ones, ensuring exclusive utilization of machine resources. While suitable for non-critical applications, it introduces downtime, making it less ideal for applications requiring high availability.

- **Rolling Update Strategy**: As the default Kubernetes strategy, it incrementally replaces application instances, facilitating continuous availability. It configures maximum unavailable and maximum surge properties to control update pace and resource utilization.

- **Canary Deployments**: By initially releasing a new version to a select group of users, canary deployments mitigate risks. Feedback acquired from this group enables validation of performance and functional objectives before broader rollout.

- **Blue-Green Deployments**: This strategy involves running two separate environments (blue for current production, green for the new version), switching traffic between them. It allows robust verification and rollback of versions without impacting live customers.

These strategies provide robust flexibility in handling various deployment scenarios, ensuring smooth integration of updates while supporting dynamic application environments.

Managing Application Configurations Kubernetes separates application code from configuration using ConfigMaps and Secrets mechanisms, enhancing security, portability, and maintainability of applications.

ConfigMaps allow configuration data to be accessed by Pods without the need to rebuild container images. They enable environment-specific customizations, storing configuration variables, command-line arguments, or entire configuration files.

```
apiVersion: v1
kind: ConfigMap
metadata:
  name: game-config
data:
  game.properties: |
    enemies=aliens
    lives=3
```

Secrets provide a safe method for dealing with sensitive information such as passwords, OAuth tokens, or SSH keys. Data is encoded in base64 within Kubernetes and should be encrypted at rest and during transit for enhanced security.

```
apiVersion: v1
kind: Secret
metadata:
  name: db-secret
type: Opaque
data:
  password: MWYyZDFlMmU2N2Rm
```

By leveraging ConfigMaps and Secrets, developers maintain clean separations between application logic and its operational parameters, fostering a secure and agile development practice.

Deploying and scaling applications in Kubernetes transcends basic container orchestration, providing robust mechanics that offer distinct flexibility and control over application lifecycle management. The declarative nature of Deployments, coupled with strategic scaling and configuration management, underscores Kubernetes as a pivotal tool in the management of complex, distributed application systems. Through a detailed understanding of deployment mechanics and scaling strategies, operators effectively automate and optimize workloads, ensuring reliable, scalable, and efficient cloud-native operations.

2.4 Service Discovery and Load Balancing

Service discovery and load balancing are two critical aspects of Kubernetes, ensuring efficient management and direction of traffic within the cluster. These mechanisms enable Kubernetes to dynamically distribute requests across different instances of services and maintain seamless communication among system components in a distributed environment.

Concept of Services in Kubernetes

Services in Kubernetes are abstractions that define a logical set of Pods and a policy by which to access them. By providing a stable endpoint for Pod sets, Services decouple Pod identities from application architectures, paving the way for service resilience and scalable deployments. Services are particularly crucial in masking the ephemeral nature of

2.4. SERVICE DISCOVERY AND LOAD BALANCING

Pods, which may be terminated or rescheduled across the cluster.

```
apiVersion: v1
kind: Service
metadata:
  name: my-service
spec:
  selector:
    app: MyApp
  ports:
  - protocol: TCP
    port: 80
    targetPort: 9376
```

This Service example coordinates access to Pods with the label app=MyApp, channeling traffic from port 80 on the Service to port 9376 on the target Pods.

Types of Services

Kubernetes provides several Service types based on how they expose applications to the network, each optimized for different use cases and environments:

- **ClusterIP**: This default service type exposes the service on a cluster-internal IP. It is accessible from within the cluster only, making it suitable for internal service-to-service communication without external traffic exposure.

- **NodePort**: Expands accessibility by exposing the service on a static port on each node in the cluster. External users can access these through <NodeIP>:<NodePort>. This setup simplifies external access with fixed node ports.

- **LoadBalancer**: Extends the NodePort functionality by creating an external load balancer (e.g., on cloud providers like AWS or GCP) that distributes incoming requests to NodePort instances, offering high availability and redundancy to the application.

- **ExternalName**: This Service maps a service to the content of the externalName field (e.g., example.com). Unlike ClusterIP, it relies on DNS names rather than specific Pod selectors or Cluster IPs, serving as a stable reference point external to the Kubernetes cluster.

```yaml
apiVersion: v1
kind: Service
metadata:
  name: my-loadbalanced-service
spec:
  type: LoadBalancer
  selector:
    app: MyApp
  ports:
  - protocol: TCP
    port: 80
    targetPort: 9376
```

The above LoadBalancer Service definition provisions an external load balancer that forwards requests to the specified Service, typically used in production for high availability of critical application endpoints.

Service Discovery Mechanisms

Kubernetes utilizes Service discovery to automatically recognize and interact with newly provisioned services, relying on two primary mechanisms: environment variables and DNS.

Environment Variables

Upon Pod startup, Kubernetes injects environment variables representing service properties. These auto-populated variables simplify service discovery for straightforward networking operations without needing additional configuration or dependency management.

DNS-Based Service Registry

A more scalable and flexible option is the built-in DNS-based service discovery provided by Kubernetes. This mechanism allows services within the cluster to appear as entries in a DNS server, resolving service names to their respective endpoint IPs and ports.

my-service.default.svc.cluster.local

The DNS implementation utilizes CoreDNS within the cluster, dynamically updating and providing DNS resolution for both ClusterIP and external services while minimizing configuration burden and facilitating service interactions.

Ingress and Egress Traffic Management

To manage fine-grained external access to services, Kubernetes uses

Ingress resources, effectively routing incoming HTTP(S) traffic to appropriate Service backends. Ingress configurations enable administrators to implement host-based or URL-based routing, SSL termination, and other traffic management features through an Ingress Controller.

```
apiVersion: networking.k8s.io/v1
kind: Ingress
metadata:
  name: example-ingress
spec:
  rules:
  - host: example.com
    http:
      paths:
      - pathType: Prefix
        path: "/"
        backend:
          service:
            name: my-service
            port:
              number: 80
```

The example configures Ingress rules to direct requests with the host example.com to my-service. This flexibility allows businesses to consolidate routing rules in a centralized location, enhancing access control over diverse application landscapes.

For egress traffic, Network Policies define which Pods are permitted to communicate out of the cluster, bolstering security by limiting unauthorized data flows.

Load Balancing Strategies

Kubernetes supports sophisticated load balancing strategies to optimize resource use and ensure consistent, responsive service delivery. These strategies can be intrinsic, as part of Service constructs, or through external load balancing extensions.

Session Affinity enables the system to bind user sessions to specific Pods. Kubernetes facilitates session affinity using Client IP, ensuring subsequent requests from the same client are directed to the same Pod, which is crucial for stateful applications that may not gracefully handle distributed session storage.

Least Connection Routing is another balancing method where traffic is directed to the server with the fewest active connections. This approach minimizes the risk of overloading a specific backend, promoting more equitable resource distribution across all available Pods.

Leveraging External Load Balancers

In cloud environments, Kubernetes can orchestrate external load balancers, such as AWS's Elastic Load Balancer or GCP's Cloud Load Balancing. By integrating directly with these services, Kubernetes extends its native capabilities with provider-specific advantages like global routing, comprehensive health checks, and advanced security features.

Advanced Service Meshes

Service meshes, such as Istio or Linkerd, provide a more advanced, transparent layer for managing service-to-service interactions and traffic policies across diverse application architectures. They extend service discovery and load balancing functionalities, offering advantages like circuit breaking, retries, and traffic mirroring without requiring changes in application code.

The service mesh architecture typically comprises a dedicated control plane and data plane, utilizing sidecar proxies co-located with application Pods to capture and manage traffic. They facilitate robust observability, security, and traffic management, decoupling these concerns from application logic.

Kubernetes' robust service discovery and load balancing mechanisms form the cornerstone of its networking capabilities, ensuring efficient, reliable, and scalable communication across services. By abstracting complex network operations, Kubernetes empowers developers to focus on application functionality rather than infrastructure concerns, making it an indispensable tool in cloud-native environments. Through these sophisticated networking practices, operators can optimize resource utilization, automate request handling, and enhance user experiences across diverse application ecosystems.

2.5 Storage Options in Kubernetes

Storage in Kubernetes is designed to support both ephemeral and persistent data needs of containerized applications, enabling users to deploy applications with varying storage requirements seamlessly. This section examines the diverse storage options available within Kubernetes, clarifying how they integrate and operate within a cluster environment.

- **Ephemeral Storage on Kubernetes**

Ephemeral storage refers to temporary storage that exists only as long as the Pod is alive. This storage type is mainly used for caching or intermediate data that does not require persistence beyond the Pod's lifecycle.

EmptyDir Volumes are typical examples of ephemeral storage in Kubernetes. When a Pod is allocated, Kubernetes creates an emptyDir volume that persists for the duration of the Pod, even if containers within the Pod are restarted. This volume offers storage shared within all containers of the Pod, supporting communication by storing data that does not need persistence across Pod restarts.

```
apiVersion: v1
kind: Pod
metadata:
  name: shared-data
spec:
  containers:
  - name: container-a
    image: busybox
    command: ["sh", "-c", "echo Hello from A > /data/message; sleep 3600"]
    volumeMounts:
    - mountPath: /data
      name: data-volume
  - name: container-b
    image: busybox
    command: ["sh", "-c", "cat /data/message; sleep 3600"]
    volumeMounts:
    - mountPath: /data
      name: data-volume
  volumes:
  - name: data-volume
    emptyDir: {}
```

In the shared-data Pod configuration, both containers interact through a shared emptyDir volume, facilitating in-Pod communication for temporary data handling.

- **Persistent Storage in Kubernetes**

Persistent storage is essential for workloads that require data to outlive the Pod lifecycle, critical for applications such as databases, logging systems, or any stateful services. Kubernetes abstracts persistent storage through several resource types:

- **PersistentVolumes and PersistentVolumeClaims**

PersistentVolumes (PVs) represent storage resources provisioned in the cluster, abstracting the underlying storage technology from the application. PVs support storage types like NFS, iSCSI, AWS EBS, Azure Disks, and more, established through a plug-in interface.

PersistentVolumeClaims (PVCs) serve as requests for the storage resources defined by PVs. The PVCs decouple storage from nodes, allowing for flexible and dynamic resource allocation, where applications define their storage needs without knowing the specifics of the provisioned storage.

```
apiVersion: v1
kind: PersistentVolume
metadata:
  name: pv-example
spec:
  capacity:
    storage: 10Gi
  accessModes:
    - ReadWriteOnce
  persistentVolumeReclaimPolicy: Retain
  hostPath:
    path: /mnt/data
```

```
apiVersion: v1
kind: PersistentVolumeClaim
metadata:
  name: pvc-example
spec:
  accessModes:
    - ReadWriteOnce
  resources:
    requests:
      storage: 8Gi
```

2.5. STORAGE OPTIONS IN KUBERNETES

In the example provided, the PVC requests storage cell pvc-example matches the resource cap provided by pv-example, resulting in the allocation of persistent storage to the claimant Pod.

- **StatefulSets and Headless Services**

StatefulSets are designed for managing stateful applications, ensuring Pods are consistently named and ordered across restarts, maintaining their unique identities. When coupled with Headless Services, they provide persistent identity and network identities crucial for stateful applications, like databases or clustered software systems.

The following YAML creates a StatefulSet using persistent storage:

```
apiVersion: apps/v1
kind: StatefulSet
metadata:
  name: web
spec:
  serviceName: "web"
  replicas: 3
  template:
    metadata:
      labels:
        app: nginx
    spec:
      containers:
      - name: nginx
        image: nginx:1.14.2
        volumeMounts:
        - name: www
          mountPath: /usr/share/nginx/html
  volumeClaimTemplates:
  - metadata:
      name: www
    spec:
      accessModes: [ "ReadWriteOnce" ]
      resources:
        requests:
          storage: 1Gi
```

Here, volumeClaimTemplates automate the creation of PVCs for each Pod in the StatefulSet, ensuring persistent storage allocation for each instance.

- **Dynamic Provisioning with Storage Classes**

One of Kubernetes' powerful features is dynamic provisioning with StorageClasses, which permit automatic provisioning of storage as required. Administrators can define multiple StorageClasses to represent different quality tiers or providers, specifying varying levels of service and performance.

```
apiVersion: storage.k8s.io/v1
kind: StorageClass
metadata:
  name: fast
provisioner: kubernetes.io/aws-ebs
parameters:
  type: io1
  iopsPerGB: "10"
  fsType: ext4
```

Using the StorageClass fast, Kubernetes can dynamically create volumes with specified performance characteristics, such as the IOPS rate or file system type dictated by the cloud provider's provisioner.

- **Volume Plugins and CSI**

Kubernetes' integration with numerous volume plugins facilitates supporting diverse storage backends, ranging from traditional NAS/SAN systems to cloud-based storage solutions. With the evolving Container Storage Interface (CSI), Kubernetes extends support to external storage systems, standardizing the development process for new storage backends, enhancing ecosystem synergies.

- **Security Considerations and Encryption**

Using configurations such as Role-Based Access Control (RBAC) and Network Policies, Kubernetes ensures robust security for storage interactions. Furthermore, for sensitive data, encryption both at rest and in transit ensures compliance with data security standards, safeguarded by implementing encrypted file systems or external KMS (Key Management Services).

-

Kubernetes provides a comprehensive framework to accommodate both ephemeral and persistent storage needs, supporting a broad spectrum of applications. By unifying various backend storage solutions through cohesive abstractions and advanced mechanisms like dynamic provisioning, Kubernetes ensures that containerized applications retain the necessary elasticity and resilience required in cloud-native environments. Understanding these storage options enables developers to optimize resource availability effectively, ensuring data persistence and reliability in distributed systems.

2.6 Networking in Kubernetes Clusters

Networking in Kubernetes is a fundamental aspect that facilitates communication within and outside of the cluster. Kubernetes adopts a distinct networking model that ensures all Pods in a cluster can communicate with each other without the need for network address translation (NAT). This seamless connectivity enables the deployment of distributed applications efficiently.

- **Core Networking Concepts**: Kubernetes networking is built upon several core concepts, including Pods, Services, and Network Policies. Each of these elements plays a critical role in managing network traffic, connectivity, and security across the cluster.

- **Pod Networking**: Kubernetes assigns each Pod a unique IP address within the cluster network. This design means Pods can communicate directly with each other using these IP addresses. Kubernetes abstracts network complexities, providing Pods with a consistent view of network resources, regardless of their physical placement within the cluster.

- **Service Networking**: While Pods have IP addresses that facilitate direct communication, these are ephemeral and may change over a Pod's lifecycle. Services provide stable IP addresses and DNS names for Pods, acting as permanent endpoints for external and internal communications.

- **Network Policies**: These policies govern the inbound and outbound traffic behavior between Pods. Network policies define rules using labels to specify which Pods can communicate, thus ensuring robust security measures are in place to protect sensitive data.

- **The Kubernetes Network Model**: The Kubernetes network model consists of two features that ensure consistency and seamless integration of networking components:
  - **Flat Network Structure**: Every Pod should have the ability to communicate with any other Pod within the cluster without NAT. This mandates a flat network topology across the cluster's nodes, often achieved through network overlays or underlays.
  - **Node Communication**: Node agents (such as kube-proxy) and other Kubernetes components must communicate with every Pod. Nodes rely on local routing setup or overlays to allow this communication, further extending the flat network throughout the cluster.

- **Implementing Cluster Networking**: Kubernetes provides several solutions through network plugins to accomplish seamless communication, including Flannel, Calico, and Weave Net, each offering specific features and configurations.
  - **Flannel** operates as a simple overlay network that distributes packets to the correct destination using encapsulation techniques like VXLAN. Ideal for straightforward use cases, Flannel manages network traffic efficiently by creating flat networks within the Kubernetes traversal realm.
  - **Calico** combines both networking and network policy enforcements, utilizing BGP (Border Gateway Protocol) for routing, ensuring fine-grained control over network policies, including deep packet inspection and namespace isolation.

```
apiVersion: projectcalico.org/v3
kind: GlobalNetworkPolicy
metadata:
  name: allow-tcp-traffic
spec:
  selector: app == 'nginx'
```

```
ingress:
- action: Allow
  protocol: TCP
  source:
    selector: app == 'client'
  destination:
    ports:
      - 80
```

The above configuration allows TCP traffic from Pods labeled as client to those labeled as nginx, illustrating Calico's network policy deployment.

- **Service Types and Communication**: Service abstraction layers in Kubernetes allow for efficient traffic distribution to Pods. The type of service—ClusterIP, NodePort, LoadBalancer, or ExternalName—dictates the communication model.

    - **ClusterIP**: Provides an internal IP for an intra-cluster service. This is the default type and supports service discovery entirely within the cluster.

    - **NodePort**: Exposes the service on identical port numbers on each node's IP address, thereby making it accessible externally through a specific node IP and NodePort number.

    - **LoadBalancer**: Integrates with cloud provider load balancers to distribute traffic across nodes and services transparently, also providing external access by default.

    - **ExternalName**: Maps a service to an external DNS name, simplifying access to resources outside of the Kubernetes environment.

- **DNS in Kubernetes**: Kubernetes employs DNS for service discovery, automatically managing DNS entries for services and Pods, using CoreDNS. It ensures that each service has an associated DNS entry, allowing Pods to connect using service names instead of IP addresses.

    Pods can resolve services by the naming convention <service-name>.<namespace>.svc.cluster.local, providing a reliable way to discover and access services across namespaces.

- **Network Security and Policies**: Network Policies in Kubernetes are essential to implementing security by allowing administrators to control traffic to and from Pods.

  Creating Network Policies involves specifying a Pod selector along with allowed traffic flows. Using the power of labels, administrators can enforce strict boundaries between services, limiting traffic movement according to the specified ingress and egress rules.

  ```
  apiVersion: networking.k8s.io/v1
  kind: NetworkPolicy
  metadata:
    name: db-restrict-policy
  spec:
    podSelector:
      matchLabels:
        role: db
    policyTypes:
    - Ingress
    - Egress
    ingress:
    - from:
      - podSelector:
          matchLabels:
            access: manager
  ```

  In this example, the Network Policy restricts traffic to Pods labeled with role: db to only allow ingress from Pods with the label access: manager, protecting sensitive data from unauthorized access.

- **Advanced Networking Integrations**: Kubernetes can extend its networking capability alongside a service mesh, such as Istio or Linkerd, to enable advanced routing, load balancing, traffic management, and observability. These service meshes introduce a dedicated control plane, finer network policies, and telemetry collection.

  By deploying sidecars alongside Pods, a service mesh intercepts network traffic without requiring changes to application code, offering centralized policy management and secure communication over distributed systems.

- : Networking is a cornerstone in Kubernetes architecture, ensuring reliable, secure, and efficient communication across distributed applications. Through its networking model, service abstraction, and cutting-edge policy mechanisms, Kubernetes provides a comprehensive framework that addresses the challenges inherent in cloud-native network management. With continued advancements and integrations, Kubernetes remains a resilient and scalable network orchestrator for modern infrastructure needs. Understanding and utilizing these components effectively can significantly enhance cluster operations, application security, and overall performance.

2.7 Kubernetes Security Essentials

Securing a Kubernetes cluster is a multi-faceted task involving the protection of its components, application workloads, and data. This section explores the essential security practices in Kubernetes, detailing strategies to safeguard against common vulnerabilities and ensuring robust security postures in cloud-native environments.

Kubernetes Security Architecture

Kubernetes' security model integrates multiple layers of defense, implementing policies and configurations to protect the cluster's core, nodes, and applications running on them. At its architecture's heart lie control mechanisms such as authentication, authorization, and admission control, each playing critical roles in guarding access and enforcing operational policies.

Authentication: Kubernetes supports multiple authentication methods, including certificates, bearer tokens, and plugins for external identity management. Implementing strong authentication mechanisms is critical to verifying the identities of users and service accounts interacting with the Kubernetes API.

```
apiVersion: v1
kind: Config
clusters:
- cluster:
    certificate-authority: /path/to/ca.crt
    server: https://<api-server-endpoint>
  name: kubernetes-cluster
```

```
users:
- name: admin
  user:
    client-certificate: /path/to/admin.crt
    client-key: /path/to/admin.key
```

Here, a kubeconfig file specifies how Kubernetes clients can authenticate against the API server using certificates.

Authorization: Upon user authentication, Kubernetes uses authorization modules such as Role-Based Access Control (RBAC) to govern permissions. RBAC assigns roles to users or groups, with roles determining actions that can be performed on resources.

```
apiVersion: rbac.authorization.k8s.io/v1
kind: Role
metadata:
  namespace: default
  name: pod-reader
rules:
- apiGroups: [""]
  resources: ["pods"]
  verbs: ["get", "watch", "list"]
```

This RBAC role restricts access, allowing only specific actions on Pod resources, enabling fine-tuned permission management.

Admission Control: Admission controllers regulate access to the cluster at the initial phases of request processing, enabling policies like PodSecurityPolicy, ResourceQuota, and NamespaceLifecycle, thus enriching Kubernetes security by validating resource requests against predefined criteria.

Securing Kubernetes Infrastructure

Infrastructure-level hardening focuses on reducing vulnerabilities within the operating system, the Kubernetes software stack, and the network.

- **Cluster Networking Security:** Deploy Network Policies to segment and restrict traffic flows between Pods, supporting defense-in-depth strategies. Network policies are particularly effective in microservice architectures by limiting service interactions to strictly necessary paths.

- **Operating System Hardening:** Regularly update and patch nodes to protect against vulnerabilities, minimize the attack surface by disabling unnecessary services, and use firewalls to block unauthorized access and secure SSH and API endpoints through restricted access controls.
- **Node Security:** Implement host-level security by employing Linux kernel security modules like AppArmor or SELinux, which provide an additional security layer by implementing access controls for applications running on cluster nodes.

Container Image Security

Securing container images is vital for maintaining cluster integrity. This encompasses building, storing, and running container images free from known vulnerabilities or misconfigurations.

- **Image Scanning:** Leverage tools like Clair or Trivy to scan container images for vulnerabilities, ensuring images adhere to security standards before running in production environments.
- **Image Signing and Trust:** Implement Docker Content Trust or Notary to ensure image provenance, allowing only trusted images to be deployed within the Kubernetes cluster.
- **Minimal Base Images:** Use minimal base images to decrease the number of vulnerabilities present in images by excluding unnecessary packages, thus reducing the attack surface.

Secret Management

Secrets in Kubernetes store sensitive data such as passwords, tokens, and keys, providing the necessary mechanism for securely managing sensitive information.

```
apiVersion: v1
kind: Secret
metadata:
  name: db-secret
data:
  username: dXNlcg==
  password: cGFzc3dvcmQ=
```

Secrets are structured as base64-encoded values, reducing the exposed risk. They should be encrypted at rest using encryption configurations within the API server settings to ensure uncompromised security.

Pod Security Practices

Securing Pods involves configuring security contexts and enforcing security policies, ensuring the applications running in Pods adhere to defined security standards.

- **Linux Capabilities:** Use security contexts to restrict Pod privileges and capabilities, ensuring minimal privileges. Examples include disallowing Pods from running as the root user or restricting access to specific host resources.

```
apiVersion: v1
kind: Pod
metadata:
  name: secure-pod
spec:
  containers:
  - name: secure-container
    image: nginx:1.14.2
    securityContext:
      runAsUser: 1000
      runAsNonRoot: true
      capabilities:
        drop:
        - ALL
```

- **Pod Security Policies (PSP):** Implement PSPs to set defaults and constrain Pod creation, limiting the resources and capabilities Pods can utilize. These policies enforce best practices, adding a layer of default compliance and defense within the cluster architecture.

Monitoring and Logging

Implementing comprehensive monitoring and logging practices enables prompt detection and response to security incidents.

- **Audit Logging:** Enable audit logging on the Kubernetes API server to capture requests and responses across cluster components, facilitating forensic analysis and anomaly detections.

- **Cluster and Application Monitoring:** Employ tools like Prometheus for monitoring KPIs and Grafana for visualizing trends, helping detect throughput anomalies or unusual resource utilization indicative of potential security threats.

Identity and Access Management (IAM)

Integrating IAM systems ensures thorough control over who can access the Kubernetes cluster and what actions they can perform.

- **Service Account Management:** Use Kubernetes service accounts to provide applications with identity credentials that are separate from the user accounts, setting specific permissions using RBAC.

- **IAM Integration for Cloud Kubernetes:** Cloud providers like AWS or GCP integrate IAM services, providing an additional layer of security through role association and permission boundaries, ensuring operations have minimal permissions required for tasks.

The Kubernetes security model demands a holistic approach, encompassing authentication, network security, container image integrity, and runtime safety practices. By implementing these essential security strategies, Kubernetes clusters can be protected against evolving threats, maintaining a robust operating environment for deploying scalable and secure applications. With continuous enhancements to the security framework, Kubernetes remains at the forefront of offering robust solutions, catering to diverse application needs in cloud-native ecosystems.

CHAPTER 2. UNDERSTANDING KUBERNETES: THE BACKBONE OF CLOUD-NATIVE

Chapter 3

Getting Started with Crossplane

Crossplane extends Kubernetes to become a control plane for provisioning and managing cloud infrastructure resources in a seamless, declarative manner. As an open-source project, it enables the management of infrastructure through Kubernetes-native APIs, supporting a wide range of cloud provider services without the need for additional tooling. By treating infrastructure as code, Crossplane integrates deeply with existing Kubernetes ecosystems, offering powerful extensibility through configurable providers and resource compositions. Setting up Crossplane involves installing it within a Kubernetes cluster and configuring it to interface with desired cloud providers, establishing a unified control plane to manage cloud resources across different environments. Understanding these initial steps is key to effectively harnessing Crossplane's capabilities for orchestrating multi-cloud operations.

3.1 What is Crossplane?

Crossplane is an open-source project that enhances Kubernetes by enabling it to manage cloud infrastructure resources as a control plane. As an extension of Kubernetes, Crossplane transforms standard Kubernetes clusters into comprehensive control planes capable of handling infrastructure provisioning and management in a declarative manner. Leveraging the robustness of Kubernetes APIs, Crossplane allows engineers to describe, allocate, and adjust cloud resources through a consistent interface, regardless of the underlying cloud provider. This section aims to delve into the architecture, functionality, and advantages of employing Crossplane in a cloud-native environment.

At its core, Crossplane integrates seamlessly with the Kubernetes ecosystem, utilizing Custom Resource Definitions (CRDs) to represent various cloud infrastructure components. This design approach ensures that users familiar with Kubernetes concepts can easily extend their existing knowledge to manage cloud resources. Crossplane's strategic use of CRDs represents various cloud services like databases, storage, compute resources, and network services, enabling declarative resource management across different cloud providers.

Here's a simple YAML that defines a resource claim for a MySQL database in Crossplane:

```
apiVersion: database.crossplane.io/v1alpha1
kind: MySQLInstance
metadata:
  name: example-database
spec:
  classSelector:
    matchLabels:
      type: production
  writeConnectionSecretToRef:
    name: db-connection
```

Crossplane's architecture is built around the concept of extensibility. It does so by plugging in various Providers, which are modular components that communicate with different cloud service APIs. Providers abstract the specifics of cloud services from users, allowing Crossplane to offer a consistent API surface for cloud management tasks. This capability extends Kubernetes' ability to manage not just application workloads, but also to provision and manage cloud provider services, directly tying them into application lifecycles.

Providers in Crossplane are a foundational element that enables its functionality by converting Kubernetes-native API calls into actions on cloud provider services. For example, provisioning a cloud SQL database or an object storage bucket can be as simple as applying the relevant YAML file to a Kubernetes cluster. The provisioned resources are often managed as if they are native Kubernetes resources.

The snippet below shows how you might define a Provider for AWS:

```
apiVersion: v1
kind: Secret
metadata:
  name: aws-provider-creds
  namespace: crossplane-system
type: Opaque
data:
  creds: YOUR_BASE64_ENCODED_AWS_CREDENTIALS

---
apiVersion: pkg.crossplane.io/v1alpha1
kind: Provider
metadata:
  name: provider-aws
spec:
  package: "crossplane/provider-aws:master"
```

Crossplane introduces a clean separation between the desired state of infrastructure (defined by users) and the actual state managed by controllers running in the Kubernetes cluster. This separation enables platform teams to define concrete infrastructure provisioning strategies and application teams to deploy their workloads on these predefined resources without worrying about the complexities of underlying infrastructure.

Cloud infrastructures managed by Crossplane are treated analogously to Kubernetes workloads. The management of infrastructure resources is transitioned into Kubernetes clusters as if they are workload objects managed by controllers. This re-use of Kubernetes' declarative nature simplifies the mastering of infrastructure management for individuals already versed in Kubernetes.

A significant advantage of using Crossplane is its support for composition, allowing users to define new kinds of infrastructure resources that encode business-specific logic and best practices. Compositions enable the creation of composite resources, where a high-level abstraction consists of multiple lower-level components, aiding organizations in maintaining consistency and enforcing infrastructure standards. Compositions are a powerful way to define reusable infrastructure patterns suitable for differing environments such as development, testing, and production.

The benefits of using Crossplane become evident when managing multi-cloud resource environments wherein different cloud providers each offer their unique infrastructure components. Through Crossplane, a unified Kubernetes-native API can manage resources across these providers without learning different service APIs or tools, and this extends Kubernetes' ecosystem the ability to craft infrastructure as code across heterogeneous cloud environments.

Crossplane's capability is augmented through community-driven providers that expand the reach and possibilities of its integration with cloud services. Apart from mainstream cloud service providers like AWS or Google Cloud, the community consistently contributes additional providers catered to specific needs or services, ensuring Crossplane's adaptability remains cutting-edge and future-ready.

By integrating closely with GitOps practices, Crossplane enables version-controlled infrastructure management. The infrastructure declaration lies alongside application code in repositories, enhancing collaboration among development and operations teams and streamlining infrastructure scaling, updates, and rollback processes. This model pushes the boundary of DevOps practices, where pipelines automate the creation and management of infrastructure alongside application deployment.

The adoption of Crossplane is further refined by custom policies and configurations that organizations can implement, ensuring only compliant infrastructure states are enforced, aligned with both technical and business mandates. This systemic management encompasses identity controls, access management, and cost governance, all fine-tuned through Crossplane's API-centric approach.

To fully leverage Crossplane's advanced features, in-depth comprehension of key Kubernetes concepts such as controllers, operators, and custom resources is crucial. Users should also engage with Crossplane's ecosystem through its documentation, tutorials, and community forums to maintain a current understanding of its evolving capabilities and best practices.

Crossplane notably increases an organization's agility in managing cloud resources, morphing the dynamism of Kubernetes into comprehensive infrastructure orchestration. Through its harmonized API, broad provider range, and capacity for detailed configuration, Crossplane accelerates the cloud-native journey, driving innovation across IT landscapes while retaining alignment with existing Kubernetes-driven workflows. Through this section, readers gain insight into Crossplane's structure and purpose, unraveling its potential to act as an orchestration framework against the backdrop of modern cloud demands.

3.2 Installation and Setup

Setting up Crossplane involves several key steps that integrate it closely with an existing Kubernetes cluster. This section provides a thorough walkthrough on installing Crossplane, configuring its initial setup, and validating that it is functioning correctly within the cluster. The process outlines how to prepare the Kubernetes environment, install Crossplane using the Helm package manager, configure necessary permissions, and validate the setup by provisioning a simple cloud resource. By understanding this setup correctly, users can ensure that Crossplane is optimized to manage cloud resources effectively.

Preparing the Kubernetes Environment

Before installing Crossplane, a functional Kubernetes cluster is required. The cluster can be hosted on any Kubernetes distributor service such as Google Kubernetes Engine (GKE), Amazon Elastic Kubernetes Service (EKS), Azure Kubernetes Service (AKS), or a self-hosted solution. It is crucial to ensure that the Kubernetes cluster is configured to enable necessary network policies, permissions, and resources such as CPU and memory to handle Crossplane workloads.

Ensure access to the cluster with `kubectl`, the Kubernetes command-line tool, installed and configured. Validate the cluster's accessibility by checking its nodes:

```
kubectl get nodes
```

```
NAME              STATUS  ROLES   AGE   VERSION
ip-192-168-20-45  Ready   <none>  10d   v1.21.0
ip-192-168-23-100 Ready   <none>  10d   v1.21.0
```

Installing Crossplane with Helm

Helm is often used to install packages into Kubernetes clusters, simplifying complex applications' setup and deployment processes. To install Crossplane using Helm:

1. **Install Helm**: Ensure Helm is installed on your local environment. Verify the installation with:

   ```
   helm version
   ```

2. **Add the Crossplane Helm repository**: This repository includes all the packages necessary for Crossplane installation.

   ```
   helm repo add crossplane-master https://charts.crossplane.io/master/
   helm repo update
   ```

3. **Install Crossplane**: Deploy Crossplane into the Kubernetes cluster in the default namespace. This process spins up several pods and CRDs that enable Crossplane's functionality.

   ```
   kubectl create namespace crossplane-system
   helm install crossplane --namespace crossplane-system crossplane-master/crossplane
   ```

4. **Verify Installation**: Check that Crossplane pods are running successfully.

   ```
   kubectl get pods -n crossplane-system
   ```

   ```
   NAME                                      READY  STATUS   RESTARTS  AGE
   crossplane-c6b6b747-56tln                  1/1   Running  0         5m
   crossplane-rbac-manager-568787b7fb-582vl   1/1   Running  0         5m
   ```

Configuring Permissions

Crossplane requires permissions to manage cloud resources, which are provided through cloud provider credentials stored within Kubernetes secrets. Here's how to configure these credentials:

1. **Create a Secret for AWS Credentials**: Assume you are integrating Crossplane with AWS.

    ```
    apiVersion: v1
    kind: Secret
    metadata:
      name: aws-credentials
      namespace: crossplane-system
    type: Opaque
    data:
      credentials: <BASE64_ENCODED_AWS_JSON_CREDENTIALS>
    ```

    The credentials data should be encoded from a valid AWS credentials JSON.

2. **Install Provider**: Use the installed Crossplane to install a provider e.g., AWS.

    ```
    kubectl crossplane install provider crossplane/provider-aws:v0.17.0
    ```

3. **Configure the ProviderConfig Resource**: Link the secret with AWS configuration to enable interaction between Crossplane and the cloud provider.

    ```
    apiVersion: aws.crossplane.io/v1beta1
    kind: ProviderConfig
    metadata:
      name: example
    spec:
      credentials:
        source: Secret
        secretRef:
          namespace: crossplane-system
          name: aws-credentials
          key: credentials
    ```

Validating the Setup with a Simple Provisioning

After a successful installation, Crossplane should be validated by provisioning a cloud resource. This ensures the setup is working correctly and that Crossplane can interact with cloud services as expected. Validate by provisioning an S3 bucket in AWS:

1. **Define the S3 Bucket Resource**

    ```
    apiVersion: s3.aws.crossplane.io/v1beta1
    kind: Bucket
    metadata:
      name: example-bucket
    spec:
      forProvider:
        locationConstraint: us-west-2
      providerConfigRef:
        name: example
    ```

2. **Apply the YAML configuration**: Use kubectl to apply this definition, observing how Crossplane manages the lifecycle of this resource.

    ```
    kubectl apply -f s3-bucket.yaml
    ```

3. **Verify Bucket Creation**: Once applied, verify using an appropriate AWS CLI tool or console to ensure that the bucket is indeed created and accessible.

Crossplane Configuration Best Practices

When configuring Crossplane, it is beneficial to utilize best practices to ensure security, efficiency, and maintainability. Consider the following:

- **Minimal Permissions**: Restrict permissions associated with cloud provider credentials strictly to those required for operations. Apply principle of least privilege.

- **Resource Limits**: Define limits for the resources Crossplane managers, ensuring clusters aren't over-provisioned.

- **Version Control**: Keep all resource configuration files under version control using a provider such as Git. This allows for tracking changes, reverting to previous states, and auditing configurations.

- **Monitoring and Logging**: Set up appropriate monitoring using Kubernetes-native tools and cloud-specific dashboards to maintain visibility over cloud resources and Crossplane's activities. Enable logging for troubleshooting when any issues are encountered.

Advanced Configuration and Optimization

Beyond the initial installation, advanced configuration optimizes Crossplane for large-scale or complex deployments:

- **Horizontal Pod Autoscaling**: Implement auto-scaling for Crossplane pods to automatically adapt to changing management workloads.

- **Namespace Isolation**: Use separate namespaces to isolate different environments (like production and development) ensuring safer swim lanes between environments and clear resource separation.

- **GitOps Integration**: Integrate Crossplane deployment with GitOps practices using tools like ArgoCD or Flux. This streamlines continuous deployment of infrastructure configurations alongside applications.

Setting up Crossplane in a Kubernetes cluster represents a strategic move towards more fluid and dynamic infrastructure management, leveraging the paradigms of Infrastructure as Code (IaC) within Kubernetes' ecosystem. Through this section, the installation journey unveils processes that establish a foundation for managing cloud resources in a scalable, consistent, and secure manner. While setting up might seem procedural, the consistency and cohesion it brings to cloud resource orchestration considerably enhance operational efficiencies and developmental cohesiveness, paving the way for enriched cloud-native applications and services.

3.3 Crossplane Providers

Crossplane Providers play a crucial role in the architecture of Crossplane by acting as the interface between Kubernetes and cloud service APIs. Providers seamlessly enable cloud resource management within a Kubernetes environment by encapsulating the details of different cloud services, exposing them through Kubernetes-native APIs. This architecture abstracts the complexity inherent in managing multiple cloud resources, translating Kubernetes operations into actions on cloud services. The extensibility and modularity provided by Crossplane are largely attributed to these providers, making them central to its functionality. This section delves into the concept of providers in Crossplane, offering a comprehensive understanding of their setup, operation, and the advantages they bring to cloud resource management.

Understanding Crossplane Providers

At a high level, providers in Crossplane are packages that extend Crossplane's capabilities to interact with cloud services. Each provider is responsible for translating API calls from Crossplane into actions on the respective cloud platform, ensuring that infrastructure resources are provisioned, configured, maintained, and deleted according to the defined system state. Providers can be considered as plugins that empower Crossplane's control plane to perform CRUD operations (Create, Read, Update, Delete) on cloud resources.

Providers support an extensive range of cloud services from leading cloud vendors such as AWS, Google Cloud Platform (GCP), Microsoft Azure, and others, as well as on-premises systems or even specialized services like Alibaba Cloud. By leveraging these providers, Crossplane can serve as a control plane for a diverse cloud ecosystem, providing uniform management capabilities across heterogeneous cloud resources.

A key feature of Crossplane providers is versioning, which enables users to select specific versions of providers that match their needs, ensuring compatibility with various APIs and features that a cloud vendor might offer.

Installing a Crossplane Provider

The procedure for installing a Crossplane provider involves adding a provider package, configuring its credentials, and applying the necessary configurations in the form of Kubernetes Custom Resource Definitions. The example below walks through installing and initializing the AWS provider.

Step 1: Install the Provider

First, install the AWS provider using Crossplane's package manager interface. This package equips Crossplane with the capacity to manage AWS services.

```
kubectl crossplane install provider crossplane/provider-aws:v0.20.2
```

The command fetches the specified version of the AWS provider and installs it into the `crossplane-system` namespace of the Kubernetes cluster. This installation creates the required CRDs that represent AWS resources within Crossplane.

Step 2: Provider Configuration

To authorize Crossplane to access AWS services, configure the necessary credentials. These credentials usually follow the AWS IAM paradigm, stored as Kubernetes secrets.

- Create an IAM user in AWS with permissions to manage AWS resources. Generate an access key ID and secret access key for this user.

- Store Credentials in a Kubernetes Secret:

```
apiVersion: v1
kind: Secret
metadata:
  name: aws-credentials
  namespace: crossplane-system
type: Opaque
data:
  credentials: <BASE64_ENCODED_AWS_JSON_CREDENTIALS>
```

Encode the JSON credentials file using base64 encoding to fill the credentials field.

- Define a ProviderConfig Resource:

Link the credentials to the AWS provider in Crossplane through a ProviderConfig resource.

```
apiVersion: aws.crossplane.io/v1beta1
kind: ProviderConfig
metadata:
  name: default
spec:
  credentials:
    source: Secret
    secretRef:
      namespace: crossplane-system
      name: aws-credentials
      key: credentials
```

The ProviderConfig resource contains metadata that ties the Kubernetes secret to Crossplane, enabling interaction with AWS services.

Interacting with Crossplane Providers

Once a provider is installed and configured, Crossplane users can define cloud services using custom resource definitions (CRDs) that the provider installs. Providers translate Kubernetes-native operations into cloud platform API interactions transparently, simplifying resource management significantly.

Example: Provisioning an RDS Instance with AWS Provider

Using the AWS provider, provision an RDS instance with a YAML configuration:

```
apiVersion: database.aws.crossplane.io/v1beta1
kind: DBInstance
metadata:
  name: example-rds
spec:
  forProvider:
    dbInstanceClass: db.t3.micro
    engine: postgres
    masterUsername: masteruser
```

3.3. CROSSPLANE PROVIDERS

```
    masterUserPasswordSecretRef:
      name: rds-password
      key: password
    writeConnectionSecretToRef:
      name: db-conn-info
    providerConfigRef:
      name: default
```

- Define the RDS resource: This YAML configuration creates an RDS instance with specified properties, such as engine type and instance class.

- Manage secrets: Store sensitive information like passwords in Kubernetes secrets, referenced in the RDS configuration.

- Apply the configuration: Use kubectl to apply the configuration, which instructs Crossplane to communicate with AWS and provision the desired RDS instance.

```
kubectl apply -f rds-instance.yaml
```

Provider Advantages and Considerations

Crossplane providers offer numerous advantages to DevOps and platform engineering teams:

- Unified Management: Providers convert multiple cloud APIs into a single Kubernetes-native API, enabling unified management of multi-cloud resources.

- Scalability: Providers let Crossplane scale cloud service orchestration along with application workloads in a highly efficient manner.

- Policy Enforcement: Providers can encapsulate policy parameters and governance rules within configuration objects, ensuring compliant resource provisioning.

- Extensibility: Organizations can develop custom providers, tailoring Crossplane interactions with in-house APIs or specific third-party services.

- **Community and Support:** Providers are actively supported and continuously improved by the Crossplane community, ensuring relevance and adaptability to cloud developments.

When employing providers, it is crucial to consider security and version compatibility:

- **Access Controls:** Employ strict IAM permissions and role-based access controls to limit provider capabilities to necessary operations.
- **Versioning:** Manage provider updates cautiously, verifying that new versions retain compatibility with existing configurations and workflows.

Crossplane providers constitute the backbone of Crossplane's cloud resource management capabilities, empowering Kubernetes to manage a broad spectrum of services across multiple cloud environments. By enabling providers, Crossplane delivers unprecedented control, scalability, and efficiency to cloud-native organizations. Understanding how providers operate and capitalizing on their capabilities allows teams to streamline operations, enforce policies, and enhance agility in managing ever-evolving cloud landscapes. This detailed exploration of Crossplane providers elucidates the pivotal role they play in consolidating cloud management under a unified, Kubernetes-native control interface.

3.4 Configuring Crossplane Workloads

Configuring workloads in Crossplane involves deploying and managing cloud infrastructure services in a declarative manner using Kubernetes-native APIs. Crossplane extends Kubernetes beyond container orchestration, enabling it to configure and manage a wide array of cloud services as workloads. This capability provides a seamless user experience for platform operators who aim to manage both application and infrastructure lifecycles. In this section, we explore how to effectively configure Crossplane workloads, offering insights into the configuration of infrastructure resources, their lifecycle management, and best practices for optimized performance and security.

Understanding Crossplane Workloads

In the Crossplane ecosystem, workloads encapsulate not only application components but also the cloud resources they rely on. This involves creating and managing resources like databases, message queues, storage solutions, networks, and more, as first-class citizens along with Kubernetes services and deployments. Crossplane uses Kubernetes Custom Resources (CRs) to represent these cloud infrastructure elements, establishing a consistent interface for defining and managing them.

By leveraging its providers and configuration tools, Crossplane translates workload definitions into concrete cloud infrastructure setups, effectively handling the orchestration, scaling, and decommissioning of these resources as part of application lifecycles.

Configuring Workloads with Compositions

Crossplane introduces the concept of Compositions, which abstracts the lower-level cloud resources into higher-level, reusable resource types. Compositions enable the creation of tailored templates fitting various use cases, encapsulating best practices and compliance necessities in the infrastructure configuration.

Step-by-Step Guide to Configuring a Simple Workload Using Compositions

Let's create and configure a workload using Compositions to provision a database service and an S3 bucket concurrently.

Step 1: Define a CompositeResourceDefinition (XRD)

A CompositeResourceDefinition declares a new composite resource type that organizes multiple granular resources under a unified abstraction. Here's an example XRD for a CompositePostgreSQLInstance.

```
apiVersion: apiextensions.crossplane.io/v1
kind: CompositeResourceDefinition
```

```
metadata:
  name: compositepostgresqlinstances.db.example.org
spec:
  group: db.example.org
  names:
    kind: CompositePostgreSQLInstance
    plural: compositepostgresqlinstances
  versions:
  - name: v1alpha1
    served: true
    referenceable: true
    schema:
      openAPIV3Schema:
        type: object
        properties:
          spec:
            type: object
            properties:
              parameters:
                type: object
                properties:
                  version:
                    type: string
                  storageGB:
                    type: integer
```

Step 2: Define a Composition Resource

A Composition specifies how composite resources should be instantiated into concrete underlying resources. For our PostgreSQL example, it might look like this:

```
apiVersion: apiextensions.crossplane.io/v1
kind: Composition
metadata:
  name: postgresql-and-s3
spec:
  compositeTypeRef:
    apiVersion: db.example.org/v1alpha1
    kind: CompositePostgreSQLInstance
  resources:
  - name: postgresqlinstance
    base:
      apiVersion: database.aws.crossplane.io/v1beta1
      kind: RDSInstance
      spec:
        forProvider:
          dbInstanceClass: db.t3.micro
          allocatedStorage: 20
          engineVersion: 13.3
  - name: s3bucket
    base:
      apiVersion: s3.aws.crossplane.io/v1beta1
      kind: Bucket
      spec:
        forProvider:
```

```
      locationConstraint: us-west-2
```

Step 3: Create an Instance of the CompositeResource

With the XRD and Composition in place, users can provision the resource using the composite resource, which Crossplane then translates into the underlying AWS RDS and S3 services.

```
apiVersion: db.example.org/v1alpha1
kind: CompositePostgreSQLInstance
metadata:
  name: example-database
spec:
  compositionSelector:
    matchLabels:
      providers: postgresql-and-s3
  parameters:
    version: "13.3"
    storageGB: 20
```

Resource Management and Operational Considerations

Declarative configuration of workloads via Crossplane provides multiple operational benefits such as easy rollback, consistency, and reproducibility. As configurations are central to successful deployments, users should take note of several key areas:

- **Version Control:** Maintain all configuration files under version control systems to track changes, mitigate errors, and collaborate seamlessly across teams.

- **Parameterization:** Utilize environment-specific configurations and templating techniques to parameterize resources within Compositions for flexible deployment across development, staging, and production environments without the need to manually alter YAML files.

- **Monitoring and Observability:** Integrate with observability stacks to monitor lifecycle events within the Crossplane environment, allowing quick identification and resolution of performance or configuration issues.

Best Practices for Configuring Crossplane Workloads

These best practices enhance workload deployment, operational efficiency, and governance structures:

- **Security:** Strictly manage access and credentials used within workloads. Utilize Kubernetes secrets and encrypt sensitive information.

- **Resource Optimization:** Align workload characteristics with cloud service specifications to optimize for cost, performance, and scalability.

- **Automation Pipelines:** Innovate CI/CD pipelines to continuously deploy and update infrastructure components as part of automated workflows, ensuring robust infrastructure resilience and agility.

- **Recovery:** Implement backup and recovery strategies within configuration scripts to safeguard critical data and facilitate rapid recovery from unsuccessful deployments or disruptions.

Crossplane's infrastructure-as-code capabilities significantly enhance the method of configuring workloads within cloud-native environments. Through resource abstraction, Compositions streamline infrastructure management, reinforcing policies, efficiency, and automation in one coherent approach. Utilizing Crossplane to orchestrate infrastructure services directly via Kubernetes leads to seamless application development and operations, providing a holistic view of applications and resources that support them. By leveraging Crossplane's powerful configuration model, organizations foster a future-proof operational strategy designed to adapt and cater to dynamic infrastructure landscapes.

3.5 Declarative Infrastructure Management

Declarative infrastructure management is a core principle in modern cloud environments, enabling organizations to define the intended state of their infrastructure through high-level declarations rather than procedural scripts. Crossplane advances this concept by extending

3.5. DECLARATIVE INFRASTRUCTURE MANAGEMENT

Kubernetes' declarative approach to cloud infrastructure, allowing diverse cloud resources to be managed alongside applications within a unified, coherent framework. Through this section, we explore the significance, methodologies, advantages, and practical implementation of declarative infrastructure management using Crossplane.

The Essence of Declarative Infrastructure Management

Declarative infrastructure management revolves around defining the desired state of infrastructure through configurations that the system autonomously realizes. Unlike imperative approaches, which require detailed step-by-step instructions, declarative models simplify resource management by abstracting away the complexity of changing and maintaining infrastructure states to match these declarations.

Crossplane leverages this paradigm by introducing everything-as-code capabilities that manage a variety of cloud services using Kubernetes Custom Resource Definitions (CRDs). This enables cloud native infrastructure to remain consistent, scalable, and easy to manage, crucial for the rapid growth and demand dynamics of modern cloud applications.

Crossplane and the Declarative Model

Crossplane utilizes Kubernetes Custom Resources to define cloud infrastructure components declaratively. Here's how Crossplane incorporates declarative management techniques:

Fundamental Concepts

- **Custom Resource Definitions (CRDs):** These serve as schema specifications for each unique type of resource you wish to manage. CRDs extend Kubernetes with additional resource kinds, representing specific infrastructure components such as databases, caches, network configurations, or any service provided by a cloud provider.

- **Control Loops:** Crossplane's controllers continuously reconcile the actual state with the desired state declared in Kubernetes resources. This ensures that any drift from the required configuration is corrected autonomously.
- **Compositions and Templates:** Compositions abstract away the complexity of resource definitions by allowing higher-level resources to be defined through templates. These templates consolidate multiple resources into reusable, shareable configurations.

Implementing a Declarative Model with Crossplane

A declarative infrastructure management model within Crossplane consists of defining the desired state in YAML files, applying these configurations, and leveraging Crossplane to enact these declarations.

Example: Provisioning a Scalable Web Application

Consider a scenario where you are required to deploy a scalable web application that consists of a front-end service, a backend API, and a database.

Step 1: Define Infrastructure as Code

Define Kubernetes resources representing each component of the application architecture. This involves the deployment of managed cloud databases, Kubernetes-managed deployments, and load balancers.

Define a MySQL Database

```
apiVersion: database.crossplane.io/v1alpha1
kind: MySQLInstance
metadata:
  name: example-mysql
spec:
  forProvider:
    version: "5.7"
    region: us-west-2
    storageType: standard
```

3.5. DECLARATIVE INFRASTRUCTURE MANAGEMENT

```
    storageCapacity: 20Gi
  providerConfigRef:
    name: aws-provider
```

Define Backend Deployment

```
apiVersion: apps/v1
kind: Deployment
metadata:
  name: backend-api
spec:
  replicas: 3
  selector:
    matchLabels:
      app: api
  template:
    metadata:
      labels:
        app: api
    spec:
      containers:
      - name: api-container
        image: example/api:latest
        ports:
        - containerPort: 8080
```

Define LoadBalancer Service

```
apiVersion: v1
kind: Service
metadata:
  name: web-service
spec:
  type: LoadBalancer
  ports:
  - port: 80
  selector:
    app: web
```

Step 2: Apply the Configurations

Using `kubectl`, apply each YAML configuration file to the Kubernetes cluster. Crossplane manages the infrastructure provisioning, while Kubernetes handles the service deployments.

```
kubectl apply -f mysql-instance.yaml
kubectl apply -f backend-deployment.yaml
```

```
kubectl apply -f loadbalancer-service.yaml
```

Benefits of Declarative Infrastructure Management

- **Consistency and Reproducibility:** Declarative configurations ensure that environments can be recreated reliably, maintaining consistency across deployments and scaling operations.

- **Abstraction of Complexity:** By defining the desired end state, Crossplane abstracts the complexity of interfacing with individual cloud service APIs, making infrastructure management both efficient and streamlined.

- **Reduced Operational Overhead:** The reconciliation loops manage state drift automatically, reducing the manual intervention typically required in reactive maintenance approaches.

- **Change Auditing and Governance:** The version-controlled infrastructure declarations provide an immutable history of changes. This transparency supports compliance and governance initiatives.

Challenges and Mitigation Strategies

While declarative infrastructure management offers substantial benefits, several challenges can emerge:

- **Complexity in Configuration Management:** Though configurations are simplified, large-scale systems may accumulate numerous YAML files. Adopting structured directories and effective templating can mitigate this.

- **Initial Learning Curve:** Understanding CRD and Crossplane's reconciliation models necessitate initial learning. Investments in training and documentation contribute to faster ramp-up times.

- **Version Management:** Aligning infrastructure declarations with software versions requires discipline in managing configuration repositories. Semantic versioning and label referencing in Kubernetes can address these needs.

The Role of GitOps in Declarative Management

GitOps practices align closely with a declarative infrastructure model by emphasizing Git as the source of truth for infrastructure configurations. With GitOps, any proposed change initiates from a git repository, followed by automated deployment pipelines that propagate these changes to the infrastructure, effectively closing the loop on continuous delivery.

Integrating Crossplane with GitOps can be accomplished by leveraging tools such as ArgoCD or Flux, which automate the application of Kubernetes configurations sourced from repositories. This integration enhances deployment consistency, rollback capabilities, and operational transparency.

Crossplane stands as a powerful instrument in governance, providing an ecosystem where infrastructure configuration dovetails seamlessly with cloud-native applications across diverse cloud environments. Its alignment with declarative infrastructure management reflects a dramatic shift toward more predictable, reliable, and efficient cloud operations. Through expert use of Crossplane's declarative model, organizations can reduce complexity, improve agility, and achieve significant operational efficiencies. This facilitates an empowered DevOps culture that fully leverages the potential that cloud technologies offer.

3.6 Crossplane API and Extensibility

Crossplane's API architecture is pivotal to its functionality and extensibility, empowering developers and platform engineers to efficiently manage cloud resources through declarative Kubernetes interfaces.

Crossplane extends Kubernetes API to interact natively with diverse cloud service providers, presenting itself as a seamless extension to the Kubernetes control plane. Moreover, its extensibility facilitates rapid customization and integration of new services and configurations, adapting to evolving cloud technologies and business needs. This section delves into the architectural framework, components, and methods for extending Crossplane, equipping users to leverage and expand Crossplane's capabilities effectively.

Understanding Crossplane API Architecture

Crossplane's architectural approach focuses on enhancing Kubernetes with additional API resources, known as Custom Resource Definitions (CRDs). These CRDs are synthesized by Providers, acting as translators or drivers for diverse cloud service APIs. Below is the architectural rundown of how Crossplane operates:

Core Components

- **Custom Resource Definitions (CRDs):** These encapsulate the schema and validation rules for the new resource types introduced by Crossplane. Through CRDs, users define desired cloud resources in a declarative format.

- **Controllers:** Controllers are specialized looped processes that observe CRDs and ensure that the desired state expressed in them aligns with the actual state of the resources. They implement the reconciliation logic, adjusting underlying resources as needed.

- **Providers:** Providers are extensions (often analogous to plug-ins) that connect Crossplane to external APIs of specific cloud services. Each provider supports a set of resources based on its targeted cloud environment.

- **Compositions:** Compositions allow resource abstraction and consolidation, empowering users to define complex infrastructures from simpler building blocks, encapsulating resource configurations, and propagating reusable templates.

- **Crossplane Runtime:** The operational backbone managing and scheduling controllers, observing Kubernetes API server to detect changes or updates to resources, and triggering processes accordingly.

Extensibility through Providers

Crossplane's extensible nature is predominantly manifested through Providers. Each Provider extends Crossplane with the capability to support a new set of resources from a given cloud service. The creation and deployment of custom Providers allow enterprises to bring in unique services or adapt existing ones, optimizing Crossplane usage for their specific needs.

Creating a Custom Provider

Developing a custom provider necessitates understanding both Crossplane's architecture and the cloud API you aim to integrate. Below is a streamlined process for creating a custom provider:

Step 1: Define Your Custom Resource and Loom Up Scaffolding

The Custom Resource Definition will represent the new resource.

```
apiVersion: apiextensions.crossplane.io/v1
kind: CustomResourceDefinition
metadata:
  name: examples.example.com
spec:
  group: example.com
  versions:
  - name: v1alpha1
    served: true
    schema:
      openAPIV3Schema:
        type: object
        properties:
          spec:
            type: object
```

Step 2: Implement Controller Logic

The controller manages the lifecycle of the custom resources. It should establish connections and manage communication with the specific cloud service API.

```
package main
import (
    "sigs.k8s.io/controller-runtime/pkg/manager"
)
func main() {
    // Initiate the manager and start the controller
    mgr, err := manager.New(...)
    // Implement reconciliation logic
}
```

Implement appropriate CRUD functions within the controller to translate CRD requests into cloud provider API calls.

Step 3: Deploy the Provider

Package and deploy your custom provider using the same Helm configurations adopted for other providers.

```
kubectl crossplane install provider crossplane/provider-example:v0.1.0
```

Enhancing Extensibility

With Crossplane's open API framework, the integration and configuration are bounded only by the cloud service APIs it connects to. This flexibility facilitates several key strategies:

- **Versioning and Upgrades:** Providers can have multiple versions, enabling gradual upgrade paths and compatibility with cloud service evolutions.

- **Edge Cases and Custom Logic:** Developing custom reconciliations for niche use cases or specific service interactions not covered by generic providers.

- **Community Engagement:** Extensible by nature, Crossplane thrives on community contributions to its library of providers, promoting shared knowledge and rapid advancement.

API Features for Advanced Management

Crossplane's advanced API features enable precise management of infrastructure states and resources:

- **Field Selectors and Labels:** Query and filter resources based on criteria to facilitate automated workflows and selective processing.

- **Resource Policies:** Implement governance policies through resource settings, maintaining compliance and operational standards.

- **Multi-tenancy Support:** Through namespace scoping and RBAC, facilitate multi-tenant environments where isolated infrastructure segments are managed independently through shared Crossplane systems.

Advantages of Crossplane's API Model

- **Cohesion with Kubernetes:** As Crossplane integrates into Kubernetes itself, it offers a unified interface that standardizes cloud resource management alongside ongoing application workflows.

- **Scalability:** By relying on Kubernetes' mature orchestration capabilities, Crossplane scales with the requirements of the infrastructure, providing elastic management of bursting, shrinking, or changing workloads.

- **Portable Abstractions:** By abstracting cloud service interactions, organizations are more agile in transitioning providers or supporting multi-cloud deployments without extensive re-engineering efforts.

- **Agility with Composable Infrastructure:** Rapid evolution of infrastructure landscapes becomes feasible due to Compositions that construct infrastructure templates dynamically, allowing users to derive new compositions from existing primitives.

Integrating Crossplane with Existing Toolchains

As Crossplane serves developers and operators alike, its integration with CI/CD pipelines is pivotal in automating infrastructure lifecycle management:

- **Implementing GitOps Flows:** Crossplane seamlessly integrates with GitOps tools to automate deployments and updates from source-control platforms.

- **Collaboration with Service Meshes:** Enhance network-level configurations with service meshes to optimize application communication across composite infrastructures.

- **DevSecOps Integration:** Integrate guarding and monitoring tools within the Crossplane deployment pipeline to enforce compliance and review, assuring secure, resilient environments.

The extensibility of Crossplane's API transforms infrastructural management within Kubernetes-enabled systems, ushering a comprehensive approach to engage and extend cloud resource configurations. With an ever-growing library of providers and composition models, Crossplane facilitates dynamic, repeatable, and controlled resource management in a scalable manner. Through its versatility and integrations, Crossplane assures that adopting cohesive cloud management strategies aligns with both existing operations and future ambitions. As Crossplane API and extensibility encourage innovation, they promote a proactive engagement with modern cloud operations, reinforcing a leading-edge posture towards digital infrastructure advancement.

3.7 Troubleshooting Common Issues

In managing infrastructure with Crossplane, users may encounter various challenges that stem from configuration discrepancies, provider-specific constraints, or integration complexities within a Kubernetes environment. Systematically troubleshooting these issues is essential to ensure resilient and efficient cloud operations. This section provides detailed insights into common problems encountered in Crossplane deployments, each accompanied by diagnostic methods and pragmatic solutions to address them effectively. By adopting a structured troubleshooting approach, administrators can enhance the reliability and performance of infrastructure orchestration.

Integration with Kubernetes and Environment Readiness

Problem: Cluster Preparation

Ensure the Kubernetes cluster is correctly configured to accommodate Crossplane. Issues can arise from insufficient resources, inadequate permissions, or incompatible Kubernetes versions.

Solution and Diagnostic Steps:

- Verify the cluster nodes and their availability by using:
  ```
  kubectl get nodes
  ```

- Confirm Kubernetes version compatibility with Crossplane requirements:
  ```
  kubectl version --short
  ```

- Check resource quotas and limits in your namespace to ensure sufficient capacity for Crossplane's components:
  ```
  kubectl describe namespace crossplane-system
  ```

- Analyze pod and service statuses post-installation:
  ```
  kubectl get pods -n crossplane-system
  ```

Problem: Helm Installation Errors

Crossplane is frequently installed through Helm, and installation issues can result in incorrect configurations or incomplete setups.

Solution and Diagnostic Steps:

- Ensure Helm is up to date using:

```
helm version
```

- Ensure adequate permissions by confirming 'kubectl' can manage cluster roles and permissions:

```
kubectl auth can-i create clusterrole --as=system:admin
```

- Debug Helm installations by running with verbose logging:

```
helm install crossplane crossplane-master/crossplane --namespace crossplane-system --debug
```

Provider Configuration and Secret Management

Problem: Incorrect Provider Credentials

Credentials used within providers must match permissions required for intended operations. An incorrect setup can lead to authorization failures.

Solution and Diagnostic Steps:

- Validate that provider credentials have the necessary permissions scoped by IAM policies (in AWS) or relevant configuration in other cloud systems.

- Examine the configured Kubernetes secrets for key errors or mismatches:

```
kubectl describe secret aws-provider-creds -n crossplane-system
```

- Re-encode credentials to validate correct Base64 encoding:

```
echo -n 'YOUR_JSON' | base64
```

Problem: Secret Reference Errors in Configurations

3.7. TROUBLESHOOTING COMMON ISSUES

Errors may arise if secret references in Crossplane resource manifests are incorrect or unavailable in the specified namespace.

Solution and Diagnostic Steps:

- Check that the secret referenced exists and matches the names or keys specified in configurations:

```
kubectl get secret -n crossplane-system
```

- Confirm Secret was correctly created from valid credentials:

```
apiVersion: v1
kind: Secret
metadata:
  name: aws-credentials
  namespace: crossplane-system
type: Opaque
data:
  credentials: <BASE64_ENCODED_JSON>
```

Reconciliation Loops and Resource States

Problem: Stalled Resource Creation or Deletion

When controllers fail to reconcile desired states, resources remain pending, preventing further actions.

Solution and Diagnostic Steps:

- Investigate controller logs for errors in resource creation or update attempts:

```
kubectl logs deploy/crossplane -n crossplane-system
```

- Use Events to identify issues pushed during reconciliation attempts:

```
kubectl describe <resource> -n <namespace>
```

- Ensure governance and policy restrictions do not block resource actions, particularly in corporate or secured cloud environments.

API and Custom Resource Management

Problem: CRD Schema Conflicts

Errors can occur when CRDs conflict with existing schemas or are improperly updated during migrations or version changes.

Solution and Diagnostic Steps:

- Ensure CRDs are installed and correctly configured for the intended API version:
  ```
  kubectl get crds
  ```

- Validate the syntactical correctness of CRDs by checking manifest and YAML integrity:
  ```
  kubectl apply -f crds.yaml --validate=true
  ```

Problem: Custom Resource Constraints

Custom resources can fail if they become inconsistent with controller expectations or valid states defined by the provider.

Solution and Diagnostic Steps:

- Track the lifecycle and status messages of custom resources:
  ```
  kubectl get <crd> -n <namespace>
  kubectl describe <crd> -n <namespace>
  ```

- Cross-reference custom resource configurations against provider-specific documentation, ensuring all mandatory fields and relationships are satisfied.

Enhancing Reliable Operations

Optimizing Crossplane for robust operations involves continuous validation and monitoring strategies alongside troubleshooting tactics.

Monitoring and Logging

- Utilize existing Kubernetes monitoring setups (Prometheus, Grafana) to visualize Crossplane operational metrics, recognizing deviations or unusual activities rapidly.

- Implement log aggregation (e.g., using Elasticsearch) to consolidate logs across providers, Crossplane, and Kubernetes for comprehensive situational awareness.

3.7. TROUBLESHOOTING COMMON ISSUES

Implementing Auditing and Governance

- Activate auditing logs to track critical changes, especially actions affecting multi-cloud environments governed through Crossplane.

- Maintain distinct environments (dev/test/prod) and enforce role-based access controls (RBAC) to limit privilege escalation and accidental disruptions.

Effectively resolving common issues in Crossplane demands a structured approach, keen attention to provider integration nuances, and persistent observability over deployed systems. By implementing these diagnostic strategies, operators can anticipate potential pitfalls, optimize responses to unforeseen events, and maintain stable, high-performance infrastructure deployments over extended scales and diverse environments. Testing and continual iteration on these practices ensure Crossplane remains a reliable asset within the Kubernetes ecosystem, enacting cloud management in innovative, adaptive ways that align with evolving organizational ambitions.

Chapter 4

Provisioning Cloud Resources with Crossplane

Crossplane empowers users to provision and manage cloud resources across multiple providers using Kubernetes-centric, declarative configurations. By leveraging Crossplane, infrastructure components such as compute, storage, and networking resources are defined and managed as code, promoting consistency, repeatability, and scalability. Users can define resource compositions to create reusable infrastructure templates, simplifying complex deployment scenarios. Crossplane providers bridge the gap between Kubernetes and cloud services, dynamically provisioning resources based on Kubernetes API interactions. Understanding how to effectively configure and utilize Crossplane to automate cloud resource provisioning enables seamless infrastructure management and enhances operational efficiency in multi-cloud environments.

4.1 Setting Up Cloud Credentials

Crossplane facilitates the management and provisioning of cloud resources across various cloud service providers via a Kubernetes-native approach. To leverage these capabilities, the initial requirement is the proper configuration of cloud credentials. This setup is crucial as it allows Crossplane to authenticate and authorize operations with your cloud provider(s). When configuring cloud credentials, users must ensure secure, efficient, and compliant practices.

Crossplane supports several major cloud providers, each with its method for credential configuration. At a high level, this process involves the creation of a Kubernetes secret that contains your cloud provider's credentials. Crossplane then references this secret to perform operations on your behalf.

To understand the cloud credential setting process thoroughly, it is essential to dissect this into clear steps for various providers. Detailed configurations for Amazon Web Services (AWS), Google Cloud Platform (GCP), and Microsoft Azure are elaborated below.

Configuring AWS Credentials

Amazon Web Services require an access key ID and a secret access key for programmatic access. Begin by navigating to the AWS Management Console and proceeding to the Identity and Access Management (IAM) section:

- **Create an IAM User**:
    - Open the IAM section and create a new user.
    - Assign a suitable name and grant programmatic access, which will enable access via an access key.
    - Attach necessary permissions or opt to use existing policies, such as 'AmazonEC2FullAccess' for compute resources or more specific policies as required.

- **Retrieve Access Credentials**:
    - Upon creating the user, AWS provides an access key ID and a secret access key. Secure these credentials; they will not be retrievable later.

4.1. SETTING UP CLOUD CREDENTIALS

- **Create Kubernetes Secret**:

  – Use the following configuration to create a Kubernetes secret in your cluster:

```
kubectl create secret generic aws-creds -n crossplane-system \
  --from-literal=credentials="[default]
aws_access_key_id=<YOUR_ACCESS_KEY_ID>
aws_secret_access_key=<YOUR_SECRET_ACCESS_KEY>"
```

Replace <YOUR_ACCESS_KEY_ID> and <YOUR_SECRET_ACCESS_KEY> with the actual credentials obtained from AWS.

Configuring GCP Credentials

For Google Cloud Platform, you will need a service account with a JSON key file. The setup process involves creating this account and assigning appropriate roles to ensure the required permissions:

- **Create a Service Account**:

  – Navigate to the GCP Console and access the IAM & Admin section.

  – Create a new service account and assign roles based on the resources you will manage. For instance, 'Cloud SQL Admin' for managing databases.

- **Generate a Key File**:

  – After creating the service account, download the JSON-format key file, which contains necessary credentials.

- **Create Kubernetes Secret**:

  – Use the key file to create a Kubernetes secret as shown:

```
kubectl create secret generic gcp-creds -n crossplane-system \
  --from-file=credentials.json=<PATH_TO_KEY_FILE>
```

Replace <PATH_TO_KEY_FILE> with the path to your downloaded JSON key file.

Configuring Azure Credentials

Azure uses an App Registration to create a service principal, which then provides necessary credentials:

- **Create an App Registration**:
    - Access Azure Active Directory and create a new registration.
    - Record the Application (Client) ID and Directory (Tenant) ID.
- **Generate a Client Secret**:
    - In the app registration screen, create a new client secret. Securely store the generated value.
- **Assign Roles**:
    - Under your subscription settings, assign appropriate roles (e.g., 'Contributor') to your service principal.
- **Create Kubernetes Secret**:
    - Store credentials within Kubernetes as follows:

```
kubectl create secret generic azure-creds -n crossplane-system \
  --from-literal=clientId=<APPLICATION_ID> \
  --from-literal=clientSecret=<CLIENT_SECRET> \
  --from-literal=tenantId=<TENANT_ID>
```

Replace placeholders with your respective application ID, client secret, and tenant ID.

Adhering to Security Practices

Securing your cloud credentials is paramount. Here are some recommended security practices:

- **Least Privilege Principle**: Assign only necessary permissions and roles to cloud credentials. Avoid granting excessive permissions that expand potential exploit avenues.
- **Credential Rotation**: Periodically rotate your credentials to reduce the risk from breached keys. Employ automated processes if possible.

- **Secrets Encryption**: Leverage Kubernetes features to encrypt secrets at rest. Also, ensure that your cluster incorporates appropriate access controls.

- **Audit and Monitoring**: Implement logging and monitoring to detect any unauthorized use of credentials. Cloud platforms offer audit tools that can alert on suspicious activities.

Handling Multiple Cloud Provider Credentials

With Crossplane's multi-cloud capabilities, users often integrate with multiple providers simultaneously. Kubernetes namespaces can help organize credentials:

- Store each provider's credentials in a separate namespace.

- Leverage Role-Based Access Control (RBAC) to manage access by defining roles and role bindings that grant necessary permissions to service accounts across namespaces.

By efficiently organizing credentials, system administrators can maintain a structured and secure environment, reducing the risks associated with multi-provider deployments.

Integrating with Crossplane Provider Configurations

Once secrets are in place, the next step involves setting up Crossplane provider configurations. These configurations let Crossplane connect to different cloud services using the credentials stored in Kubernetes secrets:

- **Create Provider Configurations**:
    - Crossplane uses CustomResourceDefinitions (CRDs) to handle provider configurations.
    - Define a ProviderConfig for each cloud provider, referencing the Kubernetes secrets.

Example for AWS ProviderConfig:

```
apiVersion: aws.crossplane.io/v1beta1
kind: ProviderConfig
metadata:
  name: aws-provider
spec:
  credentials:
    source: Secret
    secretRef:
      namespace: crossplane-system
      name: aws-creds
      key: credentials
```

Example for GCP ProviderConfig:

```
apiVersion: gcp.crossplane.io/v1beta1
kind: ProviderConfig
metadata:
  name: gcp-provider
spec:
  credentials:
    source: Secret
    secretRef:
      namespace: crossplane-system
      name: gcp-creds
      key: credentials.json
```

Example for Azure ProviderConfig:

```
apiVersion: azure.crossplane.io/v1beta1
kind: ProviderConfig
metadata:
  name: azure-provider
spec:
  credentials:
    source: Secret
    secretRef:
      namespace: crossplane-system
      name: azure-creds
      key: tenantId
```

As Crossplane reads the provider configurations and interacts with the appropriate cloud providers, it translates the declarative infrastructure manifests into API calls specific to each cloud service. This efficient translation ensures seamless operations while maintaining the desired state of resources.

Understanding how to set up cloud credentials for Crossplane is foundational for utilizing its capabilities in provisioning and managing cloud infrastructure. Through precise configuration of cloud service credentials within Kubernetes, Crossplane achieves a seamless integration that enhances operational efficiency across diverse cloud environments. As organizations move towards multi-cloud strategies, mastering the setup of credentials not only ensures secure interactions but also paves the way for robust, scalable, and controlled infrastructure management.

4.2 Understanding Crossplane Compositions

Crossplane introduces a novel approach to cloud infrastructure management through its notion of Compositions. This powerful concept allows developers to define, manage, and reuse infrastructure configurations in a declarative manner, fostering an agile and adaptable infrastructure-as-code (IaC) environment. Understanding Crossplane Compositions is integral for leveraging its full potential to automate and streamline the management of diverse cloud services.

At its core, a Composition in Crossplane is a template for cloud resources that can be instantiated with varying parameters. It allows infrastructure teams to delineate complex structures, encapsulating best practices while promoting consistency across deployments. Fundamentally, Compositions abstract resource configurations into reusable templates, which can then be instantiated with Composite Resource Claims. This encapsulation is analogous to abstracting details in software engineering, providing a higher-level interface for users.

The Structure of Compositions

Compositions are defined using YAML, specifying both the desired resources and the transformations required to instantiate them. The definition broadly consists of:

- **Composite Resource Definitions (XRDs)**: They define a new custom resource type, describing how users consume the Composition.

- **Compositions**: Templates that describe how to create and manage the actual resources defined by an XRD.

The lifecycle of a Composition begins with the definition of an XRD, followed by the configuration of the Composition itself, and concludes with the instantiation through claims.

Defining a Composite Resource

The first step in using Compositions is to define an XRD. An XRD specifies the schema for resources managed by Crossplane and serves as the blueprint for infrastructure components.

```
apiVersion: apiextensions.crossplane.io/v1
kind: CompositeResourceDefinition
metadata:
  name: compositeresources.aws.crossplane.io
spec:
  group: aws.crossplane.io
  names:
    kind: CompositeAWSResource
    plural: compositeresources
  claimNames:
    kind: AWSResourceClaim
    plural: awsresourceclaims
  connectionSecretKeys:
  - endpoint
  - username
  - password
```

In this example, the CompositeAWSResource kind represents a custom resource that users will interact with. It outlines necessary connection secrets that will supply credentials and endpoint information for accessing the resource.

Creating a Composition

Once an XRD is defined, the next step is to create a Composition that specifies how the XRD should manifest resources:

```
apiVersion: v1
kind: Composition
metadata:
  name: compositeawsresource-composite
spec:
  compositeTypeRef:
    apiVersion: aws.crossplane.io/v1
    kind: CompositeAWSResource
  resources:
  - base:
      apiVersion: ec2.aws.crossplane.io/v1beta1
      kind: VPC
      spec:
        forProvider:
          cidrBlock: 10.0.0.0/16
    patches:
```

4.2. UNDERSTANDING CROSSPLANE COMPOSITIONS

```
- fromFieldPath: "spec.parameters.region"
  toFieldPath: "spec.forProvider.region"
```

In this Composition definition, the resource defined (VPC in this example) specifies a base configuration and applies patches for user-specified parameters. The use of patches provides a flexible mechanism to adapt static templates to dynamic user inputs.

Working with Patches and Transforms

Crossplane Compositions enable a dynamic approach to resource templates through sophisticated patches and transforms. These mechanisms allow adjustments to the resource specification, promoting flexibility and reusability:

- **Patches**: They provide a way to inject data from the claim or composite resource into composed managed resources.

- **Transforms**: By transforming input values (e.g., applying string manipulations, number operations), users gain control over how data is applied within compositions.

Transform operations enhance the adaptability of Compositions to various deployment scenarios. For instance, a common use-case is adjusting naming conventions or calculating resource sizes based on user inputs.

```
apiVersion: v1
kind: Composition
metadata:
  name: compositeaws-vpc-composition
spec:
  compositeTypeRef:
    apiVersion: aws.crossplane.io/v1
    kind: CompositeAWSResource
  resources:
  - base:
      apiVersion: ec2.aws.crossplane.io/v1alpha1
      kind: Subnet
      spec:
        forProvider:
          cidrBlock: "10.0.1.0/24"
          vpcId:
            valueFromConnectionSecretKeyRef:
              name: vpc-conn
              key: id
    patches:
    - fromFieldPath: "spec.parameters.zone"
```

```
toFieldPath: "spec.forProvider.availabilityZone"
transforms:
- type: string
  string:
    fmt: "us-east-1%s"
```

In this context, a transform modifies the availabilityZone by appending the user-defined zone to a predefined format. This mechanism is crucial for harmonizing user input with standardized configuration patterns.

Operationalizing Compositions with Claims

The operational simplicity of Crossplane Compositions shines through when deploying infrastructure via claims. A Composite Resource Claim serves as an interface, allowing end-users to request composite resources without delving into the underlying complexity:

```
apiVersion: aws.crossplane.io/v1
kind: AWSResourceClaim
metadata:
  name: aws-compositeresource-sample
spec:
  compositionRef:
    name: compositeawsresource-composite
  parameters:
    region: "us-east-1"
    zone: "a"
```

Here, an AWSResourceClaim requests an instantiation of the CompositeAWSResource, with specified parameters guiding the configuration of underlying cloud resources. These claims decouple user intent from the specific implementation details, ensuring a higher degree of abstraction and ease of use.

Deployment Scenarios and Use Cases

Utilizing Crossplane Compositions offers diversified use cases across cloud environments:

- **Standardized Deployment Patterns**: Organizations can define standard deployment templates for cloud resources, ensuring consistency across environments.

- **Complex Infrastructure Automation**: Beyond single resources, Compositions facilitate the creation of complex infrastructure stacks that include VPCs, databases, and microservices orchestrated collectively.

- **Multi-Cloud Portability**: Since Crossplane Compositions abstract resource definitions, they inherently support easier movements between cloud providers.

Understanding and implementing Compositions can drastically reduce the time needed to provision and configure infrastructure, providing a substantial business advantage.

Benefits and Challenges

Embracing Crossplane Compositions presents benefits alongside challenges that users must navigate:

Advantages:

- **Reusability**: Compositions encapsulate configurations, fostering reusability across projects and teams.

- **Modularity**: By modularizing infrastructure templates, organizations can address specific needs while maintaining flexibility in configurations.

- **Consistency**: Establishes consistent infrastructure patterns promoting security, compliance, and best practices adherence.

Challenges:

- **Complexity in Dynamic Environments**: As compositions grow in complexity, managing changes and updates across different resources might require sophisticated strategies.

- **Learning Curve**: The abstraction and templating model introduces a learning curve for teams accustomed to traditional management methods.

Advanced Patterns and Strategies

To maximize the effectiveness of Crossplane Compositions, it is vital to explore advanced patterns:

- **Nested Compositions**: Compositions can be nested, allowing one composite resource to depend on another, promoting deeper abstraction layers.
- **Version Control and CI/CD Integration**: Implementing Compositions necessitates versioning strategies to manage evolution alongside CI/CD pipelines for automated deployment and testing.
- **Policy Enforcement**: Safeguarding deployments with policy enforcement mechanisms ensures compliance and adherence to infrastructure governance standards.

When enacted with foresight and sophisticated strategies, Crossplane Compositions provide an indispensable toolset for modern cloud-native operations, supporting innovative, scalable infrastructure deployments.

4.3 Managing Compute Resources

Managing compute resources efficiently in a cloud environment is crucial for maintaining performance, scaling, and cost-effectiveness. Crossplane provides an elegant mechanism to orchestrate the provisioning, management, and scaling of compute resources across multiple cloud providers using Kubernetes-native tools. This integration of Crossplane into the Kubernetes ecosystem allows users to employ a declarative approach to manage compute resources, transcending traditional infrastructure management constraints.

Compute resources refer to various components such as virtual machines (VMs), containerized applications, and Kubernetes clusters necessary for running applications in the cloud. Key aspects of compute resource management include provisioning, scaling, monitoring, and teardown. By capitalizing on the declarative configurations provided by Crossplane, developers are relieved from the intricate details of resource lifecycle management, enabling them to focus more on application development.

Provisioning virtual machines is a crucial aspect of resource management. Crossplane facilitates the provisioning of virtual machines

4.3. MANAGING COMPUTE RESOURCES

across platforms like AWS, GCP, and Azure by abstracting the underlying complexity into manageable YAML manifests. Below is an example of provisioning an EC2 instance on AWS using Crossplane.

```
apiVersion: ec2.aws.crossplane.io/v1beta1
kind: Instance
metadata:
  name: example-ec2-instance
spec:
  forProvider:
    region: us-west-2
    instanceType: t2.micro
    ami: ami-0123456789abcdef0
  providerConfigRef:
    name: aws-provider
```

In this configuration:

- The Instance type specifies an AWS EC2 instance with attributes like region, instanceType, and ami (Amazon Machine Image).

- The providerConfigRef links to the AWS provider configuration, enabling Crossplane to authenticate and authorize actions using the relevant credentials.

Similarly, here's how you could provision a VM on Google Cloud Platform:

```
apiVersion: compute.googleapis.com/v1
kind: Instance
metadata:
  name: example-gce-instance
spec:
  forProvider:
    machineType: e2-small
    zone: us-central1-a
    bootDisk:
      initializeParams:
        image: projects/debian-cloud/global/images/debian-9
  providerConfigRef:
    name: gcp-provider
```

Crossplane abstracts the GCP-specific configuration into the Instance manifest, specifying parameters such as machineType, zone, and the bootDisk image.

One of the pivotal strengths of cloud compute resources is their scalability. Crossplane compositions can be leveraged to manage both vertical and horizontal scaling of resources based on workload demand.

By defining autoscale policies within your infrastructure definitions, resources can dynamically adjust to demand without manual intervention.

Beyond individual VMs, Crossplane can manage Kubernetes clusters themselves, creating and maintaining these foundational components of modern cloud infrastructures. This capability provides organizations with the flexibility to spin up managed Kubernetes clusters on-demand using cloud providers' managed services, such as Amazon EKS, Google GKE, or Azure AKS.

Example: Creating an Amazon EKS Cluster

```
apiVersion: eks.aws.crossplane.io/v1alpha1
kind: Cluster
metadata:
  name: example-eks-cluster
spec:
  forProvider:
    region: us-west-2
    roleArn: arn:aws:iam::<AWS_ACCOUNT_ID>:role/<EKS_ROLE>
    version: "1.21"
  providerConfigRef:
    name: aws-provider
```

In this example, an EKS Cluster is instantiated with details such as the AWS region, IAM role (roleArn), and Kubernetes version.

Example: Creating a Google GKE Cluster

```
apiVersion: gke.compute.googleapis.com/v1beta1
kind: Cluster
metadata:
  name: example-gke-cluster
spec:
  forProvider:
    location: us-central1-a
    initialClusterVersion: "1.21"
    initialNodeCount: 3
  providerConfigRef:
    name: gcp-provider
```

This GKE cluster configuration highlights the location, initialClusterVersion, and initialNodeCount for a managed Kubernetes service on GCP.

Crossplane's additional capabilities augment compute resource management with features such as:

4.3. MANAGING COMPUTE RESOURCES

- Cross-Provider Compatibility: Enabling deployments spanning multiple cloud providers with seamless transitions and unified APIs.

- Resource Claims: Simplifying resource requests, allowing application developers to specify requirements without detailed provider-specific configurations.

- Automated Configuration Drift Correction: Ensuring the declared state of an infrastructure stack remains consistent with the current state by automatically correcting discrepancies.

Optimizing cloud compute resources entails consistent monitoring and fine-tuning of configurations. Crossplane integrates well with monitoring tools, enabling proactive resource management. Several strategies promote optimization, including:

- Resource Utilization Metrics: Leverage cloud-native monitoring services like AWS CloudWatch, GCP Cloud Monitoring, or Azure Monitor to track utilization metrics and set alerts for underutilized or overcrowded resources.

- Cost Management: Use reserved instances, savings plans, or spot instances where appropriate to optimize costs. Crossplane compositions can be adjusted to align with these offerings dynamically.

- Application Load Balancing: Implement load balancers within configurations to distribute traffic evenly across resources, enhancing application performance and redundancy.

Security in managing compute resources is paramount, especially with multi-cloud environments susceptible to different threat paradigms. Crossplane provides robust frameworks for integrating security best practices:

- Identity and Access Management (IAM): Configure roles and permissions diligently to ensure principle of least privilege is enforced across compute resources.

- Encryption and Data Protection: Ensure data at rest and in transit is encrypted, defined as default standards within infrastructure manifests.

- Compliance Policies: Use Crossplane policies to enforce compliance checks, aligning infrastructure deployments with organizational standards and regulatory requirements.

To illustrate Crossplane's potency in managing compute resources, consider a multi-cloud deployment involving both AWS and Azure. Envision an application evenly split between AWS EC2 instances and Azure VMs to leverage strengths of regional data centers:

- Unified Infrastructure Manifests: Abstract configuration details into Crossplane composites, defining common requirements for both AWS and Azure platforms.

- Dynamic Scaling: Enable autoscaling policies to respond to regional demands, while using Crossplane to ensure unified management across cloud boundaries.

- Cost and Performance Monitoring: Implement a centralized dashboard capturing metrics from both environments, used to inform scaling and cost optimization decisions.

Despite Crossplane's advanced capabilities, managing compute resources in a cloud environment still presents challenges. Some notable issues and techniques to address them include:

- Inter-Provider Consistency: Variations in feature offerings between providers can lead to complex configurations. Utilizing Crossplane abstractions helps smooth over these inconsistencies.

- Configuration Complexity: As configurations grow in sophistication, they may become unwieldy. Modularize configurations into manageable compositions and utilize version control for enhanced manageability.

- Evolving Cloud Features: Rapid evolution in cloud services necessitates continuous updates. Crossplane's thriving open-source ecosystem provides timely updates to interfaces and resource definitions.

Crossplane empowers organizations to manage compute resources efficiently in a multi-cloud context, delivering both flexibility and control. By leveraging Crossplane's declarative model, users streamline the provisioning and lifecycle management of compute resources, enhancing scalability, security, and efficiency. As the cloud ecosystem evolves, Crossplane stands poised to address emerging demands through robust abstractions and seamless integrations, fostering innovation and adaptability in cloud-native infrastructures.

4.4 Provisioning and Managing Databases

In modern application architectures, databases form an integral component, underpinning both transactional systems and analytical platforms. Effective database provisioning and management in a cloud environment are crucial for ensuring application reliability, performance, and scalability. Crossplane facilitates database management by adopting a Kubernetes-native declarative approach, where databases are provisioned as code. This capability not only streamlines operations but also harmonizes database management with the broader infrastructure as code (IaC) strategies.

- Cloud service providers offer a variety of database services, ranging from relational database services (RDS) to more specialized document and NoSQL databases. Each of these databases can be managed through standardized APIs, sustaining robust performance and reliability. This section explores how Crossplane can be employed for provisioning and managing databases across prominent cloud platforms, leveraging Crossplane's provider support for services such as AWS RDS, Google Cloud SQL, and Azure Database services.

For relational databases, schemas and specifications must be meticulously defined. Crossplane allows relational database instances to be declaratively instantiated and managed, ensuring consistency and repeatability.

Example: Provisioning an AWS RDS Instance

To provision an Amazon RDS instance with Crossplane, the following configuration specifies a PostgreSQL database instance:

```
apiVersion: rds.aws.crossplane.io/v1beta1
kind: RDSInstance
metadata:
  name: example-rds-instance
spec:
  forProvider:
    dbInstanceClass: db.t3.micro
    masterUsername: adminuser
    masterUserPasswordSecretRef:
      name: db-password
      key: password
    engine: postgres
    engineVersion: "13.3"
  providerConfigRef:
    name: aws-provider
```

In this manifest:

- 'dbInstanceClass' defines the compute and memory capacity.

- 'masterUserPasswordSecretRef' refers to a Kubernetes secret holding the database password.

- 'engine' and 'engineVersion' specify the type and version of the database engine.

The 'providerConfigRef' ensures Crossplane can authenticate requests to AWS.

Example: Provisioning a Google Cloud SQL Instance

For provisioning a Cloud SQL database instance on Google Cloud Platform, the configuration might resemble:

```
apiVersion: database.gcp.crossplane.io/v1beta1
kind: CloudSQLInstance
metadata:
  name: example-cloudsql-instance
spec:
  forProvider:
    region: us-central1
    databaseVersion: POSTGRES_13
    settings:
```

```
      tier: db-custom-1-3840
    providerConfigRef:
      name: gcp-provider
```

The GCP SQL instance manifest:

- Defines 'region' and 'databaseVersion' for geographic and engine versions.
- 'settings' dictates machine type and configuration essentials.

Database configurations often require additional settings based on application needs, such as storage sizes, connectivity preferences, and security settings. Crossplane enables extensive customization through its flexible specification model.

Databases on the cloud can dynamically scale storage according to application demand. Storage auto-scaling ensures that databases remain performant without manual intervention, a significant advantage in environments with fluctuating demands.

Example: Customizing Storage Options

```
spec:
  forProvider:
    allocatedStorage: 20 # in GB
    maxAllocatedStorage: 100
```

By defining 'allocatedStorage' and 'maxAllocatedStorage', users control initial and possible maximum storage capacities.

Cloud databases are often accessed over private networks to mitigate security risks associated with public internet exposure. Networking configurations include selecting appropriate subnets and security groups in AWS or defining networks and authorized subnets in GCP and Azure.

Configuring Network Access in AWS RDS

```
spec:
  forProvider:
    vpcSecurityGroupIds:
      - sg-0123456789abcdef0
    dbSubnetGroupName:
      valueFromFieldRef:
        fieldName: metadata.name
```

Here, 'vpcSecurityGroupIds' and 'dbSubnetGroupName' secure access by confining traffic within privileged network configurations.

Ensuring the security of database instances is both operationally critical and mandatory for compliance. Crossplane enables sophisticated encryption and access management strategies to protect data integrity and confidentiality.

- **Encryption**: Ensure datasets are encrypted in transit and at rest, using built-in provider functionalities accessed via configuration policies.

- **Access Controls**: Define and enforce stringent roles and permissions to limit database access, ensuring users only operate within their security clearance levels.

Automated backups and disaster recovery strategies are fundamental in database management. Cloud providers offer inherent backup capabilities that can be configured through Crossplane for scheduled or on-demand backups.

Example: Configuring Automatic Backups

```
spec:
  forProvider:
    backupRetentionPeriod: 7 # days
    backupWindow: 02:00-03:00
```

In defining 'backupRetentionPeriod' and 'backupWindow', users control when backups occur and how many days they are retained.

Continuous monitoring of database performance ensures responsiveness and operational efficiency. Crossplane integrates seamlessly with cloud monitoring services to track essential metrics:

- **Performance Metrics**: Track CPU usage, query performance, connection pools, and slow query logs.

- **Alerting Systems**: Implement alerts to notify administrators of thresholds breaches or erratic patterns, facilitating early intervention.

4.4. PROVISIONING AND MANAGING DATABASES

Optimization also encompasses deploying indexing strategies, partitioning large tables, and regular maintenance activities such as vacuum and analyze in PostgreSQL databases.

Organizations often run heterogeneous environments with varying compliance needs. Crossplane supports custom policy implementations that span across environments, providing a unified governance model.

Policy Enforcement Example

```
spec:
  enforce:
    - name: 'InstanceTypeIsStandard'
      matchLabels:
        dbInstanceClass: "db.t3.*"
```

Such policies help enforce that only a certain class of instance types is used within a particular environment.

Consider a scenario wherein an organization strategically distributes its database services across AWS and Azure to harness regional performance benefits and service-specific features.

- **Unified Access Layers**: Abstract access layers through Crossplane, ensuring that database access is consistent regardless of the underlying cloud provider.

- **Data Synchronization**: Employ data replication strategies such as AWS DMS or Azure Data Sync for real-time, cross-cloud data synchronizations ensuring high availability and redundancy.

- **Cost Efficiency and Scalability**: Dynamically adjust resources to align with load patterns using Crossplane's scaling policies, optimizing costs, and ensuring performance.

Implementing database management with Crossplane presents challenges that necessitate informed strategies:

- **Consistency and Conflict Management**: Maintain configuration consistency across environments using templated compositions.

- **Resource Constraints**: Adapt resource allocations in response to evolving demand patterns, ensuring database performance remains optimal.

- **Vendor Lock-In**: Abstract database configurations to ensure portability and resilience against cloud provider-specific constraints.

Best practices emphasize rigorous planning, balancing cost with performance, comprehensive monitoring, and proactive compliance adherence.

Crossplane revolutionizes the provisioning and management of databases in cloud environments by marrying the declarative simplicity of Kubernetes with robust multi-cloud capabilities. This synthesis empowers organizations to streamline operations, enhance security, ensure performance optimization, and align with strategic business objectives. As the demands for dynamic, scalable infrastructures proliferate, Crossplane provides a compelling framework that enables sophisticated database management informed by precision, reliability, and future-proof adaptability.

4.5 Networking and Security Resources

Networking and security are pivotal components of any cloud-based infrastructure. They ensure the secure, efficient, and reliable operation of services, protecting against unauthorized access and ensuring that resources can communicate seamlessly. Crossplane plays a crucial role in not only provisioning these resources but also integrating them into a cohesive and secure network architecture. This section explores the management of networking and security resources using Crossplane, showcasing how to implement best practices and secure cloud environments across multiple providers.

Networking Resources in Cloud Environments

Networking in the cloud involves creating networks, subnets, routing tables, and gateways that facilitate communication between resources while isolating them from unauthorized access. Crossplane abstracts these configurations into declarative YAML manifests, offering a comprehensive way to manage networking components consistently.

Example: Provisioning a Virtual Private Cloud (VPC) on AWS

```
apiVersion: ec2.aws.crossplane.io/v1beta1
kind: VPC
metadata:
  name: example-vpc
spec:
  forProvider:
    cidrBlock: 10.0.0.0/16
    enableDnsSupport: true
    enableDnsHostnames: true
  providerConfigRef:
    name: aws-provider
```

Components Explained:

- **CIDR Block**: Specifies the IP address range for the VPC.

- **DNS Support and Hostnames**: Enabled to allow resources within the VPC to resolve domain names.

This setup ensures that foundational networking is securely established, providing a framework for additional resources and services.

Example: Creating a Subnet in GCP

```
apiVersion: compute.gcp.crossplane.io/v1alpha1
kind: Subnetwork
metadata:
  name: example-subnet
spec:
  forProvider:
    ipCidrRange: 10.0.1.0/24
    region: us-central1
    network: projects/myproject/global/networks/default
  providerConfigRef:
    name: gcp-provider
```

Components Explained:

- **IP CIDR Range**: Defines a smaller subnet network range.

- **Region and Network**: Assigns the subnet within a specific region and VPC network.

Security Group and Firewall Management

Security groups and firewall rules define the permitted inbound and outbound traffic to resources, acting as a virtual firewall for instances to control traffic based on protocols, ports, and IP addresses.

Example: Configuring AWS Security Group

```
apiVersion: ec2.aws.crossplane.io/v1beta1
kind: SecurityGroup
metadata:
  name: example-security-group
spec:
  forProvider:
    description: Allow SSH and HTTP
    vpcId:
      valueFromFieldRef:
        fieldPath: metadata.name
    ingress:
    - fromPort: 22
      toPort: 22
      protocol: tcp
      cidrBlocks:
      - 0.0.0.0/0
    - fromPort: 80
      toPort: 80
      protocol: tcp
  securityGroups:
  - example-security-group
  providerConfigRef:
    name: aws-provider
```

Configurations:

- **Ingress Rules**: Permit SSH and HTTP traffic from all IPs, an essential configuration during development, but for production, specific IP ranges should be defined for enhanced security.

Example: Configuring GCP Firewall Rule

```
apiVersion: compute.gcp.crossplane.io/v1beta1
kind: Firewall
metadata:
  name: example-firewall-rule
spec:
  forProvider:
    description: Allow internal network
    direction: INGRESS
    priority: 1000
    sourceRanges:
    - 10.0.0.0/24
    allowed:
    - protocol: tcp
```

4.5. NETWORKING AND SECURITY RESOURCES

```
    ports:
    - '8080'
  providerConfigRef:
    name: gcp-provider
```

Configurations:

- **Direction and Priority**: Control rule application ordering and traffic direction.

- **Source Range and Allowed Protocols**: These ensure tightly controlled access filtering, allowing only essential connections.

Integrating Network and Security Policies

In a dynamic cloud infrastructure, enforcing network and security policies ensures that resources are aligned with organizational standards, reducing the risk of misconfigurations and security breaches.

Load Balancing and Traffic Management

Load balancers distribute incoming traffic across multiple instances, enhancing scalability and reliability. Integrating load balancers with security policies ensures end-to-end security and performance optimization.

Designing an AWS Elastic Load Balancer (ELB)

```
apiVersion: elb.aws.crossplane.io/v1alpha1
kind: ELB
metadata:
  name: example-elb
spec:
  forProvider:
    name: example-load-balancer
    listeners:
    - protocol: HTTP
      loadBalancerPort: 80
      instancePort: 80
    subnets:
    - subnet-0123456789abcdef0
  providerConfigRef:
    name: aws-provider
```

Details:

- **Listeners**: Define how the load balancer listens to connections, crucial for ensuring proper routing.

- **Subnets**: Associate specific subnets where the ELB will operate.

Traffic Management Considerations

- Implementing intelligent routing through policies, such as session persistence or weighted routing, can vastly improve application performance.

Connecting Hybrid and Multi-Cloud Networks

Organizations increasingly deploy hybrid and multi-cloud architectures necessitating reliable and secure interconnectivity solutions. Crossplane facilitates this through its provider-agnostic approach.

Implementation of a VPC Peering in AWS

```
apiVersion: ec2.aws.crossplane.io/v1beta1
kind: VPCPeeringConnection
metadata:
  name: example-vpc-peering
spec:
  forProvider:
    vpcId: vpc-1234567890
    peerVpcId: vpc-0987654321
  providerConfigRef:
    name: aws-provider
```

Details:

- **VPC and Peer VPC IDs**: Establish the connection between two VPC networks, enabling them to communicate as if within the same network.

Multi-Cloud VPN Integration

- Establish cross-provider VPN tunnels to secure communications, ensuring encrypted transmissions over public and private networks.

Enabling Security Compliance and Monitoring

Security compliance is paramount, given the stringent regulatory environments many industries operate within. Crossplane enables comprehensive monitoring and auditing of network and security configurations.

Best Practices for Security Compliance

- **Centralize Security Management**: Maintain all security group, firewall, and network configurations in a centralized repository for versioning and audit trails.

- **Automated Compliance Checks**: Integrate tools that assess configurations against compliance policies, flagging deviations automatically.

Monitoring with Integrated Tools

- Leverage cloud provider-native monitoring services like AWS GuardDuty, GCP Security Command Center, and Azure Security Center for real-time threat detection and analysis.

Challenges and Mitigation Strategies

Navigating the complexity of cloud networking and security presents challenges that require proactive strategies.

- **Configuration Drift**: Regularly audit and review configurations to ensure they align with the intended state, utilizing Crossplane's declarative model to detect drifts.

- **New Threat Vectors**: Stay informed about emerging threats, continually adapting security rules and policies within Crossplane configurations to mitigate potential vulnerabilities.

- **Complexity in Hybrid Architectures**: Employ standardized templates and reusable configurations to manage the sprawling complexity in hybrid and multi-cloud setups.

Adopting a disciplined approach to security and network management, supported by automation tools like Crossplane, plays a crucial role in maintaining the integrity and performance of cloud infrastructures.

Conclusion

Incorporating Crossplane into the management of networking and security resources empowers organizations to adopt a unified, automated, and secure approach to cloud infrastructure. This approach reduces the risk of manual errors, enhances compliance with security policies, and promotes the efficient operation of services across dispersed environments. As the cloud landscape evolves, embracing these paradigms will not only safeguard against vulnerabilities but will also harness the full potential of cloud-native technologies, driving innovation and resilience in network and security architectures.

4.6 Leveraging Crossplane Packages

Crossplane packages represent a powerful mechanism for bundling, sharing, and deploying configurations that manage cloud resources. These packages allow users to encapsulate complex infrastructure deployments into reusable and distributable units, facilitating collaboration and standardization across teams and projects. Understanding how to effectively leverage Crossplane packages is essential for maximizing the efficiency and scalability of cloud-native infrastructure management.

Crossplane packages provide a modular approach to managing infrastructure as code. They are built on top of Kubernetes Custom Resource Definitions (CRDs) and their controllers, which manage the lifecycle of cloud resources. By using packages, users can define, compose, and share custom resources and their configurations, promoting code reuse and consistency.

A Crossplane package includes the following core components:

- **CRD Definitions**: These define the custom resources that the package will provide or manage.

- **Controllers**: These manage the lifecycle of the resources defined by the CRDs.

There are several types of Crossplane packages that facilitate different use cases:

- **Provider Packages**: These packages include the infrastructure required to connect Crossplane with a specific cloud provider,

4.6. LEVERAGING CROSSPLANE PACKAGES

such as AWS, GCP, or Azure. They contain the CRDs and controllers needed to provision and manage resources on those platforms.

- **Configuration Packages**: These are higher-level packages that define a set of resources or services. They leverage provider packages to define and deploy complete infrastructure setups.

Creating a provider package involves defining the CRDs and controllers that allow Crossplane to manage resources on a specific cloud platform. Below is an example of creating a simple provider package for a fictional cloud provider:

Step 1: Define the CRD

```
apiVersion: apiextensions.crossplane.io/v1
kind: CustomResourceDefinition
metadata:
  name: exampleinstances.example.org
spec:
  group: example.org
  names:
    kind: ExampleInstance
    listKind: ExampleInstanceList
    plural: exampleinstances
    singular: exampleinstance
  scope: Namespaced
  versions:
  - name: v1alpha1
    served: true
    storage: true
    schema:
      openAPIV3Schema:
        type: object
        properties:
          spec:
            type: object
            properties:
              size:
                type: string
              image:
                type: string
```

This CRD defines an 'ExampleInstance' resource with properties like 'size' and 'image', which might correspond to instance specifications like machine type and operating system image.

Step 2: Implement the Controller

The controller for a provider package will handle the resource lifecycle events. Typically, this involves writing a custom controller using a language like Go that integrates with the relevant cloud provider APIs to perform operations defined by the CRDs.

Step 3: Package and Deploy

Once the CRDs and controllers are defined, they are bundled into a package and pushed to a registry for distribution. The package can then be installed into a Crossplane environment.

```
kubectl crossplane build package
kubectl crossplane push example-provider:latest
kubectl crossplane install provider example-provider:latest
```

Configuration packages define a set of resources that collectively make up a complete infrastructure setup. They often include references to provider packages and encapsulate common patterns or multi-resource setups.

Example: Configuration Package for a Web Application

Imagine a scenario where you need to define the infrastructure for a multi-tier web application, including a load balancer, a set of compute instances, and a database:

```yaml
apiVersion: apiextensions.crossplane.io/v1
kind: Composition
metadata:
  name: webapp-composition
spec:
  compositeTypeRef:
    apiVersion: core.example.org/v1alpha1
    kind: WebApp
  resources:
  - name: instance
    base:
      apiVersion: compute.example.org/v1alpha1
      kind: ExampleInstance
      spec:
        size: t2.medium
        image: webapp-image

  - name: database
    base:
      apiVersion: database.example.org/v1alpha1
      kind: ExampleDatabase
      spec:
        engine: postgres
        version: "13"
```

This composition package describes a 'WebApp' infrastructure, automatically deploying a VM instance and a database. The package can be reused across different environments, ensuring that the deployments are consistent and standardized.

One of the key advantages of Crossplane packages is their ability to be shared and reused across environments. Packages can be pushed to public or private registries, allowing other users or teams to easily deploy them.

Publishing a Package to a Registry

Crossplane provides commands to build and push packages to OCI-compatible registries, facilitating easy distribution:

```
kubectl crossplane build configuration
kubectl crossplane push <registry>/webapp-config:latest
kubectl crossplane install configuration <registry>/webapp-config:latest
```

Once published, the package can be easily consumed by others, speeding up the deployment process and facilitating best-practice sharing across an organization.

Integrating Crossplane packages with CI/CD pipelines enhances deployment agility and ensures that infrastructure changes are tested, versioned, and deployed as part of an automated workflow.

Creating a CI/CD Workflow for Package Deployment

A typical CI/CD pipeline for a Crossplane package might include steps for building, testing, and publishing the package:

- **Build**: The package is defined and constructed using Crossplane's build tools.

- **Lint and Test**: Validate the syntax and functionality of the package configuration.

- **Push**: If tests pass, the package is pushed to a container registry.

- **Install and Validate**: Automatically install the package in a staging environment to ensure it deploys correctly, followed by validations and checks.

Example: GitHub Actions Workflow

```
name: Crossplane CI/CD
```

```yaml
on:
  push:
    branches:
      - main

jobs:
  build:
    runs-on: ubuntu-latest
    steps:
      - uses: actions/checkout@v2
      - name: Set up Crossplane
        run: curl -sL https://raw.githubusercontent.com/crossplane/crossplane/master/install.sh | sh
      - name: Build Package
        run: kubectl crossplane build package
      - name: Push Package
        env:
          REGISTRY: <registry>
          USERNAME: ${{ secrets.REGISTRY_USERNAME }}
          PASSWORD: ${{ secrets.REGISTRY_PASSWORD }}
        run: |
          echo $PASSWORD | docker login $REGISTRY -u $USERNAME --password-stdin
          kubectl crossplane push $REGISTRY/webapp:latest
      - name: Verify Installation
        run: kubectl crossplane install configuration $REGISTRY/webapp:latest
```

Case Study: Building a Shared Resource Library

Imagine an organization that wants to standardize its cloud resource management by creating a shared library of Crossplane packages representing common infrastructure components:

- **Define Core Infrastructure Components**: Identify common infrastructure setups such as VPCs, data storage solutions, and monitoring services.

- **Package Creation**: Develop Crossplane packages for each component, encapsulating best security practices and performance optimizations.

- **Repository and Registry Management**: Store packages in a company-wide repository and push images to a dedicated OCI registry.

- **Automation and Integration**: Integrate package deployments into team-specific workflows, enabling easy adoption and auditability across projects.

While Crossplane packages offer robust capabilities, several challenges and best practices help maximize their effectiveness:

- **Version Management**: Maintain version control rigorously to track and manage changes in packages. Semantic versioning helps with compatibility tracking.

- **Security and Compliance**: Regularly audit package contents for security vulnerabilities and ensure compliance with industry regulations.

- **Documentation and Community Best Practices**: Leverage detailed documentation and community resources to ensure that packages are used effectively.

- **Testing and Validation**: Implement comprehensive testing frameworks to validate package configurations and operations across multiple cloud environments.

Leveraging Crossplane packages empowers teams to efficiently manage and deploy cloud infrastructure setups in a modular, repeatable, and standardized manner. As organizations increasingly adopt cloud-native practices, workshops, and workflows, harnessing the capabilities of Crossplane packages ensures that infrastructure is robust, scalable, and aligned with strategic business objectives. By fostering collaboration and knowledge-sharing, packages streamline cloud operations and facilitate innovation, positioning teams to navigate complex and dynamic environments with agility and confidence.

4.7 Automating Resource Management

Effective resource management in cloud environments is the linchpin for ensuring scalability, reliability, and efficiency. Automation is paramount, removing the onus from developers and administrators to manually provision, manage, and decommission resources, thus minimizing human error and expediting operations. Crossplane fundamentally embraces automation by providing tools to define and maintain cloud resources declaratively, integrating seamlessly with continuous integration and deployment (CI/CD) pipelines, and enabling dynamic responses to changes in demand. This section delves into the intricacies of automating resource management using Crossplane, highlighting its capabilities, advantages, and practical implementations.

Declarative Resource Management

Crossplane leverages the declarative model intrinsic to Kubernetes, extending this paradigm to cloud resources. This model facilitates stating the desired end-state of infrastructure without detailing the procedural steps to achieve it. Automation within this framework ensures that:

- **State Reconciliation**: The system continuously monitors resource states, making adjustments as necessary to align with the desired configuration.

- **Idempotency**: Repeatedly applying the same configuration yields consistent results, which simplifies automation workflows.

Crossplane adopts Kubernetes Custom Resources (CRs) and controllers to manage resource definitions and lifecycle events. These constructs enable automated reconciliation loops that perpetually strive to converge actual resource states with their declared specifications.

Implementing Infrastructure as Code (IaC)

Infrastructure as Code frameworks allow administrators to version control and manage resource configurations similarly to application code. Crossplane extends Kubernetes to apply IaC principles across diverse cloud environments. Here is how automated IaC is implemented with Crossplane:

Example: Automated Deployment of a Database

Consider the scenario of deploying a managed MySQL database instance on AWS:

```
apiVersion: rds.aws.crossplane.io/v1beta1
kind: RDSInstance
metadata:
  name: automated-rds-instance
spec:
  forProvider:
    region: us-west-2
    dbInstanceClass: db.t3.micro
```

4.7. AUTOMATING RESOURCE MANAGEMENT

```
    masterUsername: admin
    masterUserPasswordSecretRef:
      name: db-password
      key: password
    engine: mysql
    engineVersion: "5.7"
  providerConfigRef:
    name: aws-provider
```

This YAML blueprint for the RDS instance is stored within a version-controlled repository. Upon changes or new deployments, automation tools like Helm or ArgoCD can apply these definitions in a consistent and reliable manner.

Infrastructure Pipelines and Continuous Delivery

CI/CD pipelines are integral to automating the entire lifecycle of cloud resources, from provisioning to decommissioning. By embedding Crossplane into these pipelines, teams accelerate the feedback loop, fostering an environment where infrastructure changes are routinely validated, monitored, and improved upon.

Example: Integrating Crossplane with a CI/CD Pipeline

A CI/CD pipeline encompassing Crossplane might involve the following stages:

- **Build**: Compile configurations into a release. For instance, defining environment-specific variables into resource manifests.

- **Validate**: Use tools like kubeval or kpt to syntactically validate manifests.

- **Deploy**: Apply changes in a sequenced manner, using Helm charts to capture deployment logic.

- **Monitor & Rollback**: Leverage Prometheus and Grafana to monitor deployed changes. Automated responses can trigger rollbacks if deployments exceed predefined thresholds.

Example GitHub Actions Workflow for Crossplane

```
name: Crossplane-Pipeline
on:
  push:
```

```yaml
    branches:
      - main
jobs:
  deploy:
    runs-on: ubuntu-latest
    steps:
      - name: Checkout
        uses: actions/checkout@v2

      - name: Set up Crossplane
        run: curl -sL https://raw.githubusercontent.com/crossplane/crossplane/master/install.sh | sh

      - name: Validate Configurations
        run: |
          kubeval config/

      - name: Deploy Resources
        run: |
          kubectl apply -f config/

      - name: Monitor Deployment
        run: |
          # Placeholder for monitoring logic, e.g. query Prometheus
```

Dynamic Resource Scaling

Automation transcends simple deployment to include dynamically adjusting resources in response to demand. Solutions such as the Kubernetes Horizontal Pod Autoscaler (HPA) or custom logic written in controllers can be integrated with Crossplane to achieve this.

Implementing Dynamic Scaling for a Compute Resource

Consider an application requiring additional instances during high-traffic periods:

```yaml
apiVersion: compute.aws.crossplane.io/v1alpha1
kind: AutoScalingGroup
metadata:
  name: example-autoscaling
spec:
  forProvider:
    minSize: 1
    maxSize: 5
    desiredCapacity: 2
  providerConfigRef:
    name: aws-provider
```

In this configuration: - **Dynamic Scaling**: The ASG automatically adjusts compute capacity between minSize and maxSize, ensuring performance and cost efficiency.

4.7. AUTOMATING RESOURCE MANAGEMENT

Resource Lifecycle Management

Crossplane automates essential lifecycle events beyond initial deployments:

- **Patch Management**: Apply updates and patches automatically, ensuring systems remain compliant with security standards.
- **Orphan Resource Detection and Cleanup**: Schedules automated scans to detect unused or redundant resources, optimizing costs by deprovisioning them.
- **Backup and Recovery**: Define automated backup routines and disaster recovery protocols as first-class citizens within resource manifests.

Security Automation

Security is a critical aspect of resource management. Automating security tasks reduces the risk of vulnerabilities and aids compliance efforts.

Automated Security Assessments

Tools such as kube-bench or kubectl plug-ins can automate assessments of Kubernetes and cloud provider resources, generating reports and orchestrating remediation actions based on predefined criteria.

```
kubectl run security-check --image=container/bench:latest -- bash -c "kube-bench"
kubectl logs security-check
```

Best Practices for Security Automation

- **Immutable Infrastructure**: Use immutability principles to prevent unauthorized changes post-deployment.
- **Integrated Identity Management**: Automated identity policies ensure secure and compliant access control, managing lifecycle permissions through identity providers.

Challenges and Strategic Solutions

Despite the benefits, automating cloud resources can introduce challenges that require strategic solutions:

- **Configuration Drift**: Rigorous validation and reconciliation processes must be in place to address drift from the intended configuration.

- **Complexity Management**: Modularize resources and configurations to prevent complexity from hindering automation processes.

- **Cost Overruns**: Implement automated billing and resource utilization alerts to prevent unchecked resource consumption.

- **Vendor-Specific Constraints**: Cross-platform automation demands a detailed understanding of provider-specific capabilities and service limits.

Crossplane's abstraction layer helps navigate these challenges by offering a uniform interface to manage resources across diverse providers.

Automating resource management with Crossplane reveals its potential not only in reducing laborious tasks but in enhancing reliability, security, and organizational agility. Through a blend of declarative configurations, integrated pipeline processes, and dynamic scaling capabilities, Crossplane fortifies infrastructure management paradigms. As technology and cloud environments evolve, embracing automation at every stage of resource management ensures resilience and positions organizations to innovate swiftly while maintaining alignment with ever-demanding business objectives. Through automation, teams are empowered to focus more on creativity and strategic planning, knowing the foundational operations are meticulously managed and optimized.

Chapter 5

Managing Multi-Cloud Environments

Managing multi-cloud environments involves orchestrating resources and services across various cloud providers to leverage the strengths of each while avoiding vendor lock-in. A strategic multi-cloud approach enhances flexibility, reliability, and scalability by distributing workloads based on specific performance and cost requirements. Crossplane facilitates this management by orchestrating cloud resources using Kubernetes APIs, allowing seamless interactions across diversified cloud ecosystems. Key aspects include maintaining data consistency, ensuring security compliance, managing costs, and optimizing performance across all cloud platforms. Effectively managing multi-cloud environments with tools like Crossplane enables organizations to maximize resource efficiency and operational agility.

5.1 The Concept of Multi-Cloud Strategies

The transition to multi-cloud strategies represents a fundamental shift in how organizations approach cloud computing. It involves the utilization of services, capabilities, and infrastructure provided by multiple cloud vendors to diversify technological resources and mitigate potential risks associated with depending on a single provider. Below, we explore the motivations, advantages, application strategies, and considerations for a well-structured multi-cloud approach.

The primary motivation behind adopting a multi-cloud strategy lies in the need for resilience, flexibility, and avoidance of vendor lock-in. By distributing workloads across different cloud providers, businesses can ensure service reliability and continuity. In a scenario where one provider experiences downtime, applications and services can be switched or balanced to another provider, hence maintaining availability.

A crucial advantage of multi-cloud strategies is the optimization of performance by leveraging geographical presence and technological strengths of different providers. Regions with closer physical proximity to active user bases can be targeted to reduce latency. Additionally, various cloud providers excel in specific service offerings – for instance, artificial intelligence services from a particular provider might be superior to others, allowing organizations to select the best tools for their specific requirements.

Cost management is another significant consideration where enterprises can benefit from competitive pricing models across providers. By strategically distributing their workloads, businesses are positioned to take advantage of cost differences, discounts, and optimized scaling solutions offered independently by each provider. This not only helps in controlling expenses but also contributes to overall cost efficiency by selecting vendors that offer the best fit for particular tasks.

The management of a multi-cloud environment demands clear organizational strategies and governance structures to handle operational complexities. This includes maintaining compliance, orchestration of resources, and consistent application of security protocols across all environments. Utilizing a centralized control plane like Crossplane aids in mitigating complexity, providing a cohesive platform for orchestrating cloud resources using consistent Kubernetes APIs. Crossplane enables organizations to define infrastructure needs using Kubernetes custom resources, automatically translating these declarations to configurations each cloud provider can process.

```
apiVersion: compute.crossplane.io/v1alpha1
kind: CloudSQLInstance
metadata:
  name: example-sql
spec:
  forProvider:
    tier: db-custom-1-3840
    region: us-central1
  writeConnectionSecretToRef:
    name: sql-conn-details
  providerConfigRef:
    name: example-gcp
```

With this configuration, a CloudSQL instance is established in the specified region, showcasing how multi-cloud infrastructures are defined in a Kubernetes environment through Crossplane. This abstraction enables the handling of diverse cloud resource configurations under a unified framework, reducing the technical overhead involved in managing each provider's native interfaces.

Data consistency and integration in a multi-cloud setup pose crucial challenges. Data services must ensure timely synchronization across disparate systems to maintain seamless user experiences. This can involve implementing multi-master databases or data mesh architectures where source-of-truth systems are synchronized using data transformation pipelines, capable of cross-cloud replication. Here, Crossplane's ecosystem actively participates not only by provisioning the cloud resources needed but by maintaining orchestrated management of the state of these resources.

```
{
  "status": "success",
  "cloudSQL": {
    "instanceName": "example-sql",
    "region": "us-central1"
  }
}
```

The readiness to adopt a multi-cloud strategy must include robust security postures. As data traverses multiple environments, encryption both at rest and in transit is fundamental. Security teams must employ comprehensive identity and access management (IAM) strategies and utilize tools that support multi-cloud contexts, such as federated identities and cross-account IAM roles. Vigilance is pivotal for intrusion detection, logging, and regular audits that cover all operationally relevant domains under the diverse landscape of a multi-cloud deployment.

For example, adopting a comprehensive IAM policy in Amazon Web Services (AWS) can look like the following:

```
{
  "Version": "2012-10-17",
  "Statement": [
    {
      "Effect": "Allow",
      "Action": "s3:ListBucket",
      "Resource": "arn:aws:s3:::example_bucket"
    }
  ]
}
```

Such policies must be consistently applied and adapted across different cloud environments, enhancing both the security posture and operational integrity of cross-provider applications.

The operational agility that a multi-cloud strategy imparts is significant. It allows businesses to pivot quickly by onboarding new technologies, scale infrastructure in response to dynamic demands, and foster innovation by integrating novel cloud services without the restrictions inherent to a single vendor alliance.

A practical implementation of the multi-cloud strategy includes redundancy in deployment footprints across providers to fortify disaster recovery plans. Building robust pipelines using continuous integration and continuous deployment (CI/CD) practices facilitates seamless transitions in development and production environments. Such flexibility ensures application and service updates can be deployed uniformly across all clouds, minimizing disruption and enhancing end-user experiences.

Cross-provider APIs and services coordination is essential to facilitate a coherent multi-cloud strategy. RESTful APIs that respect the constraints of statelessness, cacheability, and uniform interfaces are often employed to ensure standardized communications. A service mesh can provide valuable services such as load balancing, authentication, circuit-breaking, and more, thereby abstracting complex network behavior and simplifying the orchestration of services across distributed environments.

Incorporating these tools, frameworks, and strategies creates a state of synchronized cloud resource management where operational efficiency is increased and innovation is unfettered. Thus, a multi-cloud approach becomes not merely a technical arrangement but a strategic leveraging of various cloud features to suit evolving business needs. The design and implementation of such a strategy is an ongoing process, requiring iterative refinement and adaptation in response to new cloud capabilities, updates, and corporate shifts in focus.

In essence, through a well-constructed multi-cloud strategy, organizations are empowered to transcend the limitations posed by single-provider reliance, thereby enabling operational scalability, reliable service continuity, and innovation through adaptive resource utilization. This underscores the importance of evolving cloud management practices to embrace hybrid and cross-cloud functionalities, preparing enterprises to not only meet current business objectives but to strategically pivot towards emerging opportunities as they arise.

5.2 Crossplane's Role in Multi-Cloud Management

Crossplane emerges as a pivotal tool in the arena of multi-cloud management, offering the abstraction and orchestration needed to streamline operations across various cloud providers. It extends Kubernetes control mechanisms, enabling DevOps teams to manage cloud resources using the powerful declarative approach of Kubernetes for infrastructure management. This section elucidates the functionalities of Crossplane, highlighting its integral role in harmonizing the complexities of a multi-cloud environment.

By positioning itself as an extension within the Kubernetes ecosystem, Crossplane leverages the Kubernetes API server to manage not only containerized workloads but also cloud provider resources, thereby transforming Kubernetes into a universal control plane for cloud infrastructure management. This paradigm allows resources to be modeled, scheduled, and orchestrated as Kubernetes-style resources, which Crossplane refers to as *Managed Resources*.

Managed resources in Crossplane are Cloud Service Providers (CSP) offerings wrapped into Kubernetes Custom Resource Definitions (CRDs). Through this mechanism, Kubernetes controllers manage cloud resources which mimic the approach employed to manage Kubernetes Pods, Deployments, Services, and other core objects.

```
apiVersion: database.gcp.crossplane.io/v1beta1
kind: CloudSQLInstance
metadata:
  name: sample-sql
spec:
  forProvider:
    databaseVersion: MYSQL_5_7
    region: us-central1
    settings:
      tier: db-f1-micro
      ipConfiguration:
        ipv4Enabled: true
  writeConnectionSecretsToRef:
    name: cloudsql-password
  providerConfigRef:
    name: gcp-provider
```

The above example delineates a Crossplane managed resource for a Google Cloud SQL instance. The specification illustrates aspects such as database versioning, geographic region, and other pertinent attributes configured within a Kubernetes environment. Importantly, the use of Crossplane manifests allows for the intricate integration of infrastructure code deployment pipelines, which aligns perfectly with Continuous Integration and Continuous Deployment (CI/CD) processes.

Crossplane's operational model is further enhanced through the use of *Composite Resources* (XRs) and *Composition*, which are pivotal for crafting reusable infrastructure definitions. A Composite Resource is essentially a Kubernetes Custom Resource that aggregates multiple managed resources into a single abstraction. This approach facilitates the definition of complex infrastructure patterns, encapsulating various resources across multiple cloud providers.

```
apiVersion: v1
kind: Composition
metadata:
```

5.2. CROSSPLANE'S ROLE IN MULTI-CLOUD MANAGEMENT

```
name: high-availability-db
spec:
  compositeTypeRef:
    apiVersion: example.org/v1
    kind: CompositeDatabase
  resources:
    - base:
        apiVersion: database.example.org/v1alpha1
        kind: SQLDatabase
      patches:
        - fromFieldPath: "spec.parameters.databaseName"
          toFieldPath: "spec.forProvider.dbName"
```

This illustration presents a Composition configuration, where the Composite Resource 'CompositeDatabase' orchestrates multiple underlying SQL database instances, potentially across different cloud providers, to fulfill the high-availability requirement. The 'patches' directive describes how fields from the Composite Resource should map to fields of each managed resource, allowing for dynamic and environment-specific customization.

One of Crossplane's powerful features is its ability to facilitate *Provider Agnosticism*. Developers and operators endeavor to write infrastructure configurations that are decoupled from specific cloud provider implementations. By embracing this pattern, organizations can modify service providers with minimal changes to their infrastructure source code, enhancing portability and flexibility in cloud strategies.

Crossplane providers serve as translation interfaces that convert the Crossplane Custom Resources into calls to the respective cloud provider APIs. These Providers abstract the specifics of each cloud provider's API, thus aligning with the quintessential advantage of Write Once, Deploy Anywhere (WODA).

To demonstrate, let's consider a sample Crossplane Provider configuration:

```
apiVersion: pkg.crossplane.io/v1
kind: Configuration
metadata:
  name: my-aws-config
spec:
  package: crossplane/provider-aws:v0.18.1
  imagePullSecrets:
    - name: my-registry-secret
```

This configuration specifies a Crossplane provider package for AWS.

Such a setup empowers operators to manage AWS resources using the same declarative syntax as for on-premises and other cloud resources, eliminating context-switching and reducing integration complexity.

Beyond managed resources and composition, Crossplane also empowers policy-driven infrastructure use with the aid of *Control and Policy APIs*. These APIs enforce governance through policies that control how resources are created and used. Policies can be introduced to validate configurations, such as enforcing region-specific deployments or budget controls, before resources are provisioned.

In a production environment, policy APIs might be critical in harmonizing security and compliance requirements germane to multi-cloud operations. Crossplane policies ensure governance by intercepting configuration changes and enforcing organizational rules and standards before changes are applied.

Crossplane's seamless integration with the GitOps ecosystem is a notable advantage, harmonizing well with modern DevOps practices. As infrastructure configurations are versioned and managed as code, Crossplane manifests stored in repositories via GitOps controllers like Flux or ArgoCD automate the deployment and changes to cloud resources, ensuring synchronized and reliable infrastructure states.

```
apiVersion: argoproj.io/v1alpha1
kind: Application
metadata:
  name: crossplane-managed-resources
spec:
  source:
    repoURL: 'https://github.com/my-org/my-infra-repo'
    path: 'crossplane-resources'
    targetRevision: HEAD
  destination:
    server: https://kubernetes.default.svc
    namespace: crossplane-system
```

This ArgoCD Application specification highlights how Crossplane-managed resources are maintained by automatically syncing configurations from a designated Git Repository into the Kubernetes cluster.

Ultimately, Crossplane elevates the abstraction of cloud resources into Kubernetes-native constructs, enabling fine-grained management of multi-cloud environments through the lens of Kubernetes APIs. By utilizing Crossplane's extensible architecture, organizations can architect, define, and manage multi-cloud strategies that align with their operational objectives while streamlining integration efforts with existing technology stacks.

Crossplane fosters an increased velocity in deploying applications by reducing complexity and configuration sprawl. Orchestrating through composite resource design patterns, Crossplane unifies cloud resource management in a way that significantly enhances productivity and consistency across teams tasked with building and managing cloud-native applications. Thus, Crossplane is not just a tool within the modern developer's toolkit, but a foundation upon which scalable and resilient cloud-first strategies are constructed, paving the way for innovative solutions within diverse and dynamic IT landscapes.

5.3 Defining and Managing Multi-Cloud Applications

Defining and managing applications across multiple cloud environments requires a sophisticated and strategic approach, one that incorporates comprehensive planning, robust tools, and coherent processes. In this section, we delve into the methodologies, practices, and technologies that facilitate the effective deployment and administration of multi-cloud applications, with particular attention to the role of Crossplane and Kubernetes in this domain.

A multi-cloud application strategy leverages services from multiple cloud providers, enabling businesses to capitalize on the unique offerings and geographical reach of each provider. The design phase is critical, as it involves determining the architecture necessary to deploy hybrid services efficiently, maximizing performance, resilience, and cost-effectiveness. This requires an understanding of the application components, dependencies, and the specific capabilities of each cloud environment.

Key considerations in defining multi-cloud applications include:

- Service Portability: Applications should be designed to be portable across different cloud environments, minimizing dependency on provider-specific services whenever feasible.

- Interoperability Interconnects: Network configuration and integrations across cloud environments must ensure seamless communication between application components.

- Data Governance and Compliance: Strategies to manage data sovereignty, privacy, and adherence to regulatory requirements across jurisdictions.

- Optimized Resource Allocation: Efficient utilization of resources, taking advantage of cost variations, and performance capabilities inherent to each provider.

Understanding these elements sets the foundation for deploying applications in a multi-cloud environment. Kubernetes plays a pivotal role as a container orchestration platform that abstracts infrastructure management, allowing the deployment of applications using consistent APIs across different cloud providers. Crossplane extends this capacity by managing not only containerized workloads but also cloud-native infrastructure components as described in earlier sections.

One of the primary methodologies for managing multi-cloud applications is the microservices architecture, which involves decomposing applications into modular, loosely-coupled services. Microservices encourage distributed processing and parallel development, and naturally lend themselves to deployments across multiple cloud environments. Each microservice can be isolated to the cloud provider offering the optimal balance of performance, capabilities, and cost.

```
apiVersion: apps/v1
kind: Deployment
metadata:
  name: my-microservice
  labels:
    app: my-microservice
spec:
  replicas: 3
  selector:
    matchLabels:
      app: my-microservice
  template:
    metadata:
      labels:
        app: my-microservice
    spec:
      containers:
      - name: my-microservice
        image: myregistry/my-microservice:v1
```

5.3. DEFINING AND MANAGING MULTI-CLOUD APPLICATIONS

```
ports:
- containerPort: 80
```

The example above outlines how a microservice might be deployed on Kubernetes, showcasing the declarative nature of Kubernetes resource management, which is extended to cloud infrastructure using Crossplane. The statelessness and scalability of microservices make them ideal candidates for multi-cloud deployments, further enhanced by Crossplane's ability to manage the required cloud components.

Defining hybrid connectivity is critical in multi-cloud applications to manage communication between services hosted on disparate cloud infrastructures. This involves configuring network elements such as Virtual Private Networks (VPNs), dedicated interconnects, or software-defined networking (SDN) solutions. These integrations ensure that microservices communicate efficiently with distributed elements, sustaining application performance and integrity.

Service mesh solutions such as Istio or Linkerd add an additional layer, providing features like secure service-to-service communication, failure recovery, and load balancing, all without modifying the application code. These capabilities are vital for maintaining a stable and secure application environment in a distributed setting.

```
apiVersion: networking.istio.io/v1beta1
kind: ServiceEntry
metadata:
  name: external-apis
spec:
  hosts:
  - external-api.mycompany.com
  location: MESH_EXTERNAL
  ports:
  - number: 80
    name: http
    protocol: HTTP
  resolution: DNS
```

The configuration snippet for Istio above allows secure, controlled access to external services, defining how external APIs are integrated into an application's service mesh.

Implementing Continuous Integration and Continuous Deployment (CI/CD) pipelines is vital for ensuring that application updates and infrastructure changes are automatically tested, validated, and deployed to the various cloud environments without unnecessary delays or errors. Infrastructure as Code (IaC) tools, such as Terraform or Pulumi, could be used alongside Crossplane to automate and maintain consistent cloud deployments.

CI/CD systems, such as Jenkins or GitLab CI, serve to keep development and production environments synchronous, monitoring changes in source control and automatically deploying validated changes across environments.

```
pipeline {
    agent any
    stages {
        stage('Build') {
            steps {
                sh 'make build'
            }
        }
        stage('Test') {
            steps {
                sh 'make test'
            }
        }
        stage('Deploy') {
            steps {
                sh 'kubectl apply -f deployment.yaml'
            }
        }
    }
}
```

This simplified example demonstrates how Jenkins orchestrates a CI/CD pipeline to automate the build, test, and deployment processes, illustrating the seamless transition from code commit to cloud deployment as managed by Kubernetes.

Implementing monitoring and observability is vital in managing multi-cloud applications, enabling teams to track system performance, identify bottlenecks, and resolve potential issues proactively. Tools like Prometheus for metric collection and Grafana for data visualization are commonly used within Kubernetes environments to achieve comprehensive observability.

Logs, metrics, and traces are crucial data sources, and a comprehensive observability strategy will typically include event logs, request tracing, and real-time metrics from various sources, leveraged through dashboards for rapid analysis.

Set up comprehensive alerting mechanisms integrated with operational systems, which can preemptively notify operators of anomalies in application performance, resource utilization, or network connectivity.

```
scrape_configs:
 - job_name: 'kubernetes-nodes'
   kubernetes_sd_configs:
     - role: node
   relabel_configs:
     - action: labelmap
       regex: '__meta_kubernetes_node_label_(.+)'
```

This snippet exemplifies a Prometheus configuration setup for monitoring Kubernetes nodes, capturing relevant performance indicators necessary for maintaining application reliability.

In summary, defining and managing multi-cloud applications encapsulates a variety of strategies and practices, from leveraging container orchestration and network configurations to integrating continuous delivery pipelines and implementing thorough observability protocols. Crossplane, combined with Kubernetes, emerges as a critical asset in this framework, providing an abstraction layer that simplifies the complexities of multi-cloud environments, thus enabling development teams to focus on enhancing application functionality and end-user experience. The adoption of these practices must be guided by organizational goals, technological capabilities, and operational constraints, fostering applications that are not only robust and efficient but are also aligned with evolving business landscapes.

5.4 Data Consistency and Integration Across Clouds

In a multi-cloud architecture, maintaining data consistency and ensuring seamless integration of data across various cloud platforms are critical yet challenging objectives. As organizations increasingly distribute their data and applications across multiple cloud providers to leverage their distinct capabilities, the ability to maintain consistent data views and integrations becomes a cornerstone of operational excellence. This section explores the challenges of data consistency and integration in a multi-cloud environment and outlines strategies and technologies that help overcome these challenges.

Understanding Data Consistency

Data consistency involves ensuring that data remains accurate, reliable, and up-to-date across different systems or locations. In a multi-cloud context, this means that any updates to data in one cloud provider's database should be reflected accurately and timely in the corresponding datasets in other cloud providers' environments. When managing widely distributed data, it is essential to understand the various models of data consistency:

- **Strong Consistency** guarantees that all nodes see the same data at the same time after a transaction.

- **Eventual Consistency** allows for data to be temporarily inconsistent across systems but eventually reach a consistent state.

- **Causal Consistency** ensures that operations related by cause and effect are seen by all nodes in the same order.

- **Read Your Writes** assures that once a write operation is completed by a client, all subsequent read operations will reflect the write.

In multi-cloud environments and distributed systems, many organizations opt for eventual consistency due to its lower latency and higher availability compared to strong consistency models.

Challenges in Data Consistency and Integration

A number of issues arise when addressing data consistency across multi-cloud environments:

- **Network Latency and Partitioning:** As data traverses different networks and cloud domains, latency and partitioning can introduce inconsistencies.

- **Diverse Database Technologies:** Variability between database systems and technologies across cloud providers can complicate consistency management strategies.

5.4. DATA CONSISTENCY AND INTEGRATION ACROSS CLOUDS

- **Concurrency and Transaction Coordination:** Managing concurrent data access and updates across different cloud domains can lead to race conditions and data anomalies.

- **Replication and Synchronization:** Efficiently replicating data without overwhelming network resources and ensuring synchronization pose significant challenges.

- **Compliance and Localization Requirements:** Diverse regulatory requirements can dictate data location and access policies, complicating cross-cloud data strategies.

Strategies for Ensuring Data Consistency and Integration

Several strategies and technologies can be employed to achieve data consistency and facilitate integration across clouds:

- **Distributed Database Systems:** Utilizing databases designed for distributed architecture, such as Google Spanner or Amazon Aurora Global Databases, which inherently offer cross-region replication and consistency controls.

  ```
  CREATE DATABASE example_db
    OPTIONS (instance_id = 'example-instance', database_id = 'global-db');
  ```

- **Data Synchronization Services:** Employing dedicated services like AWS Database Migration Service or Azure Data Factory for continuous data replication and synchronization across cloud environments.

- **Eventual Consistency with Conflict Resolution:** Designing applications to handle conflict resolution under eventual consistency models using techniques such as version vectors or merging algorithms to ensure correct data states.

- **Consistent Hashing and Sharding:** Implementing consistent hashing and data sharding schemes can ensure balanced and resilient data distribution across clouds, minimizing cross-region latency and accelerating data access.

  ```
  class ConsistentHashRing:
      def __init__(self, nodes=None):
          self.nodes = nodes or []
  ```

```python
        self.ring = {}
        self.__generate__hash__ring()

    def __generate__hash__ring(self):
        for node in self.nodes:
            hashed_key = self.__hash_function(node)
            self.ring[hashed_key] = node

    def __hash_function(self, key):
        return hash(key) % len(self.nodes)

    def get__node(self, key):
        hashed_key = self.__hash_function(key)
        return self.ring.get(hashed_key)

consistency_hash = ConsistentHashRing(['node1', 'node2', 'node3'])
data_node = consistency_hash.get_node('my_data_key')
```

- **Data API Gateways and Middleware:** Integration of middleware solutions and API gateways that encapsulate underlying data platforms, provide uniform data access methods, and handle consistency at the application middleware layer.

- **Event-Driven Architectures:** Leveraging event-driven paradigms with streaming platforms such as Apache Kafka or Google Pub/Sub, which can ensure real-time data updates across applications deployed over multiple clouds.

```yaml
apiVersion: kafka.strimzi.io/v1beta1
kind: KafkaTopic
metadata:
    name: crosscloud-data-sync
spec:
    partitions: 3
    replicas: 3
    config:
        retention.ms: 7200000
        cleanup.policy: compact
```

Ensuring Data Integration

Beyond maintaining consistency, integrating data across clouds forms a cornerstone of multi-cloud architectures. Integration involves amalgamating data from various systems, ensuring seamless flow and exchange of information.

Several integration approaches can be utilized:

- **Data Lakes and Warehousing Extended Across Clouds:**

5.4. DATA CONSISTENCY AND INTEGRATION ACROSS CLOUDS

Creating centralized data lakes or integrating distributed data warehouses that aggregate data from multiple cloud sources using services like Snowflake, which natively supports cross-cloud integration and processing.

- **APIs and Microservices Integration:** Developing APIs and microservices that abstract cloud service heterogeneity, ensuring uniform communication and data handling across different environments, while also delegating tasks like data transformation and enrichment.

```
type Query {
   getCloudData(id: ID!): CloudData
}

type CloudData {
   id: ID!
   providerData: String
   region: String
}
```

- **Use of Middleware and ETL Tools:** Employing middlewares such as Apache Camel or ETL tools like Talend that facilitate transformations, filtering, and integration of data from diverse sources.

The complexity of maintaining data consistency and integration across cloud environments is non-trivial and requires careful considerations of both technical choices and architectural design. Using robust distributed data systems, automated synchronization services, and abstracting integration complexities through microservices and middleware solutions can architect an environment where data remains consistent and integrated, channeling the cumulative strengths and services of a multi-cloud approach to full effect. These practices provide a comprehensive methodology to evolve data management approaches, aligning them with the nuances and demands of dynamic and diverse multi-cloud ecosystems.

5.5 Ensuring Reliability and Availability

In the multi-cloud landscape, ensuring the reliability and availability of services is paramount. Reliability refers to the system's ability consistently to perform its expected functions over time, while availability indicates the system's readiness for use whenever needed. Achieving these qualities in a multi-cloud environment involves intricate strategies that encompass architectural planning, fault tolerance mechanisms, redundancy, and real-time monitoring. This section explores these aspects in detailed context and how Crossplane can facilitate in orchestrating reliable and available cloud infrastructures.

Architectural Frameworks for Reliability

At the heart of ensuring reliability and availability in multi-cloud applications are resilient architectural paradigms. These architectural blueprints commonly encompass redundancy, fault isolation, graceful degradation, and leader-election procedures, among others.

- **Redundancy and Replica Sets**: Replication both in horizontal and vertical dimensions ensures that application components are duplicated across several cloud resources or regions, which provides seamless end-user experiences even if parts of the system fail. This holistic approach spreads instances across multiple nodes or even across cloud provider zones.

    Kubernetes Deployments, for instance, provide an inherent form of redundancy with replica sets, ensuring that a pre-defined set of application instances are always running.

```
apiVersion: apps/v1
kind: Deployment
metadata:
  name: web-server
spec:
  replicas: 5
  selector:
    matchLabels:
      app: web
  template:
    metadata:
      labels:
        app: web
    spec:
      containers:
```

5.5. ENSURING RELIABILITY AND AVAILABILITY

```
- name: web
  image: nginx:latest
  ports:
    - containerPort: 80
```

- **Service Mesh for Fault Isolation**: Introducing a service mesh such as Istio or Linkerd contributes to fault isolation, controlling traffic during failure scenarios and enabling granular redirection, retries, or circuit breaking.

    Circuit breaking paradigms permit systems to stop repeatedly failing operations, preventing cascading failures, and allowing services to recover autonomously.

```
apiVersion: networking.istio.io/v1alpha3
kind: DestinationRule
metadata:
  name: web-destination
spec:
  host: web.service.cluster.local
  trafficPolicy:
    circuitBreaker:
      simpleCb:
        errorThresholdPercentage: 50
        slowResponseThresholdPercentage: 60
        slowResponseTimeout: 5s
```

- **Load Balancing and Geo-Diversity**: Distributed load balancing dynamically matches resource availability and demand, directing traffic to the least congested or geographically favorable servers. Cloud-native load balancers or services like AWS Elastic Load Balancing (ELB), Azure Load Balancer, and Google Cloud Load Balancing are invaluable.

Ensuring High Availability

High availability involves ensuring that resources and services remain accessible even amid failures. Multi-cloud architectures inherently foster opportunities for high availability solutions:

- **Multi-Region Deployments**: Deploying resources across various geographic locations underpins high availability, protecting against regional outages or network failures. Resource mirror replicas are structured, ensuring alternative region accessibility.

- **Caching Layer**: Implementing distributed caching solutions like Redis or Amazon ElastiCache removes bottlenecks from data reads, efficiently supplying data closer to end-users while reducing load on primary databases.

- **Auto-scaling Capabilities**: Leveraging auto-scaling within cloud resources ensures the system-scale accommodates variable loads without manual interventions. Providers like AWS and GCP empower rules-driven autoscaling based on specific metrics thresholds.

```
apiVersion: autoscaling/v1
kind: HorizontalPodAutoscaler
metadata:
  name: web-server
spec:
  maxReplicas: 10
  minReplicas: 3
  scaleTargetRef:
    apiVersion: apps/v1
    kind: Deployment
    name: web-server
  targetCPUUtilizationPercentage: 60
```

Crossplane's Role in Reliability and Availability

Crossplane's contribution transcends providing APIs around managed cloud resources, instead offering comprehensive solutions aligning Kubernetes with cloud-native operations and enabling resources spanning across cloud providers and regions.

- **RAP (Reliability and Availability Policies)**: Utilizing Crossplane's Custom Resource Definitions (CRDs), organizations can encapsulate their RAP strategies, ensuring policy adherence via Kubernetes manifest language.

- **Automated Failover and Disaster Recovery**: Crossplane orchestrates seamless deployments across cloud resources, favoring geographically distributed setups. Managed resources for DNS failover or health-check monitors direct traffic to operational workloads.

Monitoring, Alerting, and Response Strategies

5.5. ENSURING RELIABILITY AND AVAILABILITY

Maintaining reliability and availability mandates vigilant monitoring and rapid response protocols that capture real-time system metrics and alert operators to unforeseen events. Key elements include:

- **Centralized Logging and Monitoring Tools**: Tools like Prometheus and Grafana under Kubernetes setups, or cloud-native services such as CloudWatch, Azure Monitor, or Stackdriver, systematically collect data for analysis and illustrate health and performance trends.

- **Alerting Systems**: Applying alerting rules that trigger notifications to responsible teams upon metric breach helps preemptively mitigate issues before impacting end users.

```
groups:
- name: example
  rules:
  - alert: HighCPUusage
    expr: node_cpu_seconds_total{mode="idle"} < 0.1
    for: 5m
    labels:
      severity: warning
    annotations:
      summary: "CPU usage is critically high"
      description: "CPU usage on instance {{ $labels.instance }} is above 90%."
```

Automated Incident Response

Reliability does not rest solely with infrastructure but encompasses preparedness through Incident Response procedures. This aims to automate recovery steps ranging from rollback deployments upon failures using CI/CD pipeline scripts, to detailed run-books guiding manual interventions.

Ensuring reliability and availability in multi-cloud environments is a multifaceted endeavor that demands harmonizing architectural innovation, strategic redundancy, real-time monitoring, and proactive incident management. By integrating native cloud possibilities with orchestrated platforms like Crossplane, organizations pivot to defend and enhance service reliability and readiness. This concerted effort underpins a resilient service delivery, effectively addressing the nuanced challenges posed by distributing operations across diverse and dynamically evolving cloud landscapes.

5.6 Cost Management and Optimization

Effective cost management and optimization are crucial components of multi-cloud strategies. As businesses leverage diverse cloud services to enhance scalability, flexibility, and performance, the complexity of managing and controlling costs increases exponentially. Organizations must employ comprehensive strategies to ensure cost-effective use of multi-cloud infrastructures. This section provides an in-depth exploration of cost management practices, optimization techniques, and tools that facilitate prudent financial oversight in a multi-cloud environment.

Understanding Multi-Cloud Cost Dynamics

The intricacies of multi-cloud cost management stem from the varied pricing structures of different cloud service providers. Each provider—whether AWS, Google Cloud, Azure, or others—offers distinct pricing models for computation, storage, networking, and additional services, making cost-effective resource utilization challenging. Core factors influencing cloud costs include:

- **Provisioning Inefficiencies:** Overprovisioned resources, unused instances, and redundant services increase costs without improving performance.

- **Data Transfer and Egress Costs:** Transferring data between cloud platforms or regions incurs costs that can accumulate significantly.

- **Billing Complexity:** Understanding and managing intricate billing mechanisms and structures across multiple vendors can be daunting.

- **Dynamic Usage Patterns:** Fluctuating demand requires agile resource management to ensure cost scales with usage.

Strategies for Cost Management and Optimization

- **Right-Sizing Resources:** Constantly evaluate and adjust compute resources (e.g., CPU, memory) to align with actual work-

5.6. COST MANAGEMENT AND OPTIMIZATION

loads. Employ automated right-sizing tools that analyze usage patterns and recommend optimal configurations.

```
apiVersion: v1
kind: Pod
metadata:
  name: optimized-pod
spec:
  containers:
  - name: my-container
    image: my-image
    resources:
      requests:
        memory: "256Mi"
        cpu: "500m"
      limits:
        memory: "512Mi"
        cpu: "1"
```

- **Utilize Preemptible or Spot Instances:** Take advantage of cost-efficient, short-lived instances like AWS Spot Instances or GCP Preemptible VMs designed for fault-tolerant and flexible applications. Implement strategies to accommodate interruption handling.

```
aws ec2 request-spot-instances \
  --instance-count 2 \
  --type one-time \
  --launch-specification file://launch-specification.json
```

- **Monitor and Analyze Usage Patterns:** Deploy cloud monitoring and analytics tools to derive insights into usage patterns, identifying periods of high and low activity, and adjusting resources accordingly.

- **Implement Budget and Cost Alerts:** Leverage cloud-native tools to set detailed budgets or projected spending limits, receiving alerts on potential overages in real-time to prevent unexpected bills. AWS Budgets, for instance, can provide detailed reports and alerts.

- **Adopt Cloud-Native Cost Management Tools:** Utilize tools provided by cloud vendors such as AWS Cost Explorer, Azure Cost Management, and Google Cloud's Cost Management, each offering comprehensive dashboards, cost allocation tags, and forecasting capabilities.

Crossplane's Role in Cost Management

Crossplane extends the Kubernetes control plane to manage cloud infrastructure with declarative configuration methodologies, allowing for the definition and management of infrastructure as code. This facilitates efficient resource utilization by enforcing policies through Kubernetes constructs, promoting cost-effective deployments.

- **Declarative Infrastructure Management:** Use infrastructure definitions that dynamically adjust to resource needs, reducing the risk of overprovisioning and inefficient resource utilization.

- **Policy-Driven Cost Optimization:** Define and apply cost-related constraints and policies, such as quotas or tags, to manage and enforce cost limits programmatically.

  ```
  apiVersion: policy.crossplane.io/v1alpha1
  kind: Policy
  metadata:
    name: cost-limits-policy
  spec:
    costBudget:
      maxMonthlySpend: 1000
      currency: USD
  ```

- **Utilize Composite Resources for Aggregate Management:** Employ Crossplane's Composite Resources (XRs) to create reusable infrastructure modules that inherently apply cost management policies irrespective of the underlying cloud provider.

Advanced Cost Optimization Techniques

- **Serverless Architectures:** Embrace serverless computing, which charges only for actual consumption rather than preallocated resources, automatically scaling with workload demand.

- **Hybrid and Reserved Instances:** Combine on-demand and reserved pricing models tailored to workload stability, balancing cost efficiency with flexibility. This approach can significantly reduce firefighting scenarios.

- **Data Archiving and Tiered Storage:** Implement tiered storage strategies using cold or archive storage for infrequently accessed data, optimizing costs for long-term data retention on services like AWS Glacier or Azure Blob Archive.

- **Automate Lifecycle Management:** Use automation scripts for periodic cleanup, resource deactivation during off-hours, and lifecycle events management to avoid unnecessary resource retention.

```
import boto3

ec2 = boto3.client('ec2')

def terminate_idle_instances():
    instances = ec2.describe_instances(Filters=[
        {'Name': 'instance-state-name', 'Values': ['running']}
    ]).get('Reservations', [])

    for reservation in instances:
        for instance in reservation['Instances']:
            # Custom logic to check instance usage
            terminate_instance(instance['InstanceId'])

def terminate_instance(instance_id):
    ec2.terminate_instances(InstanceIds=[instance_id])
    print(f"Terminated instance: {instance_id}")

terminate_idle_instances()
```

- **Containerization and Kubernetes Orchestration:** Maximize server utilization and enhance flexibility through container strategies orchestrated by Kubernetes, allowing fine-grained resource allocation.

Effective cost management and optimization in multi-cloud environments are continuous endeavors requiring detailed planning, proactive monitoring, and strategic execution of industry-proven practices. By exploiting advanced cost management tools, adopting Crossplane's policy-driven infrastructure, and utilizing comprehensive monitoring and automation strategies, organizations can harness the multi-cloud domain to its utmost potential while maintaining financial prudence. Through concerted efforts in managing resources, controlling waste, and forecasting expenses, businesses can achieve a harmonious balance between operational performance and cost-effectiveness in their cloud operations.

5.7 Security Considerations in Multi-Cloud

Operating within a multi-cloud environment presents distinct security challenges that require meticulous attention and strategic planning. As organizations distribute applications and data across multiple cloud service providers, the complexity of maintaining secure operations increases. This section delves into the security considerations vital to multi-cloud strategies, addressing identity and access management, data protection, network security, compliance, and the integration of security best practices.

Identity and Access Management (IAM)

IAM in a multi-cloud context is integral to ensuring that users and services have correct and consistent access across all cloud environments. Because each provider often has its own IAM system (e.g., AWS IAM, Google Cloud IAM, and Azure AD), organizations must establish processes that unify these disparate systems.

- **Unified Identity Federation**: Implement identity federation to centralize authentication processes across various cloud platforms. Solutions like Single Sign-On (SSO) simplify user management and enforce consistent security policies.

  ```
  gcloud alpha iam identity-providers create \
    --provider-id=my-sso-provider \
    --idp-config="{\"ssoUrl\":\"https://sso.example.com\",\"rsaPublicKeys
       ...\":[]}"
  ```

- **Role-Based Access Control (RBAC)**: Leverage RBAC to enforce fine-grained access control by defining roles and corresponding permissions, ensuring least privilege access across cloud environments.

  ```
  kind: Role
  apiVersion: rbac.authorization.k8s.io/v1
  metadata:
  ```

```
      namespace: my-namespace
      name: read-access
    rules:
    - apiGroups: [""]
      resources: ["pods", "services"]
      verbs: ["get", "list", "watch"]
```

- **Audit and Monitoring**: Establish comprehensive logging and monitoring of IAM activities to detect unauthorized access attempts or misuse.

Data Protection

Data encryption and protection mechanisms are vital for safeguarding sensitive information across cloud environments. Ensuring data integrity and confidentiality involves multi-layered approaches:

- **Data Encryption (At Rest and In Transit)**: Enforce strong encryption algorithms for data at rest using server-side encryption mechanisms available on cloud platforms and ensure end-to-end encryption for data in transit through TLS/SSL protocols.

- **Key Management Systems (KMS)**: Utilize cloud-native KMS services for seamless management of cryptographic keys, ensuring automatic key rotation and access control. Securely manage encryption keys with AWS KMS, Google Cloud KMS, or Azure Key Vault.

```
aws kms create-key --description "My Multi-Cloud Key" \
    --key-usage ENCRYPT_DECRYPT --origin AWS_KMS
```

- **Data Loss Prevention (DLP) Services**: Integrate DLP services to identify, monitor, and protect sensitive data, preventing unauthorized exposure and transmission.

Network Security

Network security within a multi-cloud environment demands the configuration of secure, resilient network architectures that can scale and protect against threats:

- **Virtual Private Networks (VPNs)** and **Dedicated Interconnects**: Configure secure VPNs and dedicated network connections to ensure protected communications between cloud environments.

- **Network Segmentation and Microsegmentation**: Utilize network segmentation to isolate workloads in distinct virtual networks and employ microsegmentation for fine-grained access control within the application layer, minimizing lateral movement.

```
apiVersion: networking.k8s.io/v1
kind: NetworkPolicy
metadata:
  name: allow-app-traffic
spec:
  podSelector:
    matchLabels:
      app: my-app
  ingress:
  - from:
    - podSelector:
        matchLabels:
          app: frontend
```

- **Firewall and Security Groups**: Implement multi-layered filtering with firewalls and cloud-native security groups that define rules to permit or restrict traffic based on protocol, IP addresses, and ports.

Compliance and Governance

Maintaining compliance across multiple cloud providers involves ensuring adherence to industry standards and regulatory requirements, which vary depending on data types and jurisdictions:

- **Compliance Frameworks**: Implement compliance frameworks like GDPR, HIPAA, or PCI DSS, and prepare audits to assess adherence to privacy and security standards.

- **Configuration Management**: Use configuration management tools to ensure consistent and approved configurations across environments, reducing the risk of non-compliance due to misconfigurations.

```
{
  "policyRule": {
    "if": {
```

5.7. SECURITY CONSIDERATIONS IN MULTI-CLOUD

```
      "field": "type",
      "equals": "Microsoft.Storage/storageAccounts"
    },
    "then": {
      "effect": "audit"
    }
  }
}
```

- **Policy Automation and Reporting**: Employ tools like Cloud Custodian or AWS Config for automated policy enforcement and reporting, allowing for constant compliance monitoring and adjustments.

Integrating Security Best Practices

Security is an evolving discipline, where best practices ensure robust and context-sensitive protection in a multi-cloud setup. Key practices include:

- **DevSecOps Integration**: Adopt DevSecOps methodologies to incorporate security into the continuous integration and continuous deployment (CI/CD) pipeline, facilitating early vulnerability detection and remediation.

- **Security as Code**: Leverage Infrastructure as Code (IaC) to integrate security policies and configurations into the deployment scripts, ensuring automated and consistent security enforcement and reducing human error.

- **Continuous Vulnerability Assessment**: Deploy automated scanning tools to identify vulnerabilities in cloud applications and infrastructure. Solutions like OWASP Dependency-Check and cloud-specific services can be embedded into CI/CD pipelines.

```
dependency-check.sh --project "Multi-Cloud Project" --scan .
```

- **Zero Trust Architecture**: Implement Zero Trust principles by continuously verifying access with minimal trust assumptions, reinforcing identity verification and microsegmentation.

Maintaining a secure multi-cloud environment relies on comprehensive and integrated approaches addressing identity and access management, data protection, network security, compliance, and security best practices. Emphasizing layered defenses, consistent policy application, and continuous security assessment united under cohesive management frameworks paves the way for a robust and durable multi-cloud strategy. By proactively adapting to the evolving threat landscape, organizations can safeguard their multi-cloud operations, reinforcing trust and delivering secure, efficient cloud services.

Chapter 6

Integrating Crossplane with DevOps Pipelines

Integrating Crossplane with DevOps pipelines streamlines infrastructure management by embedding cloud resource provisioning into continuous integration and deployment workflows. This integration fosters a unified approach, where infrastructure is treated as code, allowing for automated deployments and scalable operations. By leveraging Crossplane within DevOps processes, organizations achieve greater agility, reduced operational risk, and improved consistency across environments. This approach enables rapid iteration and feedback cycles, integrating seamlessly with existing toolchains like GitOps and CI/CD platforms. Understanding this integration's potential allows teams to enhance their DevOps practice by aligning infrastructure management with application delivery, ensuring agility and reliability.

6.1 DevOps and Infrastructure as Code

DevOps represents a cultural and operational paradigm shift that emphasizes collaboration, automation, and integration between software development and IT operations. It emerged as a response to the siloed divisions that traditionally existed between the development of application code and its deployment in production environments. By fostering a culture of shared responsibility and transparency, DevOps aims to enhance software delivery speed, quality, and consistency.

Infrastructure as Code (IaC) complements DevOps by bringing similar levels of automation and consistency to infrastructure management as have been achieved in application development. IaC allows infrastructure configurations to be managed using code versioning and collaboration tools. This codification of infrastructure facilitates automated provisioning, configuration, and management of computing resources. IaC is central to achieving the efficiencies promised by DevOps, as it enables teams to manage infrastructure similarly to applications — with rapid iteration, testing, and deployment.

Traditionally, infrastructure provisioning involved manual intervention by system administrators who configured servers and networks according to documented procedures. This manual approach was fraught with potential for error, consumed significant time, and lacked scalability. Infrastructure as Code overcomes these challenges by allowing infrastructure to be defined and maintained via high-level, human-readable configuration files. These configurations can be stored in version control systems, facilitating traceability, collaboration, and rollback capabilities.

The implementation of IaC often involves using configuration management tools and orchestration frameworks. Examples include platforms like Terraform, Ansible, Puppet, and Chef, each having unique features and capabilities. Terraform, for instance, uses its own domain-specific language to define infrastructure in configuration files, allowing users to describe cloud resources like instances, networks, and DNS records. Meanwhile, Ansible focuses on automation across various systems using simple YAML syntax, useful for configuration management and application deployment.

```
provider "aws" {
```

6.1. DEVOPS AND INFRASTRUCTURE AS CODE

```
  region = "us-west-2"
}

resource "aws_instance" "web_server" {
  ami = "ami-0c55b159cbfafe1f0"
  instance_type = "t2.micro"

  tags = {
    Name = "WebServerInstance"
  }
}
```

DevOps and IaC are inherently intertwined as both emphasize automation and the removal of manual processes that constitute bottlenecks in the software delivery lifecycle. Continuous Integration (CI) and Continuous Deployment (CD) pipelines are integral components of DevOps that leverage IaC for reliable infrastructure configuration, provisioning, and deployment.

IaC provides several benefits, including speed, simplicity, and repeatability. Automation scripts replace manual setup procedures, reducing the time needed for provisioning infrastructure from hours or days to minutes. By automating infrastructure deployment processes, organizations can quickly scale up and down their environments to meet fluctuating demand.

Infrastructure as Code enhances deployment stability and predictability by reducing the variation between different environments. Development, testing, and production environments can be provisioned using the same set of configuration files, ensuring that the same settings and resources are applied consistently. This reduces the "it works on my machine" problem, where code operates correctly in one environment but fails in another due to configuration differences.

IaC also plays a crucial role in disaster recovery and business continuity. Infrastructure configurations can be stored in version control, allowing for reverting to a known state quickly in case of failure. Moreover, the automation scripts can act as documentation, detailing every aspect of the infrastructure. This ensures that in the event of a failure, consistent environments can be reproduced with minimal effort.

The synergy between IaC and cloud computing cannot be overstated. The elasticity and scalability offered by cloud platforms are fully realized when paired with IaC. Resources can be provisioned and deallocated dynamically based on application load without needing physical intervention. This elasticity is especially beneficial for organizations with variable workloads, allowing them to optimize cost and performance.

IaC further cements its role by enabling Infrastructure Testing, which is similar to unit testing in software development. Tools such as Test Kitchen and ServerSpec can be used to validate that infrastructure as defined by code actually functions as expected. This form of testing ensures that configurations are correct and compliant before they are applied to production environments, echoing the testing practices in software development that contribute to robust application quality.

```
describe port(80) do
  it { should be_listening }
end
```

Another critical consideration is security, an area where IaC offers significant improvements. By codifying infrastructure, organizations can achieve enhanced security automation and compliance verification. Infrastructure code can undergo static analysis to detect insecure configurations before deployment. Additionally, infrastructure configurations stored in version control systems can be subjected to the same rigorous review and approval processes as application code, providing traceability and accountability.

IaC also supports the implementation of "immutable infrastructure" — a concept where servers are never modified post-deployment. Instead, any change requires a new server creation with the updated configurations. This practice minimizes configuration drift and creates reliable, predictable environments.

However, IaC and its implementation are not without challenges. Organizations need to adopt new skill sets to manage infrastructure code effectively. This involves developers acquiring knowledge of system operations and operators understanding development practices and tools. Additionally, the abstraction of complex infrastructure tasks into code can lead to increased complexity and potential errors requiring robust quality assurance processes.

Ultimately, DevOps and Infrastructure as Code together enable teams to deliver software faster and more reliably. By reducing the effort and errors typically associated with infrastructure management, teams can focus more on delivering business value through their software and leave the more repetitive, error-prone tasks to automated systems. This integration advances an agile and resilient IT landscape, crucial in today's rapidly changing technological environment.

6.2 Crossplane in CI/CD Workflows

Crossplane is an open-source control plane that extends the Kubernetes API, bringing a new paradigm for managing cloud resources through declarative configurations. When integrated within CI/CD workflows, Crossplane extends the power of Kubernetes to manage not only containerized applications but also a wide variety of multi-cloud and hybrid cloud infrastructure components. This integration enables developers and operations teams to automate cloud resource provisioning alongside their application deployments, ensuring a unified approach to software delivery and operations.

Continuous Integration and Continuous Deployment (CI/CD) are key practices within the DevOps methodology that streamline the lifecycle of application development and deployment. CI/CD pipelines automate building, testing, and deploying code changes, significantly reducing the time it takes to release new features and bug fixes. The incorporation of Crossplane into these workflows allows teams to automate infrastructure provisioning in a standard manner, leveraging the Kubernetes ecosystem's inherent capabilities.

Crossplane achieves this by using the concept of managed resources, akin to Custom Resource Definitions (CRDs) in Kubernetes, which represent external resources like databases, message queues, or cloud instances. Developers can utilize these managed resources to define the desired state of their application's infrastructure and let Crossplane reconcile that state automatically.

A typical CI/CD pipeline involves stages parallel to the software delivery lifecycle, including code building, testing, and deployment. Incorporating Crossplane into these stages will typically involve:

1. Infrastructure Setup: Define infrastructure requirements using Crossplane resources.

2. **Application Development:** Develop and verify applications against the defined infrastructure.

3. **Integration Testing:** Validate integration of components, including infrastructure managed by Crossplane.

4. **Deployment:** Deploy the application and infrastructure updates as a cohesive unit.

Setting up Crossplane within a CI/CD workflow involves several setup components, primarily focused on configuring Crossplane to work within the Kubernetes Cluster where the CI/CD pipeline executes. The following developers and DevOps engineers can manage infrastructure along with application code:

Cloud Service Providers expose various APIs that can be used to automate infrastructure provisioning. Crossplane leverages these APIs to manage resources consistently with Kubernetes native resources. This means that the same automation principles applied to container orchestration in Kubernetes can be used for cloud infrastructure provisioning.

```
apiVersion: database.aws.crossplane.io/v1alpha1
kind: RDSInstance
metadata:
  name: example-db
spec:
  forProvider:
    region: us-west-2
    dbInstanceClass: db.t3.micro
    engine: postgres
    masterUsername: postgresadmin
  providerConfigRef:
    name: example-aws-provider
```

In CI/CD systems like Jenkins, GitLab CI, or GitHub Actions, Crossplane manifests can be applied as part of the pipeline, allowing for an end-to-end automated deployment strategy that begins from code changes and culminates in fully provisioned infrastructure.

An important characteristic of Crossplane in CI/CD workflows is the concept of environment demarcation through namespaces. Kubernetes namespaces allow logical partitions in a cluster, and Crossplane extends this feature by managing the lifecycle of resources in these namespaces. Within a CI/CD pipeline, different environments (e.g., development, testing, production) can be mapped to namespaces, ensuring consistent per-environment management of resources.

```yaml
name: Deploy Infrastructure

on:
  push:
    branches: [ main ]

jobs:
  build:
    runs-on: ubuntu-latest

    steps:
    - name: Checkout code
      uses: actions/checkout@v2

    - name: Set up Crossplane
      run: |
        kubectl apply -f cluster-config.yaml

    - name: Apply Crossplane Resources
      run: |
        kubectl apply -f manifests/
```

Crossplane's capabilities in integration span beyond resource provisioning; it also includes health and drift detection mechanisms through Kubernetes' reconciliation loop. This means any divergence from the declared state due to manual changes or unexpected failures will be detected and remediated automatically, maintaining environment consistency. This auto-remediation feature is crucial for ensuring that infrastructure remains reliable and as specified during CI/CD processes, enabling continuous delivery without disruptions.

Another advantage of using Crossplane within CI/CD workflows is its customization via Composition and XRD (Composite Resource Definitions). Organizations can create reusable blueprints for application infrastructure, comprising multiple interrelated resources that are consistently deployed as part of the CI/CD pipeline. Compositions abstract the intricacies of specific cloud providers from developers, streamlining the process of specifying infrastructure dependencies.

```yaml
apiVersion: apiextensions.crossplane.io/v1
kind: Composition
metadata:
  name: composite-cluster
spec:
  compositeTypeRef:
    apiVersion: clusters.example.org/v1alpha1
    kind: CompositeCluster
```

```
resources:
- base:
    apiVersion: compute.crossplane.io/v1alpha1
    kind: KubernetesCluster
    name: k8sCluster
```

The Crossplane Compositions can interlock seamlessly with CI/CD systems through pipelines that handle parameter substitution and environment-specific values. Such composability offers a uniform interface to different resources which have beneath them layers of platform-specific logic, making it ideal for managing deployments across diverse environments.

Implementing Crossplane effectively in CI/CD pipelines requires a few considerations:

- Security: Proper secret management is vital, as access to cloud providers and sensitive data should be encapsulated within appropriate security measures within Kubernetes.

- Observability: Integrate monitoring and logging solutions to track the status of managed resources. Observability tools should align with the monitoring solutions in place for applications, providing holistic visibility over deployments.

- Abstractions vs. Transparency: While abstraction reduces complexity, too much abstraction might hide necessary details. Balancing abstraction with transparency is crucial to maintaining control over managed resources while simplifying developer's interaction with infrastructure.

- Scalability: The performance considerations regarding hundreds or thousands of resources being managed by Crossplane, especially when Kubernetes itself is managing multiple applications, should be assessed and optimized.

By automating infrastructure as closely as application code, DevOps teams can achieve unprecedented harmony between environments and codebases, enhancing the speed and reliability of software deployments. Crossplane's role in CI/CD workflows exemplifies the progression towards a landscape where infrastructure is as agile and adaptive as software development practices themselves, thus fulfilling the promise of DevOps and cloud-native solutions.

6.3 Automating Resource Deployments

Automating resource deployments is an essential aspect of modern software development and delivery, playing a pivotal role in achieving scalable, reliable, and fast deployments in cloud environments. This section details strategies for automating resource deployments with a focus on leveraging tools like Crossplane, Kubernetes, and contemporary CI/CD systems. By understanding and implementing automation strategies, organizations can significantly reduce operational overheads and streamline their software delivery processes.

Resource deployment traditionally involved manual intervention where operations teams would configure servers, networks, and databases based on given specifications. This manual approach was time-consuming and prone to human error. Automation replaces these manual processes with scripts and tools that execute predefined operations to provision resources consistently across environments.

To automate resource deployments effectively, a combination of key components is typically involved, including configuration management, provisioning orchestration, and continuous integration/deployment pipelines.

- **Infrastructure as Code (IaC):** The foundation of deployment automation, IaC involves the definition of infrastructure in code-like formats that can be executed repeatedly to achieve the same results. Using languages such as Terraform's HCL (HashiCorp Configuration Language) or Kubernetes YAML manifests, infrastructure can be defined, versioned, and managed alongside application code.

- **Provisioning Tools:** Tools like Terraform, Ansible, and Crossplane help automate the creation of compute resources, network configurations, and storage systems. They are responsible for transforming IaC definitions into actual cloud infrastructure.

- **CI/CD Pipelines:** These pipelines automate the process of building, testing, and deploying applications and infrastructure. When integrated with IaC and provisioning tools, they allow seamless and frequent deployment of both applications and their underlying infrastructure.

- **Monitoring and Logging:** Integrating automation frameworks with monitoring solutions ensures that automated deployments can be validated, and performance metrics can be gathered. This integration is essential for maintaining system health and identifying potential issues early.

Crossplane, as an extension of Kubernetes, can manage cloud resources using Kubernetes APIs, hence enabling an end-to-end automation process that spans applications and infrastructure. This unique approach utilizes Kubernetes native capabilities such as Custom Resource Definitions (CRDs) and controllers to manage the lifecycle of resources.

```
apiVersion: eks.aws.crossplane.io/v1alpha1
kind: EKSCluster
metadata:
  name: sample-eks
spec:
  forProvider:
    region: us-west-2
    version: "1.21"
    roleArnRef:
      name: sample-iam-role
  providerConfigRef:
    name: aws-provider
```

Incorporating Crossplane into a Kubernetes-centric automation strategy involves defining infrastructure components as manageable resources within Kubernetes. These resources are reconciled by Crossplane controllers to achieve the desired state specified in manifests. This seamless integration simplifies the management of complex dependencies between cloud offerings and resources under the consistent interface provided by Kubernetes.

- **Pipeline Configuration:** Configure your CI/CD tool, whether Jenkins, GitLab CI, or another platform, to trigger deployments based on code repository changes. Incorporate steps to apply IaC scripts and Crossplane manifests. This ensures that resource changes are automatically applied when the corresponding infrastructure code is modified.

- **Artifact Management:** Store and version infrastructure artifacts (such as YAML manifests or Terraform scripts) in a dedicated repository, allowing for rigorous change management and

6.3. AUTOMATING RESOURCE DEPLOYMENTS

history tracking. This repository is separate from application code to align with best practices for modular infrastructure management.

- **Environment Isolation:** Use namespace strategies within Kubernetes to separate and manage resources for different stages (development, test, production) which allows for concurrent testing of new infrastructure setups without impacting production systems.

- **Apply Configuration Changes:** Utilize Kubernetes kubectl commands, enriched by Crossplane capabilities, within pipeline scripts to apply resource definitions and configurations seamlessly, automating the transition from declaration to realization.

```
#!/bin/bash
set -e
kubectl apply -f infrastructure-manifests/
```

While automation introduces significant efficiencies, it is not without challenges. Automation complexity, security, and change management are some critical considerations that organizations must address.

- **Complexity:** As systems grow, the complexity of managing numerous automated workflows increases. It is crucial to modularize automation scripts and configurations, achieving reusability and reducing redundancy.

- **Security:** Ensure secure handling of sensitive configuration data (such as API keys and cloud credentials) using Kubernetes secrets or tools like HashiCorp Vault to encrypt and manage access.

```
apiVersion: v1
kind: Secret
metadata:
  name: cloud-credentials
type: Opaque
data:
  access-key: <base64-encoded-access-key>
  secret-key: <base64-encoded-secret-key>
```

- **Change Management:** Employ proper version control practices, change review procedures, and testing strategies to validate infrastructure configurations before deployment. Small, incremental changes help minimize risk and simplify rollbacks.

- **Monitoring and Rollback:** Integrate monitoring systems and dashboards to visualize automated deployment metrics, detect anomalies early, and implement rollback strategies using automated scripts to revert infrastructure changes swiftly.

- **Consistent Naming and Tagging:** Establish policies for naming conventions and resource tagging to enhance traceability, especially in automated deployments that span multiple environments.

- **Testing Infrastructure:** Apply the concept of test-driven development (TDD) to infrastructure. Tools like Terratest and InSpec allow for defining and running tests against cloud infrastructure, ensuring correctness and compliance.

- **Idempotency:** Ensure scripts and configurations maintain idempotency—repeated executions should not alter the final state, nor result in unintended consequences.

- **Documentation and Training:** Maintain comprehensive documentation of automation processes and invest in team training to bolster understanding and adaptability to new tools and practices.

Automating resource deployments using Crossplane and CI/CD workflows exemplifies how modern systems can transform infrastructure management. By abstracting complexity and adopting code-driven processes, teams achieve greater agility, scalability, and reliability across their software delivery lifecycle, aligning organizational goals with technological advancements.

6.4 Version Control for Infrastructure Configurations

Version control systems (VCS) have long been a cornerstone of collaborative software development, providing developers with mechanisms to track and manage changes to code over time. Extending the use of version control to infrastructure configurations is a crucial step in aligning infrastructure management with the more mature and disciplined practices found in software development. This section offers an in-depth analysis of leveraging version control for managing infrastructure configurations, focusing on its integration with tools like Git, Crossplane, and other cloud infrastructure management solutions.

Version control for infrastructure, often referred to as Infrastructure as Code (IaC) management, involves treating infrastructure configurations like software code. This approach enables tracking configuration changes, auditing modifications, and executing experiments without risk to production environments, offering a reliable and traceable methodology for maintaining the state across different environments.

The application of version control systems to infrastructure configurations addresses several challenges faced by organizations relying on manual or ad-hoc processes for managing infrastructure.

- **Change Management and History:** Version control maintains a detailed history of changes, providing insights into what was changed, by whom, and why. This information helps in understanding infrastructure evolution and in retracing steps during troubleshooting.

- **Collaboration and Isolation:** By allowing multiple team members to work simultaneously on configurations, version control facilitates collaboration without the risk of conflicts that lead to downtime. Branching and merging strategies, which are commonplace in software development, fit seamlessly into infrastructure management workflows.

- **Auditing and Compliance:** For organizations in regulated industries, automated record-keeping via a version control system simplifies compliance reporting by ensuring all changes to infrastructure are logged and can be retrieved for audit purposes.

- **Rollback Mechanisms:** By maintaining a detailed record of every change, version control enables rollback of configurations to previous states, providing a safety net against deployments that introduce errors or unforeseen issues.

Version control plays a vital role in the broader Operational Framework known as GitOps. GitOps applies Git-based workflows to operations, utilizing merge requests, branches, and commit history to manage infrastructure. This paradigm offers immediate visibility into system states and changes, encouraging a declarative and immutable infrastructure model.

Adopting version control for infrastructure involves several key steps and considerations, typically revolving around the decision of which toolsets and practices align best with the organization's objectives.

- **Choose a Version Control System:** While Git is the predominant tool due to its distributed nature and robust ecosystem, choosing the right version control system depends on specific organizational needs and ensuring compatibility with existing CI/CD and DevOps processes.

- **Define Infrastructure as Code Artifacts:** Infrastructure configurations should be defined using human-readable formats such as YAML, JSON, or HCL. These configurations encompass the complete stack setup, from compute instances and network configurations to higher-order service abstractions.

```
apiVersion: v1
kind: Namespace
metadata:
  name: production-environment
  labels:
    purpose: production
```

- **Organize Repository Structure:** A well-organized repository structure facilitates understanding and management of infrastructure configurations. Separate environments (e.g., dev, staging, production) into directory hierarchies, and consider using branch-based strategies for environment-specific configurations.

- **Automation and Deployment Pipelines:** Integrate VCS tightly with CI/CD pipelines. Automated scripts should monitor repositories for changes, automatically trigger validation tests, and deploy infrastructure updates whenever new commits are detected.

6.4. VERSION CONTROL FOR INFRASTRUCTURE CONFIGURATIONS

```bash
#!/bin/bash
set -e

# Pull the latest code changes
git pull origin main

# Apply Kubernetes resources
kubectl apply -f infrastructure/

# Verify deployment success
kubectl get all --namespace production-environment
```

Strategizing version control for infrastructure goes beyond merely storing configuration files in a Git repository. It often involves adopting sophisticated practices for improved efficiency and effectiveness:

- **Branching Strategies:** Implement branching strategies that align with different workflows and stages. For instance, use feature branches for new services, environment branches for separate configurations, and release branches for coordinated launches.

- **Pull Requests and Code Reviews:** Enforce code review processes through pull requests for infrastructure changes. This practice ensures peer verification, reducing human error and facilitating knowledge sharing within teams.

- **Tagging and Releases:** Use tagging in version control for marking significant deployments or releases. This creates a permanent reference point to return to for restoring configurations or comparing states.

- **Git Hooks for CI/CD Integration:** Utilize Git hooks for automating checks and validations, such as pre-commit hooks to lint files or pre-push hooks to validate configurations, ensuring higher quality and consistency.

```sh
#!/bin/sh
terraform fmt -check -diff -recursive
if [ $? -ne 0 ]; then
  echo "Terraform files are not properly formatted!"
  exit 1
fi
```

While version control for infrastructure offers numerous benefits, it also introduces several challenges that need to be addressed through best practices and thoughtful implementation:

- **Complexity Management:** As infrastructure scales, the complexity of managing configurations across multiple repositories and environments can increase. Modularize scripts and adopt microservice-aligned principles to reduce complexity.

- **Configuration Drift:** Version control alone does not prevent drift between the declared and actual state of the infrastructure. Use continuous validation tools to detect and correct drift, promoting the idempotency of scripts.

- **Security Concerns:** Safeguard sensitive data within configurations, such as keys and passwords, by utilizing secret management tools instead of hard-coding them within version-controlled files.

- **Training and Adoption:** Encourage team adaptation to these processes through training and establishing internal champions to guide adoption, highlighting the benefits of the approach.

Implementing version control for infrastructure configurations robustly integrates infrastructure management with software engineering practices. It introduces a pathway for safer, more collaborative, and efficient management of dynamic environments, fostering reliability, scalability, and predictability within the operations space. By drawing on best practices and expanding capabilities through tools like Crossplane and aligned services, organizations are empowered to manage infrastructure with the same dexterity and precision that have benefitted software development endeavors for decades.

6.5 Ensuring Consistency Across Environments

Ensuring consistency across different environments is a critical aspect of modern software development and operations. As applications and their underlying infrastructure are developed, tested, and deployed across a variety of environments—such as development, staging, and production—it is crucial that these environments remain consistent. This consistency helps to minimize errors, streamline the development process, and ensure that software behaves predictably when it reaches production.

The challenges associated with environment consistency arise due to configurations, dependencies, and external integrations that may differ across environments. Divergences can be caused by manual configuration processes, varying dependencies, or differences in environment provisioning scripts. These inconsistencies often lead to the "it works on my machine" dilemma, where an application functions correctly in one environment but fails in another.

Numerous strategies and technologies can be employed to maintain consistency across environments, leveraging automation, standardized configurations, and modern practices:

- **Infrastructure as Code (IaC):** One of the core techniques to ensure environment consistency is using IaC to define infrastructure in a declarative manner. Tools like Terraform, AWS CloudFormation, and Kubernetes manifests allow for infrastructure to be codified, versioned, and shared among all environments, ensuring that the same setup is used universally.

```
apiVersion: apps/v1
kind: Deployment
metadata:
  name: nginx-deployment
spec:
  replicas: 3
  selector:
    matchLabels:
      app: nginx
  template:
    metadata:
      labels:
        app: nginx
    spec:
      containers:
      - name: nginx
        image: nginx:1.19.1
        ports:
        - containerPort: 80
```

- **Configuration Management:** Tools like Ansible, Chef, and

Puppet can manage environment configurations, ensuring that the same packages, services, and configurations are maintained across all stages. This approach not only ensures consistency but also helps in automatically applying changes and patches across environments.

- **Containerization:** By packaging applications and their dependencies into containers using tools like Docker, teams can achieve a consistent runtime environment across development, testing, and production. Containers abstract the application from the underlying infrastructure, effectively eliminating environmental discrepancies.

```
FROM python:3.8-slim
WORKDIR /app
COPY requirements.txt /app/
RUN pip install --no-cache-dir -r requirements.txt
COPY . /app
CMD ["python", "app.py"]
```

Version control systems, like Git, extend their utility beyond code by also offering robust management for environment configurations through IaC files and templates. The use of templates allows configurations to be dynamically generated or applied based on environment-specific parameters while maintaining a baseline consistency.

- **Templates and Variables:** Configure infrastructure with parameterized templates using tools such as Helm for Kubernetes or CloudFormation templates for AWS. Variables can define environment-specific parameters (e.g., memory allocation, replica counts), allowing a single template to apply across multiple environments with differing parameters.

- **Semantic Versioning and Tagging:** Use versioning strategies to track and apply infrastructure changes methodically. Semantic versioning of configurations ensures clarity in changes, and tagging in VCS can effectively mark stability points and releases across environments.

```
#!/bin/bash
terraform init
terraform plan -var="environment=production" -out=tfplan
terraform apply tfplan
```

6.5. ENSURING CONSISTENCY ACROSS ENVIRONMENTS

```
# Check out code at tagged release
git checkout tags/release-1.3.0
```

To ensure consistent behavior across environments, automated testing and validation play a crucial role:

- **Infrastructure Testing:** Tools like Terraform's built-in testing suite or Terratest can validate that infrastructure components are configured correctly and consistently before they are provisioned.

- **Environment Verification:** Implement environment verification steps in CI/CD pipelines to automatically check that the necessary components, services, and configurations are in place during deployments.

- **End-to-End Testing:** Conduct end-to-end tests to verify application workflows in replicated production-like environments (e.g., staging). Use data and traffic mirroring strategies to simulate production scenarios.

- **Monitoring and Feedback:** Integrating monitoring tools such as Prometheus, Grafana, or ELK Stack provides real-time feedback on environmental health and consistency, promoting proactive maintenance.

```
from selenium import webdriver

driver = webdriver.Chrome()
driver.get('http://staging.example.com')

assert "Welcome" in driver.title
driver.quit()
```

There are several challenges and considerations organizations face while ensuring environment consistency:

- **Complex Dependency Management:** Managing dependencies in a homogeneous manner can be challenging, especially when environments utilize different versions of libraries or services. Consistent dependency declaration and lockfile management (e.g., package-lock.json or Pipfile.lock) are essential.

- **Environment-Specific Secrets and Credentials:** Separating secrets and sensitive credentials from code and configuration files is crucial. Use vaults or secret management solutions like HashiCorp Vault, AWS Secrets Manager, or Kubernetes Secrets to handle environment-specific credentials securely.

- **Resource Limitations and Scaling Differences:** Developers need to account for differences in available resources and scaling configurations across environments, which can lead to discrepancies in performance and behavior. Define resource allocations explicitly in IaC and container orchestrator configurations.

Maintaining consistency across environments forms the backbone of reliable software development and deployment processes. By leveraging the power of IaC, containerization, version control, and modern automation tools, teams can achieve an unprecedented level of consistency, reducing errors and enhancing the predictability of applications as they move through the pipeline from development to production. Consistently configured environments lead to less time spent on troubleshooting and more time dedicated to innovation and delivering business value.

6.6 Monitoring and Feedback Loops

Monitoring and feedback loops are integral components of any modern DevOps strategy, providing organizations with the real-time data and insights needed to maintain, optimize, and innovate their IT infrastructure and applications. By implementing effective monitoring and feedback mechanisms, teams can rapidly identify and address issues, understand system behaviors, and ensure alignment with business objectives. This section delves into the critical elements of monitoring and feedback loops, providing detailed exploration of tools, strategies, and best practices to effectively employ them within DevOps workflows.

The Role of Monitoring in DevOps

In a DevOps context, monitoring is not merely a tool for troubleshooting; it is a proactive process that informs decision-making, enhances security, and optimizes application performance. It involves tracking

6.6. MONITORING AND FEEDBACK LOOPS

key performance indicators (KPIs), application logs, network traffic, and infrastructure metrics to ensure that services remain reliable, available, and scalable.

Several core objectives drive the need for robust monitoring systems:

- System Health Indicators: Track CPU usage, memory consumption, disk I/O, and network throughput. Monitoring these metrics helps predict resource exhaustion before it affects system performance.

```
curl -X GET "http://localhost:9090/api/v1/query?query=100%20-%20(avg(irate(
    node_cpu_seconds_total{mode=\"idle\"}[5m]))%20*%20100)"
```

- Availability Monitoring: Measure system uptime and detect outages. Failure in detecting downtime quickly can lead to customer dissatisfaction and financial losses.

- Application Performance Monitoring (APM): Measure response times, latency, and errors in application components to ensure that applications meet performance expectations.

- Security Monitoring: Detect unauthorized access and anomaly patterns that could indicate security breaches.

- Business Metrics: Monitor application-level success metrics like transaction rates, user engagement levels, and customer conversion rates. These help align IT operations with business value.

Feedback Loops and Continuous Improvement

Feedback loops are essential to sustaining a continual improvement cycle, providing the necessary context for developers and operations teams to refine system capabilities and rectify defects. There are several types of feedback loops observable in DevOps, including:

- Telemetry Feedback: Real-time data collected from production environments flows back to developers, who use insights to improve code quality and robustness.

- **User Feedback:** Integrate mechanisms for end users to report problems or suggest enhancements directly. Bridging the distance between users and developers allows the prioritization of user-centric improvements.

- **Deployment Feedback:** Track the stability and success rates of deployments using deployment gates or canary release strategies. This provides insights into infrastructure resilience and software reliability.

```
apiVersion: apps/v1
kind: Deployment
metadata:
  name: canary-app
spec:
  replicas: 1
  selector:
    matchLabels:
      app: my-app
      version: canary
  template:
    metadata:
      labels:
        app: my-app
        version: canary
    spec:
      containers:
      - name: my-app-container
        image: my-app:canary
```

Implementing Monitoring Solutions

The successful implementation of monitoring solutions within a DevOps landscape involves a careful selection of tools, strategic planning, and integration with existing systems.

- **Tool Selection:** Choose tools that align with existing technology stacks and organizational needs. Popular tools include Prometheus, Grafana, ELK Stack (Elasticsearch, Logstash, Kibana), Splunk, and New Relic, each offering unique strengths in data gathering and visualization.

- **Instrument Everything:** Instrument code and infrastructure to emit detailed logs, tracing information, and metrics. Libraries such as OpenTelemetry facilitate standardized observability across systems.

6.6. MONITORING AND FEEDBACK LOOPS

- **Establish Baselines:** Define normal operating thresholds and baselines for all monitored systems. Baselines are crucial for recognizing aberrant or harmful behavior patterns in applications.

- **Alerting Strategies:** Design alerting systems which use thresholds and anomaly detection to notify teams of issues in a timely and accurate manner. Effective alerting strategies prevent alert fatigue by minimizing false positives.

```
groups:
- name: memory_alerts
  rules:
  - alert: HighMemoryUsage
    expr: node_memory_Active_bytes / node_memory_MemTotal_bytes * 100 > 90
    for: 5m
    labels:
      severity: warning
    annotations:
      summary: "Instance {{ $labels.instance }} high memory usage"
      description: "Memory usage has exceeded 90\% for more than 5 minutes."
```

Best Practices for Feedback Loops

To maximize the effectiveness of feedback loops, specific best practices should be adhered to:

- **Immersive Dashboards:** Implement dynamic dashboards that display telemetry data and KPIs in real-time. Tools like Grafana offer customizable dashboards that can correlate data sources to paint a holistic picture of system health.

- **Automate Responses:** Use AIOps (Artificial Intelligence for IT Operations) and automated remediation scripts to respond to common issues detected via feedback mechanisms. Automation reduces mean time to recovery (MTTR).

- **Prioritize Feedback Sources:** Not all feedback is equal; prioritize feedback sources based on their reliability and impact on business objectives. This prioritization assists in focusing attention on high-value areas.

- **Continuous Validation:** Validate the assumptions and hypotheses formed from gathered feedback continually. This ensures iterative improvements are based on accurate and relevant data.

Effective monitoring and feedback loops are not merely about the tools employed but how they contribute to a broader strategic framework for improving operational excellence and enhancing product quality. With intelligent design, consistent iteration, and strategic implementation, organizations can greatly enhance their capabilities to maintain performance, deliver value, and drive innovation in their IT and application landscapes. By implementing these practices, teams ensure their systems are resilient, reliable, and responsive to the ever-evolving challenges presented by digital transformation and rapid technological advancement.

6.7 Case Studies of Crossplane in DevOps

Exploring real-world applications and success stories provides valuable insights into how Crossplane can be effectively integrated into DevOps practices. These case studies illustrate various strategies and outcomes achieved by organizations that have leveraged Crossplane to streamline their infrastructure management, optimize workflows, and enhance the overall DevOps lifecycle.

This section examines multiple instances where Crossplane has been successfully employed, highlighting the specific problems addressed, the solutions deployed, and the evident benefits and learnings from these implementations.

Case Study 1: Agile Cloud Service Provider

Overview: An agile cloud service provider needed a streamlined mechanism to manage diversified cloud resources for their customers, consisting primarily of small to medium enterprises relying on a multi-cloud strategy. The existing system, heavily reliant on manual provisioning processes, led to inefficiencies and high operational overheads.

Challenge: The main challenge was the inefficiency in provisioning and managing resources dispersed across different cloud platforms like AWS, GCP, and Azure, each requiring distinct tools and expertise. Consistency and scalability in resource delivery were hard to maintain with the lack of a unified approach.

6.7. CASE STUDIES OF CROSSPLANE IN DEVOPS

Solution: By implementing Crossplane as a control plane, the service provider established a unified API to manage multi-cloud resources. With Crossplane, resource requests were standardized using Kubernetes custom resources, significantly simplifying multi-cloud management.

```
apiVersion: ec2.aws.crossplane.io/v1alpha1
kind: Instance
metadata:
  name: sample-instance
spec:
  forProvider:
    instanceType: t3.small
    region: us-west-1
  providerConfigRef:
    name: aws-config
```

Outcome: The integration resulted in a 40% reduction in provisioning times and a 30% decrease in operational overheads. The streamlined process allowed for the reallocation of engineering resources to focus on innovation rather than infrastructure management. Consistent use of Crossplane ensured uniform policies and compliance across provisioned resources.

Key Learning: Unified management of diverse infrastructural resources can be achieved effectively via Crossplane, reducing complexity and improving operational efficiency.

Case Study 2: Fintech Startup Scaling Operations

Overview: A fast-growing fintech startup was facing challenges with maintaining agility while scaling infrastructure to meet customer demands. The startup, offering real-time financial data services, required robust scalability and rapid provisioning of resources without compromising operational quality.

Challenge: Infrastructure provisioning delays were becoming bottlenecks for new feature deployments. The existing system lacked the automation needed for rapid scaling, resulting in customer dissatisfaction due to delayed services.

Solution: Crossplane was integrated to automate the provisioning process, defining composable infrastructure components through Crossplane's Composition and XR (Composite Resource) Definitions, leveraging infrastructure as services.

```yaml
apiVersion: apiextensions.crossplane.io/v1
kind: CompositeResourceDefinition
metadata:
  name: composite-database
spec:
  group: database.example.org
  names:
    kind: CompositeDatabaseCluster
    plural: compositedatabases
  claimNames:
    kind: Database
    plural: databases
  versions:
  - name: v1alpha1
    schema:
      openAPIV3Schema:
        type: object
        properties:
          engine:
            type: string
          version:
            type: string
```

Outcome: The use of Crossplane allowed the startup to provision and configure the infrastructure needed for new deployments automatically. This fostered a rapid deployment cycle and tackled the latency issues, leading to improved customer experience and retention. The system scaled efficiently to handle increased load with minimal manual intervention.

Key Learning: Crossplane can play a vital role in streamlining operations, enhancing the delivery of complex services by automating infrastructure and embracing a service-oriented architecture.

Case Study 3: Healthcare Provider Ensuring Compliance

Overview: A healthcare provider adhered to stringent regulatory frameworks and required secure, compliant infrastructure solutions that could adapt to changes in regulation and tech-driven transformation. Stagnant infrastructure limited their ability to implement new IT initiatives effectively.

Challenge: The main challenge was aligning technology upgrades with regulatory compliance and security without causing interruptions to critical services. Traditional approaches of maintaining compliance were labor-intensive and error-prone.

Solution: Crossplane was deployed to manage infrastructure lifecycle, integrating with compliance policies directly within the control plane. It allowed dynamic policy inclusion and enforcement, thus guaranteeing infrastructure met compliance requirements.

```
apiVersion: policies.crossplane.io/v1alpha1
kind: InfrastructurePolicy
metadata:
  name: secure-compliance-policy
spec:
  properties:
    encryptionEnabled: true
    auditLogging: enabled
    networkIsolation: true
  providerConfigRef:
    name: standard-compliance
```

Outcome: The healthcare provider achieved a significant reduction in the time needed for compliance checks and insurance, from days to hours. Automated compliance validation facilitated deployment pipelines, supporting faster innovation cycles within a regulated environment.

Key Learning: Automating infrastructure management and embedding compliance through Crossplane results in secure and adaptable environments without compromising on regulation adherence.

General Insights on Crossplane Integration

Summarizing these real-world cases reveals several insightful patterns and best practices:

- **Unified Schema Management:** Using Crossplane's Kubernetes-based management framework, organizations can define infrastructure with consistent APIs and configuration languages, eliminating fragmentation and promoting uniform resource management.

- **Scalability and Flexibility:** Crossplane supports rapid scaling and adapts to changes effortlessly. It abstracts underlying cloud complexities, thus empowering developers to self-service and provision infrastructure within guidelines.

- **Cost Efficiency:** By reducing manual interventions and automating cross-platform integrations, organizations have realized cost savings, allowing budgets to be reallocated for innovative projects rather than routine infrastructure expenses.

- **Security and Compliance:** Crossplane's flexibility in embedding policy-driven governance frameworks enables secure, compliant infrastructure, crucial for industries with stringent regulatory requirements.

These case studies illustrate that Crossplane is not just an infrastructure automation tool but a comprehensive platform that harmonizes DevOps practices, enhances productivity, and supports the dynamic demands of modern IT environments, transforming theoretical benefits into tangible organizational advantages.

Chapter 7

Security and Compliance in Cloud-Native Infrastructure

Security and compliance are critical in cloud-native infrastructure, where applications are distributed and dynamically orchestrated. These environments demand robust identity and access management, secure container deployments, and adherence to regulatory standards across multiple cloud platforms. Effective security practices involve integrating security controls into the DevOps lifecycle, implementing automated compliance checks, and ensuring data protection. By leveraging tools and practices tailored for cloud-native architectures, organizations can proactively manage risks and ensure compliance, while maintaining the flexibility and scalability that cloud-native technologies offer. Understanding these aspects is essential for safeguarding cloud-native environments against evolving security threats and meeting compliance requirements.

7.1 Understanding Cloud-Native Security Challenges

The transition to cloud-native architectures introduces a variety of complex security challenges that are unique to this technological paradigm. Cloud-native environments are characterized by their use of containers, microservices, and orchestrators like Kubernetes. These components facilitate flexibility and scalability but also create unique security issues that must be addressed systematically.

Cloud-native security challenges stem primarily from the ephemeral and dynamic nature of resources within these environments. The frequent instantiation and destruction of containers, coupled with the complexity of microservices interactions, demand robust security mechanisms.

One of the most prominent challenges in cloud-native security is securing containers. Containers enable developers to package applications and their dependencies into a unified and portable unit. However, the very same features that provide convenience and efficiency can also lead to security vulnerabilities if not properly managed. Security in containerized environments consists of multiple layers, including image integrity, runtime protection, and secure networking.

Image Scanning and Integrity Verification: Before containers are even deployed, ensuring the security of container images is essential. Image scanning involves analyzing the contents of a container image for vulnerabilities, misconfigurations, and outdated dependencies. Tools such as Clair, Anchore, and Trivy can be integrated into continuous integration/continuous deployment (CI/CD) pipelines to automate this process. Scanning should be a mandatory step before an image is pushed to or pulled from a container registry.

```
# Example: Using Trivy to scan a Docker container image
$ trivy image my-application:latest
```

Upon execution, Trivy outputs a list of vulnerabilities present in the image, including descriptions, severity ratings, and potential remediation

7.1. UNDERSTANDING CLOUD-NATIVE SECURITY CHALLENGES

steps.

Library	Vulnerability ID	Severity	Vulnerability Description
openssl	CVE-2021-3711	CRITICAL	A buffer overflow ...
glibc	CVE-2021-33574	HIGH	An integer overflow ...
...	...	...	...

Image integrity should also be managed through cryptographic signatures. Docker Content Trust, for example, allows users to verify image provenance by signing images. Signing ensures that images have not been tampered with and come from a trusted source.

```
# Enable Docker Content Trust
$ export DOCKER_CONTENT_TRUST=1
# Sign an image
$ docker trust sign my-application:latest
```

Runtime Security: Protecting containers at runtime is critical due to the persistent threat of exploitation after deployment. Tools like Falco can be used to detect suspicious activity or deviations from expected behavior in running containers. Falco utilizes eBPF (Extended Berkeley Packet Filter) to monitor system calls and enforce security policies.

```
# Example: A simple Falco rule to detect shell activity in containers
- rule: Terminal shell in container
  desc: Notifies if a shell is run inside a container
  condition: container.id != host and proc.name = bash
  output: "Shell activity detected in container (user=%user.name userlogin=%user.login)"
  priority: WARNING
  tags: [container, shell]
```

Dynamic Infrastructure: The dynamic nature of cloud-native environments, where resources are frequently created and destroyed, complicates traditional security practices. In Kubernetes, for instance, the management of secrets is crucial. Kubernetes provides a built-in mechanism to store and retrieve secrets, but they require additional controls for robust security management.

Securing secrets involves encrypting them at rest and utilizing access control policies to restrict unauthorized access. Kubernetes can integrate with external secret management tools like HashiCorp Vault to enhance security. Additionally, role-based access control (RBAC) policies within Kubernetes should enforce the principle of least privilege, ensuring that entities have only the permissions required for their tasks.

```
# Example: A simple RBAC role in Kubernetes
apiVersion: rbac.authorization.k8s.io/v1
kind: Role
metadata:
  namespace: default
  name: pod-reader
rules:
- apiGroups: [""]
  resources: ["pods"]
  verbs: ["get", "list", "watch"]
```

Network policies are also used in Kubernetes to restrict traffic between pods. These policies, defined using the NetworkPolicy resource, control communications at the IP/port level, mitigating the risk of lateral movement within a compromised cluster.

Networking and Service Meshes: Microservices often communicate over networks that span various cloud environments, making secure communication integral. Encrypted communication can be achieved using Transport Layer Security (TLS). Service meshes like Istio provide tools to manage secure communication between microservices through automatic TLS encryption, traffic policies, and mutual authentication.

Service meshes decouple networking and security concerns from application code, allowing unified management of security policies across microservices. This abstraction provides consistent security across heterogeneous environments.

Shared Responsibility Model: A fundamental aspect of cloud security is the shared responsibility model, which delineates security responsibilities between cloud providers and their customers. In a cloud-native environment, responsibilities are further segmented, so both parties must clearly understand their roles in maintaining security. Cloud providers secure infrastructure aspects like physical servers and networking, while customers must secure applications, data, and deployment configurations.

Security Posture and Policy Enforcement: The enforcement of security policies and continuous monitoring of security posture are necessary to ensure compliance with security practices. Policy as Code (PaC) introduces the concept of defining and managing security policies using software practices and infrastructure as code (IaC).

7.1. UNDERSTANDING CLOUD-NATIVE SECURITY CHALLENGES

Tools like Open Policy Agent (OPA) facilitate policy definition and enforcement across a range of systems, embedding policies directly into code environments.

```
# Example: A simple OPA policy for Kubernetes
package kubernetes.admission

deny[reason] {
  input.request.kind.kind == "Pod"
  input.request.operation == "CREATE"
  not input.request.object.spec.containers[_].securityContext.runAsNonRoot
  reason := "Containers must not run as root user."
}
```

The presented policies dynamically adjust with the environment; they can be updated and version-controlled like any other code. Such practices significantly reduce human error and ensure security consistency across deployments.

The design principles for cloud-native applications are significantly impacted by the necessity to bake security into every component. The security mechanisms must adapt to potential scale demands and continuously changing configurations, presenting ongoing challenges in threat modeling and risk management.

Cultural and Process Considerations: In cloud-native environments, security needs to evolve from being a stage in the deployment process to an ongoing concern embedded in the development lifecycle—a philosophy integral to DevSecOps practices. Cross-functional teams must be equipped to handle security responsibilities. This transformation augments traditional security roles with development and operational insights, leading to streamlined processes and enhanced security outcomes.

Establishing a security-first culture requires training, awareness, and commitment at all organizational levels. Development teams must be aware of secure coding practices, while operations teams should be proficient with the technical tools necessary for monitoring and incident response.

Threat Detection and Incident Response: Futuristic threat detection systems in cloud-native environments leverage artificial intelligence (AI) and machine learning (ML) to identify anomalous patterns and potential threats proactively. Proactive systems analysis enables dynamic infrastructure to mitigate risks before they manifest into full-blown issues. Effective incident response strategies entail not only reacting to incidents but also learning from them to fortify defenses against future breaches.

Security within cloud-native systems is multifaceted, encompassing cooperation across various technological and organizational domains. As these environments continue to evolve, so too must the security practices that protect them, fostering innovation while safeguarding data and functionality.

7.2 Implementing Identity and Access Management

In cloud-native environments, effective identity and access management (IAM) is crucial for safeguarding systems and data. IAM encompasses the policies, tools, and technologies that govern who can access resources within a computing environment, and under what conditions. The capabilities of cloud-native technologies heighten the need for robust identity verification mechanisms and stringent access controls to mitigate security risks.

IAM in cloud-native infrastructure delivers granular management of access rights, aligning with the principles of least privilege and zero trust. These principles necessitate that access rights are minimal and only granted based on explicit verification rather than implicit trust. This section provides a detailed examination of IAM components critical to cloud-native security, including user authentication, authorization mechanisms, and the secure management of secrets and keys.

User Authentication: Authentication is the initial step in the IAM process, verifying the identity of users or services attempting to access resources. In cloud-native systems, identity providers (IdPs) are often leveraged to streamline authentication processes. Popular protocols such as OAuth 2.0 and OpenID Connect (OIDC) enable building secure, federated authentication systems.

OAuth 2.0 serves primarily as a framework for authorization, allowing third-party services to exchange user information without exposing credentials. OpenID Connect extends OAuth 2.0 by providing identity

7.2. IMPLEMENTING IDENTITY AND ACCESS MANAGEMENT

verification capabilities. Implementing OAuth 2.0 requires defining roles such as resource owner, client, authorization server, and resource server, with explicit interactions between each.

To integrate OAuth 2.0 within cloud-native environments, platforms like Kubernetes can utilize external IdPs to manage authentication. For instance, setting up a simple OAuth workflow with Google as an identity provider within a Kubernetes cluster might involve defining authentication configurations.

```
# OAuth 2.0 setup in Kubernetes with Google as IdP
apiVersion: v1
kind: ConfigMap
metadata:
  name: oauth-config
  namespace: kube-system
data:
  client-id: YOUR_GOOGLE_CLIENT_ID
  client-secret: YOUR_GOOGLE_CLIENT_SECRET
  redirect-uri: https://your-kubernetes-cluster/api/oauth2callback
```

This configuration enables Kubernetes to delegate authentication requests to Google, where users would authenticate using their Google credentials.

User Authorization: Once a user is authenticated, authorization determines the actions they can perform and the resources they can access. Authorization mechanisms define these entitlements through roles and policies, often managed using role-based access control (RBAC) or attribute-based access control (ABAC).

In Kubernetes, RBAC policies allow administrators to define roles and bind them to users or groups, specifying the resource types and operations permitted.

```
# Example of RBAC in Kubernetes for allowing read-only access to deployments
apiVersion: rbac.authorization.k8s.io/v1
kind: Role
metadata:
  namespace: default
  name: deployment-reader
rules:
- apiGroups: ["apps"]
  resources: ["deployments"]
  verbs: ["get", "list", "watch"]
---
kind: RoleBinding
apiVersion: rbac.authorization.k8s.io/v1
metadata:
  name: read-deployments
```

```
  namespace: default
subjects:
- kind: User
  name: example-user
  apiGroup: rbac.authorization.k8s.io
roleRef:
  kind: Role
  name: deployment-reader
  apiGroup: rbac.authorization.k8s.io
```

This RBAC configuration grants the user example-user read-only access to deployment resources within the default namespace, ensuring the user cannot modify or delete deployments.

ABAC, although not widely adopted in Kubernetes, offers more flexibility by evaluating access requests against a policy that combines multiple attributes from the user, action, resource, and environment.

Policy Management: Policy management in IAM involves articulating access controls in alignment with organizational security requirements and procedures. A Policy as Code approach enhances policy management by encoding security policies within software tools, ensuring they are consistent, reusable, and version-controlled.

In cloud-native deployments, Open Policy Agent (OPA) enables policy enforcement via policy bundles which are deployed and observed by services in infrastructure, facilitating automated policy checks with environments.

```
# Example OPA policy: Enforcing tagging for cloud resource creation
package policy

deny[msg] {
  input.kind == "Resource"
  input.operation == "CREATE"
  not input.object.metadata.labels["environment"]
  msg := sprintf("Resource '%s' creation denied: must include 'environment' tag.", [
      input.object.metadata.name])
}
```

OPA policies can detect missing annotations such as environment tags, preventing the creation of untagged resources, thereby maintaining compliance and governance across cloud-native resources.

Secret and Key Management: Securely managing secrets and encryption keys is essential in IAM, as these entities control access to sensitive data. Hard-coding secrets within application code or configura-

7.2. IMPLEMENTING IDENTITY AND ACCESS MANAGEMENT

tions exposes them to significant security risks. Cloud-native environments must employ secret management solutions that facilitate secure storage, access, and audit of these sensitive items.

Kubernetes Secrets is integrated to manage sensitive data. However, additional layers like using HashiCorp Vault or AWS Secrets Manager can enhance protection, auditing, and management efficiency.

```
# Creating a Kubernetes Secret
apiVersion: v1
kind: Secret
metadata:
  name: db-password
type: Opaque
data:
  password: $(echo -n "my-secure-password" | base64)
```

Here, the database password is added to Kubernetes as a base64-encoded secret, allowing applications running within the cluster to securely access it.

Integration of IAM with Microservices: In cloud-native architectures, microservices might independently manage their identities, requiring consistent IAM practices. Distributed identity management systems such as SPIFFE (Secure Production Identity Framework for Everyone) and SPIRE (SPIFFE Runtime Environment) offer standards for giving services unique identities. SPIFFE defines service identities independently of deployment environment constraints, providing a secure method for service-to-service authentication.

Zero Trust Architecture: The adoption of a Zero Trust architecture further evolves IAM within cloud-native environments. Zero Trust principles require continuous verification of user, service, and device identity, applying strict access controls based on up-to-date intelligence across the cloud-native network topology.

Integrated with a zero trust model, IAM builds adaptive access controls contingent on context and intelligence, utilizing telemetry data and other runtime signals to dynamically adjust permissions, thus protecting the environment against modern cyber threats.

Audit and Reporting: IAM systems should provide robust auditing and reporting capabilities to verify that access controls comply with policies and that no unauthorized activities occur. Logs of access attempts, who performed them, and their success must be diligently maintained. Aggregating logs using centralized logging systems, such as the ELK stack (Elasticsearch, Logstash, and Kibana), simplifies the auditing process across distributed systems, enabling better visibility and accountability.

To implement a compliant logging system, ensure IAM platforms produce logs in standardized formats that allow automated aggregation and parsing necessary for reliable reporting and audit trails.

IAM in cloud-native environments forms an integral part of a comprehensive security strategy. By implementing strong authentication procedures, correctly configuring authorization mechanisms, securely managing secrets, and leveraging sophisticated identity management tools, organizations achieve both operational efficiency and secure access to sensitive resources. The dynamic and scalable nature of cloud-native technologies necessitates ongoing vigilance and adaptation of IAM practices to effectively protect infrastructure against evolving security threats while supporting business agility.

7.3 Securing Containerized Environments

Securing containerized environments is a critical aspect of modern cloud-native infrastructure, as they facilitate seamless application deployment, scalability, and microservices architecture. Containers encapsulate applications and their dependencies, offering consistency across different computing environments. However, their use poses unique security challenges due to their dynamic and ephemeral nature, and the specific architectural components involved, such as container runtime, orchestration, and network interfaces.

To secure containerized environments effectively, it is vital to understand the security implications at various stages, including image creation, runtime operation, orchestration, and network interactions.

Securing Container Images: Container images are the building blocks of any containerized application. Ensuring their security is paramount as they form the foundation upon which applications run. Unsecure images can act as vectors for malicious activity, so it is imperative to:

- **Use Trusted Base Images:** Always start with minimal, trusted base images sourced from official repositories. Reducing the number of packages decreases the potential attack surface.

- **Image Vulnerability Scanning:** Implement automated scanning of images for known vulnerabilities as part of the CI/CD pipeline using tools like Trivy, Clair, and Anchore.

```
# Scanning a Docker image for vulnerabilities
$ trivy image my-application:latest
```

- **Image Hardening:** Customize images for specific application needs, removing unnecessary components and privileges. Use multi-stage builds to further minimize the final image size.

```
# Multi-stage Dockerfile example
FROM golang:1.16-alpine AS builder
WORKDIR /app
COPY . .
RUN go build -o main .

FROM scratch
COPY --from=builder /app/main /app/main
ENTRYPOINT ["/app/main"]
```

- **Digital Signatures and Content Trust:** Validate image integrity using cryptographic signatures. Docker Content Trust can be utilized to sign images and confirm they have not been tampered with.

Runtime Container Security: Containers in production are subject to constant security threats. The runtime environment must implement continuous security monitoring:

- **Least Privilege Execution:** Run containers with the minimum necessary privileges. Use security features like user namespaces to prevent containers from accessing host resources. Ensure containers run as non-root users whenever possible.

```
# Dockerfile: setting user to non-root
USER 1000
```

- **Runtime Monitoring Tools:** Employ monitoring tools like Falco to detect abnormal activities within containers. Falco uses system call tracing to alert on deviations from expected behavior.

    ```
    # An example Falco rule for detecting unauthorized SSH attempts
    - rule: Unexpected outbound connection
      desc: Detects unauthorized outbound connections from containers
      condition: >
        container and
        evt.type = "connect" and
        evt.arg.resolves_domain == "true" and
        not fd.name in (localhost, trusted-endpoints)
      output: "Outbound connection to untrusted domain (user=%user.name
             domain=%fd.name)"
      priority: CRITICAL
    ```

- **Limiting Resource Usage:** Specify limits on CPU and memory to mitigate the risk of Denial-of-Service (DoS) attacks. Kubernetes, for example, allows setting limits and requests at the pod level.

    ```
    # Example Kubernetes resource limits configuration
    apiVersion: v1
    kind: Pod
    metadata:
      name: my-app
    spec:
      containers:
      - name: my-app-container
        image: my-application:latest
        resources:
          limits:
            memory: "256Mi"
            cpu: "500m"
          requests:
            memory: "128Mi"
            cpu: "250m"
    ```

Orchestration Security: Securing the orchestration layer is crucial in deploying and scaling containerized applications. Kubernetes, being the dominant orchestrator, offers robust security features:

- **Role-Based Access Control (RBAC):** Implement RBAC to enforce fine-grained access controls, ensuring users and services have only the necessary permissions.

    ```
    # Example Kubernetes RBAC role and binding for a read-only user
    apiVersion: rbac.authorization.k8s.io/v1
    kind: Role
    ```

7.3. SECURING CONTAINERIZED ENVIRONMENTS

```
  metadata:
    namespace: default
    name: pod-reader
  rules:
  - apiGroups: [""]
    resources: ["pods"]
    verbs: ["get", "list", "watch"]
  ---
  apiVersion: rbac.authorization.k8s.io/v1
  kind: RoleBinding
  metadata:
    name: read-only-binding
    namespace: default
  subjects:
  - kind: User
    name: read-only-user
    apiGroup: rbac.authorization.k8s.io
  roleRef:
    kind: Role
    name: pod-reader
    apiGroup: rbac.authorization.k8s.io
```

- **Network Policies:** Kubernetes Network Policies allow you to control traffic between pods. They are used to enforce security constraints at the network layer, limiting pod exposure.

```
  # Example Kubernetes network policy to allow traffic only to the frontend
        pod
  apiVersion: networking.k8s.io/v1
  kind: NetworkPolicy
  metadata:
    name: frontend-policy
    namespace: default
  spec:
    podSelector:
      matchLabels:
        role: frontend
    policyTypes:
    - Ingress
    - Egress
    ingress:
    - from:
      - podSelector:
          matchLabels:
            role: backend
```

- **Pod Security Policies:** Enforce security constraints at the pod level, such as preventing privileged containers, enforcing read-only root file system, and blocking host network access.

```
  # Example Kubernetes pod security policy
  apiVersion: policy/v1beta1
  kind: PodSecurityPolicy
  metadata:
```

```
      name: restricted
    spec:
      privileged: false
      allowPrivilegeEscalation: false
      runAsUser:
        rule: MustRunAsNonRoot
      seLinux:
        rule: RunAsAny
      supplementalGroups:
        rule: MustRunAs
        ranges:
        - min: 1
          max: 65535
      fsGroup:
        rule: MustRunAs
        ranges:
        - min: 1
          max: 65535
      volumes:
      - configMap
      - emptyDir
      - persistentVolumeClaim
```

Networking Security: Securing network traffic in containers involves encrypting communication and controlling traffic flow:

- **Encryption of Data in Transit:** Configure TLS for all communications involving containers. Service meshes like Istio can simplify secure inter-service communication by automatically handling aspects like TLS management, certificates, and rotation.

- **Service Meshes:** Utilize service meshes to increase security layer abstraction. Tools such as Istio provide service authentication, authorization, and encryption transparently to applications.

- **Microsegmentation and zoning:** Implement policies restricting communication to essential services only, reducing the attack surface and containing potential breaches within isolated zones.

Emerging Technologies and Considerations: New tools and methodologies continually evolve alongside container orchestration environments:

- **eBPF for Monitoring and Security:** The extended Berkeley Packet Filter (eBPF) is a powerful kernel-level technology for building high-performance monitoring tools. eBPF can be leveraged for network profiling, intrusion detection, and advanced threat prevention for containerized environments.

- **Securing Supply Chain:** As supply chains grow in complexity, adopting practices like image signing, vulnerability scanning, and provenance tracking become vital to prevent introducing malicious code into container images.

- **Automated Security Testing:** Integrate security testing tools into CI/CD pipelines to automatically check for common vulnerabilities, ensuring that changes do not introduce new security issues.

Containerized environments represent a paradigm shift in how applications are deployed and managed, driving transformational changes in security practices and infrastructure design. To effectively secure these environments, it's imperative to adopt a holistic approach that encompasses the entire lifecycle of container deployment, from image creation to production monitoring, providing a constant shield against a wide array of threats. This comprehensive security strategy ensures that containerized environments remain resilient and secure, thus safeguarding organizational assets and data against ever-evolving adversaries.

7.4 Compliance in Multi-Cloud Deployments

Ensuring compliance in multi-cloud deployments presents a significant challenge for organizations leveraging multiple cloud service providers (CSPs) to optimize resources and capabilities. The ability to seamlessly operate across different cloud environments is crucial for businesses seeking agility and scalability; however, this multi-cloud strategy introduces complex compliance issues. Each cloud platform has diverse compliance requirements, regional regulations, and security controls that must be consistently managed.

Effective compliance in multi-cloud environments demands a holistic approach encompassing governance, risk management, data protection, and monitoring. This section elaborates on key strategies to manage compliance efficiently while navigating the complexities inherent in multi-cloud architectures.

Understanding Regulatory Frameworks: In a multi-cloud framework, organizations must contend with overlapping regulatory requirements. Key regulations that commonly impact cloud deployments include:

- **General Data Protection Regulation (GDPR):** Provides guidelines for data protection and privacy for individuals within the EU. It emphasizes data localization, user rights, and rigorous data processing standards.

- **Health Insurance Portability and Accountability Act (HIPAA):** U.S. regulations protect medical records and establish stringent stipulations for handling healthcare information.

- **Payment Card Industry Data Security Standard (PCI DSS):** Governs organizations that handle branded credit cards, enforcing high standards for security and privacy.

Compliance with these frameworks requires a clear understanding of which data is governed by specific regulations and ensuring consistent application across all deployed cloud services.

Policy Management and Governance: Implementing a robust governance framework is essential for defining, enforcing, and monitoring compliance policies. Adopting Policy as Code (PaC) practices allows automated management of compliance policies across multi-cloud environments, enhancing accuracy and reducing manual errors.

Tools like HashiCorp Sentinel and Open Policy Agent (OPA) embed policy enforcement into the continuous deployment pipeline, ensuring compliance throughout the entire application lifecycle.

```
# Example OPA policy enforcing encryption for all cloud storage buckets
package compliance.storage

deny[msg] {
  input.method == "CreateBucket"
```

7.4. COMPLIANCE IN MULTI-CLOUD DEPLOYMENTS

```
    not input.encrypted
    msg := sprintf("Bucket '%s' creation denied: encryption not enabled.", [input.name])
}
```

Unified Identity and Access Management (IAM): Centralized IAM solutions streamline user and resource access management across multi-cloud environments. Integrating with identity federation services like AWS IAM, Azure Active Directory, and Google Cloud Identity simplifies user authentication and enforces consistent security policies.

Organizations should adopt a Zero Trust approach, continuously validating user identities and access requests regardless of location, thus fostering a robust security posture across distinct cloud boundaries.

Data Protection and Sovereignty: Maintaining control and visibility over data is a cornerstone of compliance in multi-cloud setups. Organizations need to ensure data is encrypted both in transit and at rest, and metadata is similarly protected.

Employ encryption key management practices that comply with applicable regulations, such as using AWS Key Management Service (KMS), Azure Key Vault, or Google Cloud Key Management to manage cryptographic keys effectively.

Data sovereignty must be addressed by mapping storage and processing locations to regulations to ensure compliance without falling afoul of cross-border restrictions.

Infrastructure and Configuration Management: Infrastructure as Code (IaC) tools like Terraform, CloudFormation, and Ansible support creating repeatable, version-controlled infrastructure templates. By adopting IaC, organizations ensure that deployment configurations adhere to compliance standards, reducing the risk of configuration drift.

```
# Example Terraform configuration for creating an S3 bucket with encryption
resource "aws_s3_bucket" "my_secure_bucket" {
  bucket = "my-compliant-bucket"

  server_side_encryption_configuration {
    rule {
      apply_server_side_encryption_by_default {
        sse_algorithm = "AES256"
      }
    }
  }
}
```

```
    }
}
```

Regular audits and compliance checks are imperative, ensuring that configurations remain within prescribed guidelines across all cloud platforms.

Monitoring and Logging: Continuous monitoring and comprehensive logging form the backbone of compliance strategies. Integrated logging tools, such as Amazon CloudWatch, Azure Monitor, and Google StackDriver, provide insights across cloud services, supporting anomaly detection and incident response initiatives.

Creating a unified logging strategy across clouds is vital for correlating events accurately and maintaining an audit trail compliant with standards like PCI DSS.

```
# Example Terraform setup for enabling CloudWatch logs on AWS
resource "aws_cloudwatch_log_group" "log_group" {
  name = "/aws/lambda/my-secure-function"
  retention_in_days = 14
}

resource "aws_lambda_function" "lambda_secure_example" {
  function_name = "my-secure-function"
  role = aws_iam_role.iam_for_lambda.arn
  handler = "index.handler"
  source_code_hash = filebase64sha256("lambda_function_payload.zip")

  environment {
    variables = {
      LOG_GROUP_NAME = aws_cloudwatch_log_group.log_group.name
    }
  }

  logs_config {
    log_group_name = aws_cloudwatch_log_group.log_group.name
  }
}
```

Cloud Security Posture Management (CSPM): CSPM solutions deliver visibility into multi-cloud environments, automatically detecting security risks and compliance issues. By continually assessing cloud services against policies and regulations, CSPMs ensure compliance is proactively managed.

These platforms also recommend remediation actions, streamlining corrective measures and allowing businesses to focus on core activities.

Managing Service-Level Agreements (SLAs): Developing and adhering to stringent SLAs is essential for meeting compliance requirements across multiple CSPs. SLAs must define metrics of accountability, service uptime, data availability, and incident response procedures.

Clarifying expectations and responsibilities within SLAs fosters transparency and lays the groundwork for effective compliance management and enforcement.

Deploying compliance in multi-cloud environments requires vigilance, coordination, and effective utilization of platforms and practices that adhere to and enforce industry standards. By leveraging tools that enhance visibility, facilitate automated management, and foster a policy-driven approach, organizations achieve consistent compliance across distributed cloud resources, reducing risks and ensuring proactive management. This comprehensive strategy is indispensable for maintaining regulatory adherence and safeguarding sensitive data in an ever-evolving technological landscape.

7.5 Best Practices for Data Protection

In cloud-native environments, data protection is pivotal, given the dynamic and distributed nature of modern applications. Ensuring data security involves robust strategies for safeguarding data at rest, in transit, and during processing. This section delves into best practices that organizations should adopt to secure data within cloud-native architectures, focusing on encryption, access controls, backup, and recovery, as well as breach detection and response.

Data Encryption: Encryption is the cornerstone of data protection, rendering data unintelligible to unauthorized parties. In cloud-native environments, encryption should be applied both in transit and at rest.

1. **Encryption at Rest:** Data stored in databases, archives, and file systems should be protected using strong encryption algorithms such as AES-256. Most cloud service providers offer built-in encryption tools and services:

- **Amazon S3 Server-Side Encryption (SSE):** Enables automatic encryption of data at rest using AWS's managed keys or custom keys through AWS Key Management Service (KMS).

```
# Enable Amazon S3 server-side encryption with AWS managed keys
resource "aws_s3_bucket" "secure_bucket" {
  bucket = "my-secure-s3-bucket"

  server_side_encryption_configuration {
    rule {
      apply_server_side_encryption_by_default {
        sse_algorithm = "AES256"
      }
    }
  }
}
```

- **Azure Storage Service Encryption (SSE):** Utilizes Azure's encryption features to protect data stored in Azure blob storage.

2. **Encryption in Transit:** Protect data while it's being transferred between client and server or between services within a system. Employ protocols such as Transport Layer Security (TLS) or Secure Sockets Layer (SSL) to encrypt data in transit. Ensure that TLS is implemented correctly by regularly updating cryptographic libraries and supporting only secure cipher suites.

```
# Example NGINX configuration for enabling TLS
server {
    listen 443 ssl;
    server_name myapp.example.com;

    ssl_certificate /etc/ssl/certs/myapp-cert.pem;
    ssl_certificate_key /etc/ssl/private/myapp-key.pem;

    ssl_protocols TLSv1.2 TLSv1.3;
    ssl_ciphers 'ECDHE-ECDSA-AES256-GCM-SHA384:...';

    location / {
        proxy_pass http://backend;
    }
}
```

Access Controls: Implementing strict access control measures ensures only authorized users and services can access sensitive data.

1. **Role-Based Access Control (RBAC):** Define roles for users and allocate permissions based on the principle of least privilege. Use IAM services provided by cloud providers for granular access control:

- **AWS IAM:** Allows creating policies that define permissions and attach them to IAM roles.

7.5. BEST PRACTICES FOR DATA PROTECTION

```
# Example JSON policy for an S3 bucket read-only access
{
    "Version": "2012-10-17",
    "Statement": [
        {
            "Effect": "Allow",
            "Action": [
                "s3:GetObject"
            ],
            "Resource": [
                "arn:aws:s3:::my-secure-s3-bucket/*"
            ]
        }
    ]
}
```

2. **Attribute-Based Access Control (ABAC):** Extends RBAC by using multiple attributes such as user identity, resource, and environment conditions to dynamically allow or deny access.

3. **Multi-Factor Authentication (MFA):** Integral to protecting access to sensitive data. Enforce the use of MFA for accessing critical systems, adding a layer of security beyond usernames and passwords.

Backup and Recovery: Robust backup and recovery strategies ensure data resilience against accidental deletions, corruption, and ransomware attacks.

1. **Regular and Automated Backups:** Implement automated backup routines that run at regular intervals, ensuring data is always recoverable. Cloud providers offer services tailored for this:

- **AWS Backup:** Provides automated data backup across AWS services.

```
# Example AWS Backup setup for an S3 bucket
resource "aws_backup_vault" "example" {
  name = "example_backup_vault"
}

resource "aws_backup_plan" "example" {
  name = "example_backup_plan"

  rule {
    rule_name = "example_rule"
    target_vault_name = aws_backup_vault.example.name
    schedule = "cron(0 12 * * ? *)" # Daily at noon
    lifecycle {
      delete_after_days = 365
    }
  }
}
```

2. **Disaster Recovery Plans:** A documented disaster recovery (DR) strategy is essential, outlining the steps to recover from data loss events. Consistently test the DR plan to ensure that recovery procedures work as expected.

Data Classification: Understand the sensitivity of data to apply appropriate protection measures. Classify data based on its value and impact, creating tailored policies for handling different classes of data.

1. **Public, internal, confidential, and restricted** are typical classification levels; each level dictates the level of protection and handling requirements.

2. **Custom Policies:** Using Policy as Code (PaC) principles, encode data protection policies using services such as Open Policy Agent to ensure consistent enforcement.

```
# Example OPA policy enforcing data encryption at storage
package data_compliance

default allow = false

# Allow access only if encryption is enabled
allow {
  input.kind == "storage"
  input.encryption.enabled
}
```

Audit and Monitoring: Document and log data access and changes to generate an audit trail that helps in managing compliance and identifying potential data breaches.

1. **Structured Logging:** Implement logging of all data access and modification activities, maintaining enough details to support audit processes. Tools like Elasticsearch Stack (ELK) or Fluentd can be deployed for managing logs across cloud-native environments.

2. **Intrusion Detection Systems (IDS):** Deploy IDS solutions that monitor incoming and outgoing communications for suspicious activities. Host-based IDS solutions like OSSEC or network-based systems like Snort are effective in alert generation and anomaly detection.

Data Masking and Tokenization: They are techniques for anonymizing data, making it less sensitive if intercepted.

1. **Data Masking:** Involves substituting or obscuring sensitive data values with shells or proxies to render them non-identifying. Use data

masking for non-production environments, ensuring sensitive data is protected in development workflows.

2. **Tokenization:** Protects data by replacing sensitive information with non-sensitive equivalents, called tokens, which are mapped back to their original values when needed.

Breach Detection and Response: Although protection measures reduce risk, readiness for handling data breaches is critical.

1. **Incident Response Plan:** Develop a detailed incident response (IR) plan outlining procedures and responsibilities when responding to a data breach. This plan should include processes for containment, eradication, recovery, and learning.

2. **Real-Time Alerting:** Implement systems for real-time alerting to detect breaches quickly and efficiently, minimizing potential impact. Utilize SIEM (Security Information and Event Management) systems like Splunk for comprehensive log analysis and threat intelligence.

3. **Post-Breach Analysis:** Conduct in-depth post-breach analysis to identify weaknesses and improve defenses, enhancing both technology setups and organizational processes.

By employing these best practices, organizations protect their data assets comprehensively, ensuring resilience against external attacks and internal threats while maintaining regulatory compliance. These strategies form a robust security posture, fostering trust and reliability in cloud-native infrastructures amidst evolving cybersecurity threats.

7.6 Automating Security with DevSecOps

The integration of security throughout the software development lifecycle is a fundamental shift in approach known as DevSecOps. This approach empowers development teams to make security a shared responsibility, ensuring it is embedded within every phase of the DevOps pipeline. By automating security tasks, companies can achieve faster deployment cycles while maintaining robust security postures. This section explores the components and practices essential for automating security within a DevSecOps framework, including continuous integration and deployment (CI/CD), threat modeling, security testing, and security as code.

Principles of DevSecOps: At its core, DevSecOps aims to integrate security measures within DevOps processes, emphasizing three key principles:

- **Shift Left:** Move security considerations earlier in the software development process, allowing developers to detect and fix vulnerabilities during the code development phase rather than post-deployment.

- **Automation:** Automate security testing and monitoring to reduce human error, improve efficiency, and facilitate continuous security analysis. This involves using various security tools integrated into the development pipeline.

- **Collaboration:** Foster a culture of collaboration between development, operations, and security teams to align their goals and work together more effectively. This reduces silos and enhances communication.

Integration of Security in CI/CD Pipelines:

- **Static Application Security Testing (SAST):** Conduct SAST within CI/CD pipelines to identify vulnerabilities in the source code without executing programs. Tools like SonarQube, Checkmarx, and Fortify can automate static analysis upon code commits.

```
# Example configuration for scanning Java code with SonarQube
mvn sonar:sonar -Dsonar.projectKey=my_project \
-Dsonar.host.url=http://localhost:9000 \
-Dsonar.login=your_sonarqube_token
```

- **Dynamic Application Security Testing (DAST):** DAST involves security testing of live applications to uncover vulnerabilities such as XSS and SQL injection. This can be automated using tools like OWASP ZAP and Burp Suite.

7.6. AUTOMATING SECURITY WITH DEVSECOPS

```
# OWASP ZAP Docker command for scanning a web application
docker run -i owasp/zap2docker-stable zap-full-scan.py \
-t http://myapp.example.com -r zap_report.html
```

- **Software Composition Analysis (SCA):** Identify vulnerabilities in third-party libraries and dependencies through tools like Black Duck, Snyk, and Whitesource. Integrate these into the CI/CD workflow to prevent known vulnerabilities from entering production.

```
# Snyk CLI command to scan a project for vulnerable packages
snyk test --org=my-org --file=package.json
```

Infrastructure as Code (IaC) Security: Protecting the infrastructure code used to deploy environments is essential within DevSecOps practices. Integrate security checks early in IaC processes to uncover misconfigurations.

- **IaC Security Tools:** Use tools like Terraform for infrastructure provisioning, integrated with security scanning tools such as Checkov, TFSec, or AWS Config, which scan code for security violations or non-compliances.

```
# Example Checkov command to scan Terraform IaC files
checkov -d /path/to/terraform/directory
```

Security as Code: Encode security policies and configurations as version-controlled code, allowing automation, collaboration, and consistent application across environments.

- **Policy as Code (PaC):** Use tools like Open Policy Agent (OPA) or HashiCorp Sentinel to write and enforce security policies.

```
# Example OPA policy encoding network access rules
package access_control

deny[msg] {
  input.role != "admin"
  input.action == "delete"
  msg := "Only admins can perform delete operations."
}
```

Continuous Monitoring and Feedback: Automation in security monitoring offers real-time insights and quick detection of anomalies.

- **Security Information and Event Management (SIEM):** Utilize SIEM solutions like Splunk, ELK Stack, or IBM QRadar to aggregate and analyze logs, generating alerts for suspicious activities.

- **Automated Incident Response:** Design automated playbooks using solutions like Palo Alto Cortex XSOAR to automate response actions, such as isolating compromised systems or notifying responsible teams immediately upon detecting security incidents.

Threat Modeling and Code Reviews: Perform automated threat modeling and integrate security reviews into the development process for proactive threat identification.

- Use tools like Microsoft Threat Modeling Tool to assess potential threats and vulnerabilities during design phases, enabling targeted security hardening.

- Implement automated code reviews using pull request automation tools within version-controlled environments (e.g., GitHub Actions, GitLab CI/CD) to ensure adherence to security best practices and coding standards.

```
# Example GitHub Actions pipeline for automated code review
name: Security Review

on: [pull_request]

jobs:
  review:
    runs-on: ubuntu-latest
    steps:
      - uses: actions/checkout@v2
      - name: Run static analysis
        uses: github/codeql-action/analyze@v1
```

Cultural Adoption and Team Alignment: The successful implementation of DevSecOps requires changes in organizational culture and mindset.

- **Training and Awareness:** Conduct regular training on secure coding practices, threat awareness, and the concepts of DevSecOps for all stakeholders involved in software development and operations.

- **Cross-Functional Teams:** Formulate cross-functional teams with representatives from development, operations, and security to facilitate ongoing communication and collaboration.

- **Metrics and KPIs:** Establish clear security metrics and key performance indicators (KPIs) to measure the success of DevSecOps initiatives, such as the number of vulnerabilities identified and mitigated, time to detect security issues, and time to resolve incidents.

By embedding security automation within the development framework, organizations create resilient environments, prioritize incremental improvements, accelerate the velocity of deployments, and build a culture of security awareness. Implementing these DevSecOps practices proactively addresses security demands within evolving cloud-native applications, enhancing the robustness and reliability of software systems while maintaining the agility and speed expected in competitive technological landscapes.

7.7 Incident Response and Remediation

Incident response and remediation are critical components of a comprehensive security strategy, particularly within cloud-native environments where threats can propagate rapidly due to their dynamic and interconnected nature. Efficiently managing security incidents involves not only detecting and responding to security breaches but also minimizing damage and recovering systems to a secure operational state. This section elucidates best practices for establishing an effective incident response strategy, utilizing modern tools and frameworks, and emphasizes the importance of continual learning and improvement in handling incidents.

Establishing an Incident Response Framework: An incident response framework provides a structured approach to managing security incidents. It generally encompasses the following phases:

- **Preparation:** This foundational phase focuses on establishing an incident response capability. Develop and document an incident response plan (IRP) that outlines roles, responsibilities, communication protocols, and escalation processes. Regular training and simulation exercises should be conducted to ensure readiness.

    - Develop a communication plan that identifies stakeholders, such as IT, legal, and communication teams, and defines internal and external communication workflows.

- **Identification:** Use monitoring tools and automation to identify potential security events quickly. Integrate Security Information and Event Management (SIEM) systems like Splunk, QRadar, or the Elastic (ELK) Stack to collect and analyze security alerts, enabling rapid identification of abnormal activities.

```
# Example Elasticsearch query to detect multiple failed login attempts
GET /logs/_search
{
  "query": {
    "bool": {
      "must": [
        { "match": { "event.type": "login_attempt" }},
        { "range": { "event.timestamp": {"gte": "now-15m"}}}
      ],
      "filter": [
        { "term": { "event.outcome": "failure" }},
        { "minimum_should_match": 5 }
      ]
    }
  }
}
```

- **Containment:** Once an incident is confirmed, efforts shift to containing the breach to prevent further damage. This phase may involve both short-term and long-term containment strategies.

    - Immediate containment: Disconnect affected systems from the network or isolate specific nodes within a cloud architecture to prevent lateral movement.
    - Long-term containment: Apply patches or temporary workarounds to affected systems, ensuring continuity of critical functions while eradicating vulnerabilities.

7.7. INCIDENT RESPONSE AND REMEDIATION

```
# Example script for isolating a compromised Kubernetes pod
kubectl label pods compromised-pod connectivity=isolated
```

- **Eradication:** Neutralize the root cause of the incident to prevent recurrence. This may involve removing malware, closing vulnerabilities, or deploying patches. Conduct thorough system audits to ensure complete removal of threats.

```
# Example script for clearing known malware on Linux endpoints
find / -type f -name 'malware_example' -exec rm -f {} \;
```

- **Recovery:** The goal of recovery is to restore affected systems and services to full operation. Validate that systems are clean and securely configured. Rebuild systems from known good backups and carefully monitor them for signs of reinfection or lingering vulnerabilities.

```
# Restore a VM from a backup image on AWS
aws ec2 create-image --instance-id i-1234567890abcdef0 --name "restored-instance"
```

- **Lessons Learned:** Conduct post-incident analysis to document findings and refine response strategies. Share insights with stakeholders and update the incident response plan to incorporate lessons learned.

Integration with Automation and Orchestration: Modern incident response incorporates security orchestration, automation, and response (SOAR) technologies to streamline processes and reduce response times.

- Utilize tools like Splunk Phantom, Cortex XSOAR, or IBM Resilient to automate repetitive tasks such as alert enrichment, evidence collection, and vulnerability scanning.

```
# Example SOAR automation playbook entry for Phishing email analysis
{
    "name": "Analyze Phishing Email",
    "tasks": [
        {
            "type": "email_header_analysis",
            "inputs": { "email_id": "{{emails.incident_id}}" },
            "outputs": [{ "key": "analysis_result", "target": "{{analysis_outcome}}" }]
        }]
```

```
    },
    {
      "type": "threat_intel_enrichment",
      "inputs": { "indicator": "{{analysis_result.indicators}}" },
      "outputs": [{ "key": "threat_level", "target": "{{intel_outcome}}" }]
    }
  ]
}
```

Building a Cyber-Resilient Culture: The organizational culture is paramount to anticipating incidents and driving effective response:

- **Training and Simulation:** Conduct regular training sessions, workshops, and incident simulation exercises for teams to improve readiness and effective decision-making during real incidents.

- **Security Awareness:** Cultivate a security-first mindset across all organizational levels. Encourage proactive reporting of suspicious activities and foster open communication around security risks.

- **Cross-Department Collaboration:** Promote collaboration between IT, security, operations, and executive leadership to align on incident management priorities and maintain business openness.

Quantifying and Prioritizing Risks: For effective incident response planning, adopt a risk-driven approach:

- **Risk Assessment Frameworks:** Employ risk assessment frameworks like NIST SP 800-30 or ISO/IEC 27005 to quantify risks and assess the potential impact of security incidents.

- **Prioritization Model:** Develop a risk prioritization model that evaluates incidents based on severity and potential business impact. Allocate resources efficiently according to the priority levels of incidents.

By adopting a focused and refined incident response framework that eschews the reactive for the proactive, and that emphasizes preparedness and automation, organizations are better equipped to navigate the complex landscape of cloud-native threats. This approach requires a perpetual commitment to training, collaboration, and the continuous evolution of incident management strategies to ensure resilience against the challenges of tomorrow's security landscape.

Chapter 8

Monitoring and Observability for Crossplane Managed Environments

Monitoring and observability are essential for maintaining the health and performance of environments managed by Crossplane. These practices involve capturing and analyzing metrics, logs, and traces to gain insights into system behavior and resource utilization. By integrating monitoring tools with Crossplane, operators can create detailed dashboards, set up alerting systems, and ensure proactive management of cloud resources. Observability not only aids in diagnosing issues but also plays a crucial role in capacity planning and optimizing resource allocation. Effectively leveraging these capabilities enhances operational visibility, enabling teams to maintain system reliability and improve performance across multi-cloud deployments.

8.1 Principles of Observability in Cloud-Native Systems

Observability in cloud-native systems is the practice of instrumenting data in such a way that one can understand the internal states of a system merely by observing its external outputs. This capability is essential for maintaining and ensuring the health, performance, and reliability of complex, distributed systems typical in modern cloud environments. Key principles of observability are metrics, logs, and traces, which collectively enable a comprehensive view into the operation of a system.

The core motivation for observability is the desire to quickly detect and resolve issues, improve system performance, and facilitate continuous integration and deployment strategies prevalent in cloud-native setups. Observability must be designed and implemented meticulously, considering the intrinsic characteristics of distributed and dynamic environments such as ephemeral nodes, network partitions, and orchestrator-induced failures.

Metrics: Metrics are numerical representations of data measured over intervals of time. They are typically used to track a system's performance, utilization, and other operations statistics. In cloud-native environments, key metrics include CPU and memory utilization, request counts, latency, error rates, and more.

To effectively leverage metrics, here's an example of how you would typically collect and visualize them using Prometheus, a leading open-source monitoring solution, coupled with Grafana for visualization:

```
# Start Prometheus
./prometheus --config.file=prometheus.yml

# prometheus.yml configuration file
global:
  scrape_interval: 15s

scrape_configs:
  - job_name: 'node'
    static_configs:
      - targets: ['localhost:9090']
```

Prometheus collects metrics from monitored targets by scraping HTTP

8.1. PRINCIPLES OF OBSERVABILITY IN CLOUD-NATIVE SYSTEMS

endpoints at specified intervals. Metrics are then queried and visualized using tools such as Grafana:

```
# Install Grafana using Helm for Kubernetes
helm repo add grafana https://grafana.github.io/helm-charts
helm install grafana grafana/grafana --namespace monitoring

# Access Grafana
kubectl port-forward service/grafana -n monitoring 3000:80

# Default login for Grafana is admin/admin
```

Logs: Logs are structured messages that describe discrete events in a system's operation. Unlike metrics, logs provide contextual information that is invaluable for troubleshooting and post-mortem analysis. Cloud-native environments harness centralized logging solutions to handle the steel flow of log data stemming from multiple components and microservices.

Fluentd is a popular log collector that unifies data collection and consumption for better use and understanding of log data:

```
# Configuration snippet for Fluentd to collect logs
<source>
  @type tail
  path /var/log/syslog
  pos_file /var/log/td-agent/tmp/syslog.pos
  tag syslog.*
  <parse>
    @type syslog
  </parse>
</source>

# Fluentd aggregates logs into a centralized store, such as Elasticsearch.
<match syslog.**>
  @type elasticsearch
  host elasticsearch.local
  port 9200
  logstash_format true
</match>
```

Traces: Traces provide a view into the path of execution through a system, offering insights into latency bottlenecks and service dependencies. Distributed tracing is vital for tracking requests across the diverse landscape of microservices typical in cloud-native setups.

OpenTracing, as a standard, defines a set of consistent, expressive APIs that enable observability across service boundaries. Here is an example using Jaeger for tracing applications:

```
# Deploy Jaeger using Helm
helm repo add jaegertracing https://jaegertracing.github.io/helm-charts
helm install jaeger jaegertracing/jaeger

# Enable tracing in application
import io.opentracing.util.GlobalTracer;
import io.jaegertracing.Configuration;

Configuration config = new Configuration("myservice");
GlobalTracer.register(config.getTracer());
```

Traces collected thus facilitate identifying latency issues, measuring call counts between services, and understanding the interaction patterns between different services within the application architecture.

Integrating Observability Components: Coordinating metrics, logs, and traces is often necessary to gain a comprehensive understanding enveloping preparation, unexpected behavior detection, and resolution paths in cloud-native systems. Tools like Fluent Bit for log forwarding, Prometheus for time-series metrics, and OpenTelemetry for unified traces are often combined in a coherent observability strategy.

Prometheus, Fluent Bit, and OpenTelemetry export telemetry data back to a single observability stack like Grafana or an enterprise solution that supports correlated views for improved clarity and insight. By employing this trifecta of observability data, operators can make more informed decisions and anticipate system failures more effectively.

Challenges and Best Practices: The principles of observability must contend with the inherent challenges of cloud environments, such as their dynamic nature, inherently transient states, and complex service interactions. Best practices for implementing effective observability include:

- Establishing a Unified Logging and Monitoring Strategy: Integrate all layers of observability—application logs, performance metrics, system traces, and more—into a cohesive strategy to see how data correlates across systems.

- Implementing an Observability Pipeline: Use pipelines for collecting, transforming, and shipping telemetry data efficiently, maintaining high availability and resilience.

- Prioritizing Data Quality and Consistency: Ensure that your data is accurate, consistent, and timely. High cardinality and unique values like identifier tags should be used judiciously.

- Automating Instrumentation and Data Collection: Use automated tools and frameworks for tracking changes and collecting data to reduce manual effort and avoid human error.

In the cumulative consideration of metrics, logs, and traces, observability becomes a proactive tool empowering developers and operators to sensibly pilot systems through thick and thin scenarios. Implementing these principles effectively affords businesses the ability to scale efficiently, mitigate potential risks, and ultimately deliver a more reliable web of services catering to end-users seamlessly.

8.2 Integrating Crossplane with Monitoring Tools

Integrating Crossplane with monitoring tools is a critical step in ensuring the effective tracking and oversight of resources managed within cloud-native environments. Crossplane, as a Kubernetes-based control plane for cloud-native applications, enables the management of applications and infrastructure through Kubernetes-like APIs. Ensuring visibility over these resources demands seamless integration with well-established monitoring tools to provide insights into resource states, performance metrics, and system health.

The integration involves the use of metrics, logging, and tracing tools alongside Crossplane, allowing operators to monitor the state of cloud resources and services that are dynamically provisioned and managed through Crossplane manifests.

Role of Crossplane in Cloud Native Monitoring: Crossplane enables users to create and manage cloud infrastructure through Kubernetes Custom Resource Definitions (CRDs). Unlike static resource management, Crossplane deals in an inherently dynamic environment where resources are created, modified, and destroyed based on declarative specifications. Such environments necessitate sophisticated monitoring to understand resource availability, performance, cost, and interactions with dependent systems.

Prometheus for Metrics Collection: Prometheus can be integrated with Crossplane to track infrastructure metrics such as CPU, memory, disk usage, network I/O, and more. The Prometheus Operator for Kubernetes facilitates the monitoring of Kubernetes-based systems, and Crossplane can be connected using the Prometheus metrics server which scrapes metrics from pods, including any managed by Crossplane.

```
# Deploy Prometheus Operator via Helm for Kubernetes
helm repo add prometheus-community https://prometheus-community.github.io/helm-
    charts
helm install prometheus prometheus-community/kube-prometheus-stack --namespace
    monitoring

# Configuring Service Monitor for Crossplane
apiVersion: monitoring.coreos.com/v1
kind: ServiceMonitor
metadata:
  name: crossplane-metrics
  labels:
    release: prometheus
spec:
  selector:
    matchLabels:
      app: crossplane
  endpoints:
  - port: http-metrics
    interval: 30s
```

The above ServiceMonitor configuration specifies that Prometheus should monitor endpoints relevant to Crossplane, every 30 seconds, capturing essential operational metrics. These metrics can be visualized using Grafana dashboards.

Grafana Dashboards for Resource Visibility: Grafana is employed to visualize the metrics scraped by Prometheus. By creating dashboards tailored to Crossplane-managed resources, operators can gain insights into resource utilization, performance anomalies, and trends over time, aiding in proactive resource management.

```
{
  "dashboard": {
    "title": "Crossplane Resources",
    "rows": [
      {
        "title": "CPU and Memory Usage",
        "panels": [
          {
            "type": "graph",
            "target": {
              "expr": "cpu_usage_seconds_total{job='crossplane'}"
```

8.2. INTEGRATING CROSSPLANE WITH MONITORING TOOLS

```
        }
      },
      {
        "type": "graph",
        "target": {
          "expr": "memory_usage_bytes{job='crossplane'}"
        }
      }
    ]
  }
  ]
}
```

The above JSON configuration creates a Grafana dashboard displaying essential CPU and memory metrics of Crossplane-managed services. These panels offer high-level visibility yet can be customized further to meet specific monitoring needs.

Integrating Fluent Bit for Log Aggregation: Fluent Bit serves as a robust solution to aggregate logs from Kubernetes pods, including Crossplane-managed applications. Capturing logs is crucial for understanding system events and behaviors.

```
# Deploy Fluent Bit via Helm for log forwarding
helm repo add fluent https://fluent.github.io/helm-charts
helm install fluent-bit fluent/fluent-bit --namespace logging

# Configuration for Fluent Bit to process Crossplane logs
[SERVICE]
    flush 5
    daemon off
    log_level info

[INPUT]
    Name tail
    Path /var/log/crossplane/*.log
    Multiline on
    Parser docker

[OUTPUT]
    Name stdout
    Match *
```

In this configuration, Fluent Bit reads logs produced by Crossplane components and sends them to a central logging service, such as an Elasticsearch cluster, for further analysis and visualization using tools like Kibana.

Tracing with OpenTelemetry: Distributed tracing, enabled through OpenTelemetry and tools like Jaeger or Zipkin, provides a detailed view of request paths and latencies in systems where Crossplane-managed resources form part of a broader service architecture.

```
# Configure OpenTelemetry Collector for seamless tracing
apiVersion: opentelemetry.io/v1alpha1
kind: OpenTelemetryCollector
metadata:
  name: crossplane-tracing
spec:
  config:
    receivers:
      jaeger:
        protocols:
          grpc:
          thrift_http:
    exporters:
      logging:
      jaeger:
        endpoint: "jaeger-collector.monitoring.svc.cluster.local:14250"
        insecure: true
    service:
      pipelines:
        traces:
          receivers: [jaeger]
          exporters: [logging, jaeger]
```

This configuration outlines how OpenTelemetry receivers, processors, and exporters are orchestrated to capture and route trace data through the system, offering granular visibility into service interactions.

Challenges and Considerations: Integrating Crossplane with monitoring systems involves addressing several challenges:

- Scalability: Monitoring must scale as the managed infrastructure grows, ensuring that increased resource allocations do not lead to monitoring overhead.

- Data Volume: The sheer volume of metrics, logs, and traces can overwhelm systems if not processed efficiently; filtering, processing, and aggregating data is crucial.

- Resource Efficiency: Monitoring workload must not unduly consume resources or impact the performance of production systems.

- Security: Ensure that sensitive information collected through logs and metrics does not expose critical vulnerabilities and complies with privacy regulations.

Integrating monitoring tools with Crossplane is an integral operation for sustaining the operability, performance, and dynamic scaling of cloud-native environments. Through effective use of telemetry data, operators gain insights into resource states and health, enabling proactive management and optimization of complex systems.

8.3 Building Dashboards for Cloud Resource Visibility

Dashboards are pivotal in enhancing visibility into the operational aspects of cloud-managed environments, such as those orchestrated by Crossplane. These visualization tools assemble complex sets of data into intuitive interfaces that facilitate real-time monitoring, diagnostics, and performance analysis. Building effective dashboards involves leveraging key observability data, such as metrics and logs, to provide clear and actionable insights into resource utilization and health.

Purpose and Benefits of Dashboards: Dashboards present an aggregate view of system and application states, offering the capability to visualize data trends, identify anomalies, and troubleshoot issues promptly. In cloud environments, dashboards are especially critical due to the dynamic nature of workloads and infrastructure, where resource configurations, health status, and performance metrics can fluctuate rapidly.

- **Real-time Data Visualization:** Dashboards enable the real-time display of critical operational data, offering immediate insights into current system statuses and allowing quick identification of anomalies or degradations.

- **Historical Insights and Trend Analysis:** By visualizing historical data trends, dashboards assist in understanding system behavior over time, assisting in capacity planning and performance tuning.

- **Integration with Monitoring Tools:** Dashboards unify data from multiple sources—metrics, logs, traces—into coherent visual displays, streamlining information flow from observability tools such as Prometheus, Grafana, Elastic Stack, and others.

Components of Effective Dashboards: Crafting a useful dashboard requires careful selection of components that collectively offer a holistic view of the environment:

- **Graphs and Charts:** Line graphs, bar charts, pie charts, and histograms are used to display time-series data, categorical distributions, and more.
- **Heatmaps:** Useful for visualizing utilization patterns, heatmaps can illustrate resource usage intensity over time and help detect cyclical patterns.
- **Alerts and Thresholds:** Indicator widgets that change colors or icons when predefined conditions or thresholds are breached.
- **Data Annotations:** Features allowing operators to correlate events with observed data trends, providing context and facilitating causality analysis.

Designing Dashboards for Crossplane Resources:

Integrating Crossplane-managed resources into dashboards involves a series of steps, including data collection, processing, and visualization specific to the resource types managed through Crossplane.

Setting Up Data Collection: In a Crossplane environment, resources are managed as Kubernetes objects, and relevant metrics can be gathered automatically by existing Kubernetes monitoring solutions such as Prometheus.

```
# Adding custom metrics export for Crossplane
kubectl annotate deployments -n crossplane-system crossplane \
  prometheus.io/scrape='true' \
  prometheus.io/port='8080'
```

This annotation ensures that metrics are scraped from Crossplane instances, which can then be fed into dashboard tools for visualization.

Building Dashboards with Grafana:

1. **Data Source Configuration:** Configure Grafana to connect to Prometheus as a data source for time-series metrics. This setup allows Grafana to pull data regarding Crossplane-managed

8.3. BUILDING DASHBOARDS FOR CLOUD RESOURCE VISIBILITY

resources, such as virtual networks, databases, Kubernetes clusters, and more.

```
{
    "name": "Prometheus",
    "type": "prometheus",
    "url": "http://prometheus-server:9090",
    "access": "proxy",
    "isDefault": true
}
```

2. **Creating Visualizations:** Once your data source is configured, begin creating visualizations tailored to your requirements:

- **Resource Utilization Panel:** Create a panel displaying the CPU, memory, and IOPS utilizations of instances managed by Crossplane.

```
{
    "title": "Resource Utilization",
    "type": "graph",
    "targets": [
        {
            "expr": "crossplane_cpu_usage_seconds_total",
            "legendFormat": "CPU Usage"
        },
        {
            "expr": "crossplane_memory_usage_bytes",
            "legendFormat": "Memory Usage"
        }
    ]
}
```

- **Status Overview Panel:** Displays the current status of critical Crossplane objects such as provisioning states, which aids in understanding the current service composition and any pending modifications.

```
{
    "title": "Status Overview",
    "type": "singlestat",
    "targets": [
        {
            "expr": "sum by(status) (crossplane_provisioning_status)",
            "legendFormat": "{{status}}"
        }
    ]
}
```

Advanced Dashboard Features:

1. **Alert Management:** Incorporate alert conditions within your Grafana dashboard to trigger notifications or visual cues when anomalies are detected. For instance, setting an alert when resource usage surges past a threshold.

   ```
   {
     "panel": "Resource Utilization",
     "alert": {
       "conditions": [
         {
           "type": "query",
           "params": ["A", "5m", "now"],
           "evaluator": "gt",
           "threshold": 80,
           "reducerType": "avg",
           "operator": "and"
         }
       ],
       "notifications": [
         {
           "uid": "alert-channel"
         }
       ]
     }
   }
   ```

2. **Embedding Live Annotations:** Enable annotations to mark significant events such as deployments, configuration changes, and policy updates that coincide with observed metrics on the dashboard. These annotations help elucidate cause-effect relationships and trends.

   ```
   {
     "type": "annotations",
     "list": [
       {
         "tags": ["deployment"],
         "time": 1617852340000,
         "text": "Deployed new version of database service."
       }
     ]
   }
   ```

3. **Security and Access Control:** Implement proper roles and permissions to secure dashboard access, ensuring only authorized users can view or modify sensitive data. Grafana's role-based access control facilitates administration of data safety and compliance.

Integration with Other Visualization Tools:

8.3. BUILDING DASHBOARDS FOR CLOUD RESOURCE VISIBILITY

Beyond Grafana, other visualization tools such as Kibana, Datadog, and Splunk can also be integrated for building dashboards, each providing unique capabilities and interfaces suited for different operational preferences and requirements.

When using Kibana, particularly in conjunction with the Elastic Stack setup, the following steps are paramount:

- **Configure Elasticsearch and Kibana to process Crossplane logs and metrics.**

- **Create index patterns for incoming Crossplane data streams, allowing you to create visualizations in Kibana's dashboarding interface.**

```
{
  "index_patterns": ["crossplane-*"],
  "settings": {
    "number_of_shards": 3
  }
}
```

Indexes facilitate quick retrieval and visualization of large volumes of data, catering to operations that require detailed temporal analysis.

Conclusion to Dashboard Strategy:

Designing and implementing effective dashboards for cloud resource visibility within Crossplane-managed environments requires thoughtful consideration of the data collection, processing, and display mechanisms. Dashboards should offer comprehensive and precise insights, facilitating seamless oversight and management of resources throughout their lifecycle. Operators leverage these dashboards not just for monitoring, but as lenses into the continual evolution and operation of the system landscape, making them indispensable assets in the realm of cloud-native architectures. Properly integrated with robust notification systems and data annotation, dashboards empower teams to make informed, timely decisions, ensuring system reliability and resilience.

8.4 Setting up Alerts and Notifications

The implementation of alerts and notifications is a critical component of managing cloud-native infrastructures, particularly in environments orchestrated by Crossplane. Alerts enable proactive responses to system anomalies, performance degradations, or security incidents by notifying operators in real-time. Properly configured alerts help reduce mean time to resolution (MTTR), maintain service uptime, and ensure compliance with service level objectives (SLOs). An effective alerting strategy should be comprehensive and precise, mitigating false positives while capturing significant issues in operational environments.

Fundamentals of Alerts and Notifications: Alerts are signals triggered when specific conditions or thresholds—set through rules or policies—are breached within a monitored system. Notifications, subsequently, deliver these signals to relevant stakeholders via preferred communication channels such as email, SMS, or integration with incident management tools like PagerDuty or Slack.

- **Alert Types:**
    - **Threshold Alerts**: Triggered when a metric exceeds a predefined value, such as high CPU utilization.
    - **Anomaly Detection**: Employing machine learning models to predict anomalies based on historical data patterns.
    - **Event-based Alerts**: Triggered by discrete occurrences or system events, like pod restarts.
    - **Resource State Change Alerts**: Raised when critical resource configurations change unexpectedly.
- **Notification Channels**: Integration with email systems, messaging platforms, or custom webhooks to disseminate alert information promptly.

Configuring Alerts with Prometheus and Alertmanager:

Prometheus paired with Alertmanager forms a robust framework for alerting mechanisms in Kubernetes-based environments, including those managed by Crossplane.

8.4. SETTING UP ALERTS AND NOTIFICATIONS

1. **Defining Alert Rules in Prometheus:**

Alert rules define the specific conditions under which alerts are triggered in Prometheus. These rules are expressed in PromQL, the query language of Prometheus, and are stored in YAML configuration files.

```
groups:
- name: crossplane-alerts
  rules:
  - alert: HighCPULoad
    expr: cpu_usage_seconds_total{job="crossplane"} > 0.8
    for: 5m
    labels:
      severity: critical
    annotations:
      summary: "High CPU load on crossplane components"
      description: "CPU load has exceeded 80% for more than 5 minutes"
```

In this configuration, a rule is defined to trigger an alert named 'HighCPULoad' if the CPU load exceeds 80% for more than 5 minutes, with an associated label of severity 'critical'.

2. **Integrating Alertmanager for Notifications:**

Alertmanager handles alert notifications and deduplication, routing, and silencing.

```
global:
  smtp_smarthost: 'smtp.example.com:587'
  smtp_from: 'alertmanager@example.com'

route:
  receiver: 'global-email'

receivers:
- name: 'global-email'
  email_configs:
  - to: 'oncall@example.com'
```

This Alertmanager configuration sets up email notifications to be sent to the on-call team using a specified SMTP server whenever alerts are triggered.

Advanced Alerting Strategies:

1. **Multi-stage Alerting System:**

A multi-stage alerting system can be configured to send initial alerts of low severity followed by escalated alerts if a condition persists or worsens. This approach helps prevent alert fatigue and ensures attention is paid to genuine issues.

```
# Prometheus alert rules for multi-stage alerts
groups:
- name: resource-usage
  rules:
  - alert: ResourceThresholdWarning
    expr: memory_usage_bytes{job="crossplane"} > 0.75
    for: 2m
    labels:
      severity: warning
    annotations:
      summary: "Memory usage near capacity"
  - alert: ResourceThresholdCritical
    expr: memory_usage_bytes{job="crossplane"} > 0.9
    for: 5m
    labels:
      severity: critical
    annotations:
      summary: "Critical memory usage"
```

In this setup, a warning is triggered when memory utilization exceeds 75%, and a critical alert is issued if the situation escalates to 90%.

2. **Integration with Incident Management Systems**:

Leveraging external incident management systems such as PagerDuty offers enhanced alerting capabilities, including automatic escalation policies, on-call rotations, and post-incident analysis.

```
# Alertmanager configuration for PagerDuty
route:
  receiver: 'pagerduty-service'

receivers:
- name: 'pagerduty-service'
  pagerduty_configs:
  - service_key: 'your-pagerduty-service-key'
    send_resolved: true
```

3. **Alert Evaluation Frequency and Timing**:

Alert evaluation intervals should be set based on the nature and criticality of metrics being monitored. Shorter intervals are suitable for high-priority alerts, while longer intervals can be used for less critical situations to reduce noise.

```
# Example Prometheus scraping interval for high-priority metrics
scrape_interval: 15s
```

4. **Silencing and Inhibition Rules:**

8.4. SETTING UP ALERTS AND NOTIFICATIONS

Silence mechanisms and inhibition rules provide the ability to temporarily disable alerts during planned maintenance windows or when certain conditions justify a gluing of lower-priority alerts.

```
# Alertmanager silence example
silences:
- matcher:
    alertname: 'HighCPULoad'
  startsAt: '2020-10-01T18:00:00Z'
  endsAt: '2020-10-01T19:00:00Z'
  comment: 'Scheduled maintenance'
```

Inhibition rules can be set to avoid alert cascades when high-priority alerts suppress notifications from lower-priority conditions during ongoing incidents.

Considerations and Challenges in Alert Configuration:

- **Avoiding Alert Fatigue**: Balance between necessary alerts and overwhelming volume is delicate. Review alert thresholds and conditions to prevent alerts from becoming neglected due to volume.

- **Data Accuracy and Reliability**: Alerts based on inaccurate telemetry data lead to false positives or missed incidents. Ensure robust data pipelines and regular calibrations.

- **Scalability**: As infrastructure scales, alerting systems must accommodate the additional volume without performance degradation. Distributed alerting setups can mitigate scaling issues.

- **Security and Compliance**: Alert configurations may inadvertently expose sensitive information if logs and messages are poorly managed. Implement access controls and encryption standards.

- **Response Planning and Automation**: Define procedures for responding to specific alerts, and explore automatic remediation where feasible to preemptively resolve issues (e.g., auto-scaling resources in response to utilization alerts).

Establishing a resilient alerts and notifications system enables comprehensive oversight and operational responsiveness within cloud-native environments managed by Crossplane. By refining alerting rules, integrating efficient notification pathways, and adopting advanced alerting strategies, organizations can better manage the complexities of dynamically orchestrated systems, thereby improving uptime and enhancing user satisfaction.

8.5 Analyzing Logs and Traces

Analyzing logs and traces forms the backbone of diagnostics, system analysis, and troubleshooting in cloud-native environments. These activities are essential for gaining insights into the behavior and performance of microservices, applications, and infrastructure components managed through platforms like Crossplane. Logs provide detailed chronological records of system activities, while traces offer an end-to-end view of request execution paths across distributed systems. Together, they empower developers and operators to understand, optimize, and secure complex architectures.

Understanding Logs: Logs are structured or unstructured records that document discrete events as they occur within systems. They capture a wide array of information, including errors, warnings, informational messages, and debugging details. In Kubernetes environments, logs can originate from application components, system services, and orchestration frameworks. Analyzing these logs involves parsing, organizing, and filtering data to extract meaningful insights.

- **Log Collection and Centralization:**

    Log data gathered from diverse sources should be centralized to facilitate efficient analysis. Fluent Bit, Fluentd, and Logstash are popular tools for log collection and aggregation. These agents gather logs from nodes and containers and forward them to a centralized storage or processing location, often Elasticsearch for storage and retrieval.

    ```
    # Deploy Fluent Bit as DaemonSet to collect container logs
    kubectl apply -f https://raw.githubusercontent.com/fluent/fluent-bit-
        kubernetes-logging/master/fluent-bit-daemonset.yaml

    # Fluent Bit configuration example
    [SERVICE]
    ```

8.5. ANALYZING LOGS AND TRACES

```
        Flush 5
        Daemon Off
        Log_Level Info

    [INPUT]
        Name tail
        Tag kube.*
        Path /var/log/containers/*.log
        Parser docker

    [OUTPUT]
        Name es
        Match *
        Host elasticsearch.logging.svc.cluster.local
        Port 9200
        Logstash_Format On
```

This setup deploys Fluent Bit to collect logs from Kubernetes pods and forwards them to an Elasticsearch cluster for storage.

- **Structured Logging:**

    Adopting structured logging practices enhances the queryability and usability of log data. By structuring logs in JSON format, analysts can perform precise searches and filter operations based on keys like timestamps, request IDs, severity levels, or user IDs.

```
{
    "timestamp": "2023-10-01T15:23:45Z",
    "level": "error",
    "message": "Failed to connect to database.",
    "service": "orders-service",
    "trace_id": "abcdef1234567890"
}
```

Understanding Traces: Traces provide comprehensive visibility into the execution path of a request as it traverses through various components in a distributed system. This end-to-end visibility highlights service dependencies, latency contributions, and errors passed between services.

- **Distributed Tracing with OpenTelemetry:**

    OpenTelemetry serves as a framework for capturing, processing, and exporting trace data from distributed systems into backend analysis tools like Jaeger. The OpenTelemetry SDKs allow instrumenting applications to generate tracing telemetry that reveals latency hotspots and execution bottlenecks.

```
# OpenTelemetry configuration in a Java application
import io.opentelemetry.api.trace.Span;
import io.opentelemetry.api.trace.Tracer;
import io.opentelemetry.api.GlobalOpenTelemetry;

public class OrderService {
    private static final Tracer tracer = GlobalOpenTelemetry.get().getTracer
        ("orders", "1.0.0");

    public void processOrder() {
        Span span = tracer.spanBuilder("OrderProcessing").startSpan();
        try {
            // Business logic
        } finally {
            span.end();
        }
    }
}
```

- **Visualizing Traces with Jaeger:**

  Jaeger is a popular tracing backend that provides visualization tools for viewing latency compositions and request journeys. Deployed alongside OpenTelemetry, Jaeger collects and displays traces in a comprehensible manner.

  ```
  # Deploy Jaeger as part of tracing stack
  kubectl create namespace monitoring
  helm repo add jaegertracing https://jaegertracing.github.io/helm-charts
  helm install jaeger jaegertracing/jaeger --namespace monitoring
  ```

- **Analyzing Trace Data:**

  Trace data provides detailed insights into system latency patterns, service dependencies, and potential fault points. Analysts evaluate the timings associated with each span of a trace to detect performance bottlenecks and deduce the root causes of latency.

Analyzing Logs and Traces Together: Integrating logs and traces offers a comprehensive view of system behavior, enabling analysts to reconstruct incidents with greater accuracy. This synergy assists in correlating failures across logs and tracing the exact paths affected within request executions.

- **Correlation and Contextualization:** By employing unique identifiers such as trace_id and span_id, analysts can correlate

8.5. ANALYZING LOGS AND TRACES

log entries with trace spans, enriching the diagnostic context and uncovering latent relationships among system components.

- **Root Cause Analysis:** During incident investigations, trace data highlights failed service interactions and errors passed along service paths, while logs provide contextual information related to state transitions and exceptions.

- **Visualization and Dashboards:** Tools like Kibana and Grafana can integrate logs and traces into unified dashboards, allowing for cross-referenced insights which include overlaying logs onto trace timelines or constructing queryable visualizations for in-depth analysis.

```
{
    "title": "Order Service Overview",
    "panels": [
        {
            "type": "traces",
            "target": {
                "service": "orders-service",
                "operation": "OrderProcessing"
            }
        },
        {
            "type": "logs",
            "target": {
                "index": "orders-service-log-*",
                "query": "trace_id:abcdef1234567890"
            }
        }
    ]
}
```

Challenges and Best Practices:

Analyzing logs and traces in cloud environments presents numerous challenges, but adopting best practices helps mitigate these issues:

- **Volume and Noise Reduction:** Manage the high volumes of data by implementing filtering strategies that prioritize critical logs and trace paths.

- **Latency vs Throughput:** Balancing the granularity of tracing with performance overhead is crucial. Lightweight sampling methods may be employed when full retention is impractical.

- **Security and Sensitivity:** Logs and traces often contain sensitive data. Employ rigorous access controls, encryption, and make auditing an integral part of the analysis process to ensure data security.

- **Structured Logging Standards:** Adopting standardized logging frameworks across services improves consistency and supports automation in log parsing.

- **Automating Analysis Workflows:** Automation using machine learning and AI is advancing into enhancing root cause detection, anomaly prediction, and pattern recognition in logs and trace data.

The effective analysis of logs and traces delivers profound insights into distributed system performance and behavior. Constructing reliable logging and tracing infrastructures complemented with structured processes ensures organizations maximize return on their investments in cloud-native observability systems, empowering operational teams with the capabilities to maintain system reliability, security, and performance.

8.6 Capacity Planning and Optimization

Capacity planning and optimization are crucial processes in managing cloud-native environments, such as those orchestrated by Crossplane. They involve predicting future resource requirements and optimizing the use of current resources to ensure efficient operation and cost-effectiveness. These processes help maintain performance levels, support scaling operations in tandem with demand, and prevent resource wastage or bottleneck scenarios.

Understanding Capacity Planning: Capacity planning is the practice of determining the infrastructure resources required to meet future workloads without compromising on performance or efficiency. It involves forecasting demand, planning for growth, and allocating resources to meet anticipated needs, all while keeping costs under control.

8.6. CAPACITY PLANNING AND OPTIMIZATION

- **Forecasting Demand:**

    Proper demand forecasting is the bedrock of capacity planning. It requires a detailed analysis of historical usage data to predict future infrastructure needs. This typically involves the following steps:

    - **Analyzing Historical Usage:** Leveraging historical data to identify patterns, peaks, and troughs in resource usage. Tools like Prometheus can be used to aggregate historical data and Grafana for visualization.

        ```
        # Prometheus query example to fetch historical memory usage
        rate(memory_usage_bytes{instance="app-instance"}[1h])
        ```

    - **Identifying Trends:** Using predictive analytics to identify upward, downward, or cyclical trends that may impact future capacity requirements. Regression analysis and time-series forecasting models, such as ARIMA or Holt-Winters, can be valuable here.

    - **Estimating Future Load:** Based on identified trends, estimate the future load characteristics to determine resource requirements. This involves considering aspects such as user growth, potential new features, and marketing activities.

- **Evaluating Current Resource Utilization:**

    Efficient capacity planning involves assessing the current resource utilization to identify underutilized capacity that can potentially support future workloads.

    - **Utilization Metrics:** Monitor key metrics like CPU, memory, disk I/O, and network throughput to gauge how resources are currently being used. This can involve creating utilization dashboards in Grafana.

        ```
        {
            "title": "Resource Utilization Dashboard",
            "panels": [
                {
                    "type": "graph",
                    "title": "CPU Utilization",
                    "targets": [
        ```

```
        {
            "expr": "rate(cpu_usage_seconds_total{job='crossplane
               '}[5m])"
        }
    ]
},
{
    "type": "graph",
    "title": "Memory Utilization",
    "targets": [
        {
            "expr": "memory_usage_bytes{job='crossplane'}"
        }
    ]
}
    ]
}
```

- **Resource Saturation Points:** Identify components nearing saturation to determine the need for scaling operations or provisioning additional resources.

Strategies for Capacity Optimization: Optimizing capacity involves fine-tuning resource utilization to get the most out of available infrastructure while minimizing costs and enhancing performance.

- **Auto-Scaling:**

  Auto-scaling dynamically adjusts resource allocation in response to changing demand. Kubernetes provides built-in mechanisms for auto-scaling pods, nodes, and clusters, allowing seamless scaling based on predefined metrics.

  - **Cluster Auto-Scaling:** Automatically adjusts the number of nodes in a cluster to maintain the balance between performance and cost. A typical configuration in Kubernetes can be implemented as follows:

    ```
    # Enable cluster autoscaler in Kubernetes
    kubectl apply -f cluster-autoscaler-config.yaml

    # Sample YAML configuration for cluster autoscaler
    apiVersion: autoscaling/v1
    kind: ClusterAutoscaler
    metadata:
      name: example-cluster-autoscaler
    spec:
      minNodes: 1
      maxNodes: 10
    ```

8.6. CAPACITY PLANNING AND OPTIMIZATION

- **Horizontal Pod Auto-Scaling (HPA):** Kubernetes HPA automatically scales the number of pod replicas based on observed CPU utilization or other custom metrics. HPA can be configured with a YAML manifest:

```
apiVersion: autoscaling/v1
kind: HorizontalPodAutoscaler
metadata:
  name: example-hpa
spec:
  scaleTargetRef:
    apiVersion: apps/v1
    kind: Deployment
    name: example-deployment
  minReplicas: 2
  maxReplicas: 10
  targetCPUUtilizationPercentage: 70
```

- **Vertical Pod Auto-Scaling (VPA):** Automatically adjusts the CPU and memory requests/limits for pod containers, ensuring that individual pod instances utilize resources efficiently.

- **Resource Optimization:**

Optimizing resource configurations and parameters ensures efficient allocation and reduces unnecessary overhead.

- **Right-Sizing Resources:** Periodically review resource allocations for over-provisioning or underuse, refactoring settings in deployment manifests. Tools such as resource profiling and audit logs provide insights into optimal allocations.

- **Tuning Garbage Collection and Memory Management:** Optimizing garbage collection strategies and memory allocation parameters reduces wastage and improves the throughput of Java and other garbage-collected languages.

- **Cost Management and Savings:**

Using cloud cost management tools to monitor expenses associated with infrastructure usage in real-time can help identify saving opportunities and reduce overspending.

– **Instance Usage Reports:** Regularly assess virtual machine or compute instance usage reports to identify cost anomalies or unused resources.

Challenges and Best Practices in Capacity Planning and Optimization:

- **Predicting Bursts and Spikes:** Handling unpredictable traffic or demand spikes requires strategies such as buffer allocations and pre-scaling. Leveraging machine learning algorithms for anticipatory scaling can be beneficial.

- **Cross-Cloud Portability:** In multi-cloud environments facilitated by Crossplane, ensure consistent configurations and policies across different cloud service providers to maintain seamless capacity planning.

- **Efficient Utilization of Spot Instances:** Utilizing preemptible or spot instances for non-critical workloads can increase cost efficiency while maintaining flexibility.

- **Cascading Failure Risks:** Ensure that scaling operations do not lead to resource contention or cascading failures that degrade system performance.

- **Regular Review Cycles:** Implement regular review cycles for capacity planning and optimization strategies, especially following significant infrastructure or application changes.

Through comprehensive capacity planning and optimization, organizations can ensure that their cloud-native architectures are both resilient and cost-effective. Careful planning, augmented by intelligent analytics and predictive capabilities, enables enterprises to accommodate future demands while minimizing waste and maximizing return on investment. As systems continue to evolve and grow increasingly complex, the ability to deftly manage resources across distributed environments becomes an invaluable asset for maintaining competitive and operational excellence.

8.7 Feedback Loop for Continuous Improvement

The establishment of a feedback loop for continuous improvement is pivotal in enhancing the performance and reliability of cloud-native environments managed by platforms like Crossplane. Such a feedback loop facilitates the integration of operational insights into developmental processes, ensuring that systems evolve and adapt in response to real-world conditions and performance metrics. Continuous improvement processes harness observability data to boost system reliability, optimize performance, and streamline operational workflows, all of which are key to maintaining competitive advantage and operational resiliency in ever-changing technological landscapes.

Concept of Feedback Loops: In a computing context, feedback loops refer to the system mechanisms that continuously gather, assess, and feed operational data back into the development cycle. This process is characterized by three main stages: observation, analysis, and action.

- **Observation**: The initial phase involves monitoring system behavior through data collection. This includes gathering metrics, logs, traces, and user feedback critical for assessing system performance and identifying anomalies.

- **Analysis**: During this stage, the collected data is analyzed to identify trends, detect issues, and uncover opportunities for optimization or innovation. Advanced data analytics and machine learning techniques are often employed here to derive actionable insights.

- **Action**: Based on the analysis, strategic decisions and improvements are implemented to enhance system efficiency, reliability, and user satisfaction. Feedback is acknowledged, prioritizing changes that deliver the most value.

Components of Effective Feedback Loops: Establishing a robust feedback loop involves integrating multiple elements to ensure that observations translate into continuous improvement.

- **Integrated Observability Framework**:

  An effective feedback loop harnesses a coherent observability framework that integrates metrics, logs, and traces, often leveraging open-source solutions like Prometheus, Fluent Bit, and OpenTelemetry, alongside visualization tools such as Grafana and Kibana.

  ```
  # Integrating Prometheus and Grafana for metric observation
  helm install prometheus prometheus-community/kube-prometheus-stack
      --namespace monitoring
  helm install grafana grafana/grafana --namespace monitoring
  ```

  Each component collects specific data types necessary for holistic monitoring:

  - **Metrics** provide quantitative insights into resource performance and usage.
  - **Logs** deliver a record of event-driven data and system behavior.
  - **Traces** highlight request paths and latencies, offering a detailed view of distributed transaction performances.

- **Automated Data Processing and Analysis**:

  Using data processing pipelines, such as those built with Apache Kafka or Elk Stack, continuous data streams are processed in real-time. Machine learning models can be trained to predict performance anomalies or to characterize patterns, making it possible to gain deeper insights from data analysis.

  ```
  # Sample machine learning workflow in Julia for anomaly detection
  using CSV, DataFrames, MLJ

  # Load the dataset
  data = CSV.read("metrics.csv", DataFrame)

  # Define and train the model
  model = @load IsolationForest verbosity=1
  mach = machine(model, data)
  fit!(mach)

  # Predict anomalies
  probs = predict(mach, data)
  ```

- **Continuous Integration and Deployment (CI/CD)**:

8.7. FEEDBACK LOOP FOR CONTINUOUS IMPROVEMENT

Feedback loops are bolstered by CI/CD pipelines that automate the testing and deployment of updates. Changes inspired by observability insights can be rapidly implemented and validated, facilitating more agile responses to operational needs.

```
# GitLab CI/CD sample pipeline for Kubernetes
stages:
  - build
  - test
  - deploy

build_job:
  stage: build
  script:
    - docker build -t registry.example.com/myapp:latest .

test_job:
  stage: test
  script:
    - docker run registry.example.com/myapp:latest test

deploy_job:
  stage: deploy
  only:
    - master
  script:
    - kubectl apply -f k8s/deployment.yaml
```

Benefits of Implementing Feedback Loops:

- **Enhanced System Reliability**: By continuously refining processes and configurations based on real-world data, systems can achieve greater stability and resilience against failures.

- **Improved Performance**: Insights from observability data help identify bottlenecks, enabling targeted optimizations that improve performance metrics such as latency and throughput.

- **Accelerated Development Cycles**: The continuous flow of feedback into development cycles quickens the pace of iteration, encouraging innovation and rapid rollout of features.

- **User Experience Optimization**: Feedback loops incorporate user feedback effectively, aligning system improvements with user needs and enhancing satisfaction.

Challenges in Establishing Feedback Loops:

- **Data Overload**: Large volumes of data may lead to analytical bottlenecks. Utilizing efficient filtering mechanisms and focusing on key performance indicators (KPIs) can mitigate this.
- **Accuracy and Precision**: Ensuring data accuracy and precision is paramount. Poor quality data can lead to incorrect analyses and misguided actions.
- **Resource Allocation**: Balancing resources between feedback loop processes and primary operational needs requires careful planning.
- **Security and Compliance**: Handling sensitive data collected in feedback loops necessitates robust security measures and adherence to compliance standards, such as GDPR or HIPAA.

Case Study Example: Implementing Feedback Loops in Crossplane Managed Environments

A hypothetical example showcases the implementation of feedback loops within a Crossplane-managed environment where the feedback process is used to optimize cloud resource allocations:

- **Data Collection and Metrics Aggregation**:
    - Deploy Prometheus and OpenTelemetry to monitor resource metrics and trace application requests, identifying utilization trends and service latency.
- **Automated Analysis and Anomaly Detection**:
    - Implement an anomaly detection model to spot abnormal resource consumption which could indicate leaking memory, inefficient code paths, or unstable resource provisioned.
- **Strategic Decision-Making and Optimization**:
    - Redefine auto-scaling and resource limits in Kubernetes based on observed data.
    - Adjust Crossplane resource definitions to optimize the cost and performance balance, following real-time insights from collected metrics and traces.

8.7. FEEDBACK LOOP FOR CONTINUOUS IMPROVEMENT

- **Iterative Deployment and Feedback Integration**:
    - Utilize CI/CD pipelines to iteratively deploy updates with changes, continuously integrating new insights and learnings into future development cycles.

Through these structured feedback loops, organizations can better adapt and align their cloud infrastructure to meet dynamic demands, improving efficiency and providing greater value to stakeholders. Employing these methodologies, engineering teams and operational personnel not only enhance system capabilities but also cultivate an environment that proactively evolves based on empirical insights, ensuring continued relevance and functional adaptability in the competitive landscape of software services.

CHAPTER 8. MONITORING AND OBSERVABILITY FOR CROSSPLANE MANAGED ENVIRONMENTS

Chapter 9

Scaling and Optimizing Cloud-Native Infrastructure

Scaling and optimizing cloud-native infrastructure involve enhancing application performance and resource efficiency to meet dynamic demand while controlling costs. Key strategies include horizontal and vertical scaling, employing auto-scaling mechanisms to adjust resources in real-time, and leveraging performance tuning techniques. Optimizing resource utilization requires monitoring workloads, analyzing usage patterns, and right-sizing instances to align operational needs with cost-effective deployment. Ensuring high availability and resilience through architectural best practices further underscores the importance of a scalable, optimized cloud setup. Implementing these strategies empowers organizations to maintain competitive agility and efficiency in cloud-native environments.

9.1 Understanding Scalability in Cloud-Native Systems

Scalability is a fundamental attribute of cloud-native systems, enabling them to efficiently accommodate varying workloads and user demands. It consists of two principal types: horizontal scaling and vertical scaling. Understanding these concepts is crucial for operating in dynamic cloud environments, where resource allocation plays a pivotal role in optimizing performance and controlling costs.

Horizontal scaling, often referred to as scaling out, involves expanding the number of instances in a system to handle increased load. This process distributes incoming tasks or requests across multiple instances, providing a means for parallel processing and enhancing system throughput. In contrast, vertical scaling, or scaling up, increases the resources of a single instance, such as its CPU or memory, to improve its processing capability. Both approaches have distinct implications in terms of architecture, cost, and complexity, and they should be judiciously applied based on specific application needs and operational contexts.

In cloud-native environments, such as those orchestrated using Kubernetes, the scalability mechanisms are advanced and automated, offering elasticity to seamlessly cope with fluctuating demands. This elasticity is a key consideration when designing and deploying applications on cloud platforms, as it ensures that resources are dynamically allocated to meet traffic demands without manual intervention.

Below is an example illustrating how Kubernetes employs horizontal pod autoscaling:

```
apiVersion: autoscaling/v2beta2
kind: HorizontalPodAutoscaler
metadata:
  name: example-hpa
spec:
  scaleTargetRef:
    apiVersion: apps/v1
    kind: Deployment
    name: example-deployment
  minReplicas: 2
  maxReplicas: 10
  metrics:
  - type: Resource
    resource:
```

9.1. UNDERSTANDING SCALABILITY IN CLOUD-NATIVE SYSTEMS

```
    name: cpu
    target:
        type: Utilization
        averageUtilization: 50
```

This YAML configuration shows a HorizontalPodAutoscaler targeting a deployment named example-deployment. The setup automatically adjusts the number of replicas between 2 and 10 based on CPU utilization, aiming for an average utilizing goal of 50%.

Auto-scaling is a valuable technique in managing workloads effectively. When integrating auto-scaling strategies, it is essential to consider factors such as:

- the granularity of monitoring,
- responsiveness to rapid changes in demand, and
- integration with existing load balancers.

Vertical scaling can also be advantageous in scenarios where individual instance performance is critical and horizontal scaling might incur prohibitive communication overhead. Cloud providers often facilitate vertical scalability through services that allow easy resizing of instances with minimal disruption to service.

It is important to understand the inherent limitations of vertical scaling, as there is a maximum capacity to which an instance can be scaled before performance improvements plateau or additional scalability results in diminishing returns. Furthermore, from an economic standpoint, vertical scaling can disproportionately increase costs as larger instances are generally priced at a premium.

In the context of Kubernetes, while Horizontal Pod Autoscalers handle horizontal scaling effectively, vertical scaling can also be automated through tools such as the Vertical Pod Autoscaler. This tool examines historic resource consumption and sets resource requests for containers dynamically.

For example, the following demonstrates a Vertical Pod Autoscaler configuration:

```
apiVersion: autoscaling.k8s.io/v1
kind: VerticalPodAutoscaler
```

```
metadata:
  name: example-vpa
spec:
  targetRef:
    apiVersion: "apps/v1"
    kind: Deployment
    name: example-deployment
  updatePolicy:
    updateMode: "Auto"
```

Here, the Vertical Pod Autoscaler automatically updates the resource requests to optimize the performance of example-deployment. This auto-tuning of resource requests based on historic data illustrates the potential for vertical scaling in cloud-native environments.

The choice between horizontal and vertical scaling should be informed by the specific demands of the application, infrastructure constraints, and cost implications. While horizontal scaling is generally preferred due to its innate ability to enhance fault tolerance and availability, vertical scaling can be a more straightforward solution for less distributed systems where scaling complexity should be minimized.

An overarching benefit of implementing effective scalability strategies is the ability to provide rapid responsiveness to user demands, ensuring that applications remain both performant and economically efficient. However, achieving such scalability necessitates a comprehensive understanding of the architectural constraints and resource demands inherent to the cloud-native paradigm. Developers and system architects need to continually assess the resource profiles of their applications, leveraging tools and services provided by cloud vendors to ensure optimal resource allocation.

For instance, in scenarios where workloads are bursty or unpredictable, proactive auto-scaling policies can provide significant performance and cost benefits. By defining policies in advance with appropriate thresholds and performance indicators, systems can dynamically adjust their resource allocations in real-time, maintaining optimal operational efficiency without necessitating manual oversight.

Furthermore, scalability does not only focus on raw computational resources. It encompasses the scaling of various system components such as storage, networking, and data access, which are often pivotal in maintaining overall system performance. As the application landscape evolves increasingly towards microservices architectures, the complexity of scaling these disparate yet interdependent components grows. This necessitates robust observability and monitoring systems to provide insights into how each component can be independently or collectively scaled.

These challenges underscore the strategic importance of a well-defined scalability plan in cloud-native environments. With advanced orchestration platforms and sophisticated monitoring tools, organizations can effectively implement both horizontal and vertical scaling strategies, striking a balance between performance, reliability, and cost-efficiency.

In practice, an optimal scaling solution is often hybrid, combining elements of both horizontal and vertical scaling. This hybrid approach allows for the unique advantages of each strategy to be realized while mitigating their respective drawbacks. A key aspect is automating the scaling mechanisms to ensure that they are responsive and adaptive to the application and infrastructure needs dynamically.

As applications continue to decentralize through microservices, orchestration frameworks like Kubernetes not only simplify the implementation of these scaling strategies but also add layers of abstraction to enhance portability and management ease. This abstraction further solidifies the role of scalability as a core tenet of cloud-native design and execution.

By adopting a principled approach to scalability, cloud-native systems can achieve significant gains in performance, availability, and cost management. Understanding the nuances and implications of both horizontal and vertical scaling is thus indispensable in the modern computing landscape, as it empowers organizations to leverage cloud resources optimally and sustain ever-growing workloads effectively.

9.2 Auto-Scaling Strategies and Implementations

Auto-scaling is a cornerstone technology in cloud-native systems, offering dynamic resource management by automatically adjusting computing power to meet the fluctuating demands of workloads. This capability is of paramount importance for maintaining application performance and cost-efficiency, particularly in environments characterized by unpredictable load patterns. Several strategies exist to achieve effective auto-scaling, each with distinct implementation considerations and benefits.

Primarily, auto-scaling can be categorized into horizontal auto-scaling and vertical auto-scaling. Horizontal auto-scaling involves adjusting the number of instances or nodes in response to workload changes. This is typically manifested through adding or removing virtual machine instances, containers, or other scalable units based on predefined metrics such as CPU usage, memory consumption, or queue length.

To illustrate horizontal auto-scaling in a Kubernetes environment, a basic implementation can be achieved using the Horizontal Pod Autoscaler (HPA), which scales the number of pod replicas automatically based on observed CPU utilization or other select metrics. The following snippet demonstrates a horizontal scaling setup using CPU utilization as the scaling metric:

```
apiVersion: autoscaling/v2beta2
kind: HorizontalPodAutoscaler
metadata:
  name: php-apache
spec:
  scaleTargetRef:
    apiVersion: apps/v1
    kind: Deployment
    name: php-apache
  minReplicas: 1
  maxReplicas: 10
  metrics:
  - type: Resource
    resource:
      name: cpu
      target:
        type: Utilization
        averageUtilization: 80
```

In this example, the HorizontalPodAutoscaler is configured to maintain CPU utilization at roughly 80%. It dynamically adjusts the pod count between 1 and 10 replicas in pursuit of this target, thus ensuring that the deployment remains responsive to changes in load.

Vertical auto-scaling differs by modifying the resource limits or requests of an existing instance type instead of altering the instance count. This technique adjusts the computing power of instances rather than their quantity, making it a straightforward yet crucial approach when changes in the workload occur within constraints that do not necessitate a shift in architecture or instance quantity.

An example configuration for a VerticalPodAutoscaler is provided below:

```
apiVersion: autoscaling.k8s.io/v1
kind: VerticalPodAutoscaler
metadata:
  name: php-apache-vpa
spec:
  targetRef:
    apiVersion: "apps/v1"
    kind: Deployment
    name: php-apache
  updatePolicy:
    updateMode: "Off"
```

In the above snippet, the VerticalPodAutoscaler is configured to target the php-apache deployment, with its updateMode currently set to "Off." This indicates that while the VPA can suggest changes to the resource requests, it will not automatically update them, thereby providing insights while maintaining operational control.

Beyond horizontal and vertical strategies, cluster auto-scaling is pivotal in cloud environments that utilize container orchestration systems such as Kubernetes. Cluster auto-scalers manage the resizing of the node pool within a cluster to provide the necessary capacity for pod scheduling based on resource requests and limits.

The complexity of auto-scaling implementations necessitates meticulous planning and consideration of several factors including, but not limited to:

- **Metric Selection**: Deciding on the right metrics is fundamental. While CPU and memory usage are the most prevalent, other indicators like request rate, error rate, or custom application performance metrics provide finer control.

- **Thresholds and Cooldown Periods**: Establishing appropriate thresholds to trigger scaling actions, along with cooldown periods, helps in reducing oscillations or thrashing, where the system continuously scales in and out due to fluctuating metrics rather than sustained load changes.

- **Scaling Policies and Limits**: Defining scaling boundaries (e.g., maximum and minimum instance count) ensures that the system remains within synthetically controlled parameters, preventing unnecessary over-allocation or under-provisioning of resources.

- **Cost vs. Performance Balance**: Auto-scaling should aim not only at maintaining performance but also at optimizing cost. Over-provisioning can lead to unnecessary expenses, while under-provisioning can result in performance degradation.

- **Integration with Load Balancers**: Coordinating scaling actions with network components such as load balancers ensures that newly spawned instances are integrated into the application flow seamlessly.

Different cloud platforms offer auto-scaling services such as Amazon EC2 Auto Scaling, Google Cloud's Instance Group Autoscaler, and Azure Virtual Machine Scale Sets. Although their overall goals align, the specific configurations, capabilities, and pricing models vary significantly among these providers.

For instance, within the AWS ecosystem, policies can be configured to scale instances based on CloudWatch alarms or predictive scaling to estimate future capacity requirements based on historical data. This predictive scaling offers a sophisticated approach enabling preemptive adjustments to coincide with expected load changes.

```
{
  "AutoScalingGroupName": "my-auto-scaling-group",
  "LaunchConfigurationName": "my-launch-configuration",
  "MinSize": 1,
  "MaxSize": 5,
  "DesiredCapacity": 3,
  "DefaultCooldown": 300,
  "AvailabilityZones": ["us-west-2a"],
  "HealthCheckType": "EC2",
  "Tags": [
    {
      "Key": "Environment",
      "Value": "Production",
      "PropagateAtLaunch": true
    }
  ]
}
```

The JSON example configures an AWS Auto Scaling Group, specifying minimum, maximum, and desired instance counts, along with cooldown periods and availability zones.

Integration of auto-scaling features is enhanced by utilizing container orchestration features provided by platforms like Kubernetes or employing infrastructure automation tools such as Terraform or AWS CloudFormation. These facilitate the seamless alignment of auto-scaling configurations with existing infrastructure, ensuring uniform management and deployment processes.

Once an operational auto-scaling framework is set up, ongoing monitoring and analysis remain critical. Regular audits on performance metrics will reveal how effectively the auto-scaling policies align with operational requirements. Additionally, adjusting thresholds in response to changing usage patterns and ensuring that scaling actions are timely and do not compromise system reliability is crucial.

Auto-scaling not only ensures optimal use of resources but also offers resilience by adapting to workload dynamics without human intervention. In rapidly evolving environments where user engagement and data volumes fluctuate, auto-scaling plays an integral role in maintaining both the cost-efficiency and fidelity of services.

Ultimately, the development of a robust auto-scaling strategy encapsulates a holistic view of the entire cloud infrastructure—to manage resource elasticity, accommodate escalation of service demands, and maintain operational continuity while managing expenditure efficiently. It requires an interplay of technology, processes, and insights, driving businesses to achieve competitive agility in a cloud-native era.

9.3 Optimizing Resource Utilization

Optimizing resource utilization in cloud-native systems is critical for ensuring that applications perform efficiently while minimizing costs. The quintessential challenge is aligning resource allocation closely with application demands without under-provisioning, which might degrade performance, or over-provisioning, which increases costs. This section explores techniques and strategies for enhancing resource utilization in cloud environments, focusing on metrics and methods that enable fine-tuned management of computational resources.

Effective resource optimization begins with accurate monitoring and analysis of workloads. Monitoring tools should provide insights not only into resource consumption rates (such as CPU, memory, and disk I/O) but also into application-specific metrics such as throughput or request-response times. Monitoring solutions like Prometheus, Grafana, and cloud-native services (e.g., AWS CloudWatch, Azure Monitor) offer the foundational insights needed for informed decision-making.

Cloud resource utilization can be optimized using several approaches:

- **Right-Sizing Instances**: One of the primary methods of optimizing resources is to right-size instances, that is, adjusting the capacity of compute resources to match the workload precisely. Right-sizing should be based on historic usage patterns, understanding of peak demand events, and identifying periods of low activity.

    For instance, deploying services on Kubernetes allows specific configuration of resource requests and limits which the scheduler uses to allocate pods to nodes. Consider the following configuration for setting these parameters:

    ```
    apiVersion: v1
    kind: Pod
    metadata:
      name: nginx
    spec:
      containers:
      - name: nginx
        image: nginx
        resources:
          requests:
            memory: "256Mi"
            cpu: "500m"
          limits:
            memory: "512Mi"
            cpu: "1000m"
    ```

    In this YAML file, the spec defines resource requests and limits for CPU and memory, providing the Kubernetes scheduler with crucial information to efficiently distribute workloads across nodes.

9.3. OPTIMIZING RESOURCE UTILIZATION

- **Load Balancing and Traffic Routing**: Effective use of load balancing can prevent resource straining in a specific part of the infrastructure. By spreading incoming requests evenly across a pool of resources, load balancers ensure no single node becomes a bottleneck.

```
{
    "id": "my-http-lb",
    "name": "MyHttpLoadBalancer",
    "backendService": "my-backend-service",
    "rules": [
        {
            "pathMatcher": "my-matcher",
            "defaultService": "default-backend-service",
            "pathRules": [
                {
                    "paths": ["/images"],
                    "service": "image-backend-service"
                }
            ]
        }
    ],
    "hosts": ["www.example.com"]
}
```

The JSON configuration demonstrates setting up an HTTP load balancer with path-based routing to distribute traffic across various backend services.

- **Efficient Scheduling and Placement Policies**: Optimizing scheduling algorithms and placement strategies can significantly increase resource utilization. Policies that consider affinity and anti-affinity rules, taints, tolerations, and other criteria aid in resource-efficient scheduling.

- **Utilizing Spot and Preemptible Instances**: Spot instances on AWS and preemptible VMs on Google Cloud offer spare capacity at reduced rates, which can be leveraged for non-critical or batch-processing tasks. These are suitable for elastic workloads that can handle interruptions gracefully.

```
{
    "Name": "EC2SpotFleetRequest",
    "TargetCapacity": 5,
    "IAMFleetRole": "arn:aws:iam::123456789012:role/service-role/
        AmazonEC2SpotFleetRole",
    "LaunchSpecifications": [
        {
            "InstanceType": "c3.large",
            "SpotPrice": "0.05",
```

```
    "ImageId": "ami-0abcdef1234567890"
   }
  ]
}
```

This JSON template configures a request for an EC2 Spot Fleet, specifying Spot instance details including bid price and instance type.

- **Strategic Use of Auto-Scaling**: Implementing intelligent auto-scaling strategies can optimize resources dynamically. Such strategies ensure that resources scale up during peak load times and down during low demand, following the measured metrics.

- **Optimizing Storage Utilization**: Beyond compute resources, storage optimization involves techniques like data compression, deduplication, tiered storage solutions, and object lifecycle management policies to balance performance and cost.

In addition to these strategies, the application design itself plays a pivotal role in optimized resource utilization. Cloud-native applications designed with stateless microservices, asynchronous processing, and effective caching strategies can reduce unnecessary resource consumption and enhance performance.

For instance, the implementation of caching strategies using services such as Redis or Memcached allows frequent data retrieval operations to be served from fast-access memory stores rather than disk-backed databases. This drastically cuts down response times and alleviates database load.

On the system architecture front, concepts such as Service Mesh (Istio, Linkerd) and Serverless architectures present opportunities for optimization by abstracting core responsibilities like network management, scaling, and provisioning.

Service Mesh implementations provide observability, traffic management, and security features out-of-the-box, allowing developers to focus on business logic rather than infrastructural concerns. They ensure that east-west traffic within data centers is securely and efficiently managed, optimizing resource utilization by reducing latency and improving throughput.

Serverless computing abstracts server management responsibilities from the developers, allowing fine-grained auto-scaling based on actual utilization metrics. This paradigm virtually removes unnecessary allocation, only charging for active resource usage, thus driving efficient utilization.

Resource optimization often entails a feedback loop where monitoring insights lead to iterative configuration tuning or application modifications. The integration of self-learning AI systems can automate this optimization cycle, providing predictions and recommendations based on workload models and current operational metrics.

Furthermore, leveraging CI/CD pipelines for deploying infrastructure as code ensures that resource configurations remain consistent, auditable, and version-controlled, thus minimizing the risks associated with manual resource management and enabling rapid iteration when tuning resource allocations.

Ultimately, optimizing resource utilization in cloud-native environments demands a holistic approach. It requires continuous interaction between engineering and operations teams to marry application demands with infrastructure capabilities seamlessly. By employing a combination of monitoring, proactive management, strategic planning, and advanced technological frameworks, organizations can achieve a balanced state where applications run efficiently and are responsive to business change, all while conserving financial resources. This strategic alignment fosters operational excellence, adaptability, and resilience in an ever-evolving cloud landscape.

9.4 Performance Tuning for Cloud Applications

In cloud computing, performance tuning is essential to ensure that applications not only function correctly but do so with speed and efficiency. Performance tuning involves identifying bottlenecks and optimizing computing resources, data flow, and algorithms to enhance application responsiveness, throughput, and resource usage efficiency. Cloud environments provide dynamic resources that can be scaled out or up with ease; however, it remains crucial to fine-tune applications to utilize these resources optimally.

The process of performance tuning encompasses multiple facets: application architecture, network configurations, data handling, resource management, and service orchestration. Approaching performance tuning systematically involves the following steps:

- **Profiling and Monitoring**: The initial step in performance tuning is to understand the current state of the application. This is achieved through rigorous profiling and monitoring. Profiling helps to identify the parts of the application that consume considerable time and resources, whereas monitoring provides insights into system metrics over time.

- **Identifying Bottlenecks**: Using profiling tools like JProfiler, VisualVM, or Py-Spy, and monitoring platforms such as Prometheus or Datadog, developers can pinpoint bottlenecks in CPU, memory, disk I/O, or network throughput. These tools often integrate seamlessly with cloud services, providing detailed metrics.

- **Optimizing Code and Algorithms**: Once the bottlenecks are identified, reviewing the code is a crucial next step. Enhancing algorithms or changing data structures can often lead to significant performance improvements. Using more efficient libraries and avoiding redundant calculations are also common practices.

  Consider the following Python example before and after optimization:

  ```
  # Before optimization
  def calculate_square(numbers):
      result = []
      for number in numbers:
          result.append(number * number)
      return result

  # After optimization using list comprehension
  def calculate_square_optimized(numbers):
      return [number * number for number in numbers]
  ```

The optimized version uses list comprehension, which is more efficient and concise.

- **Leveraging Asynchronous Processing**: In cloud applications, particularly web services, latency can be reduced

9.4. PERFORMANCE TUNING FOR CLOUD APPLICATIONS

by utilizing asynchronous programming models or background processing. This is especially useful for tasks that do not require immediate user feedback. Languages like JavaScript (using async/await), Python (using asyncio), or Java (using CompletableFuture) provide strong support for asynchrony.

Example of asynchronous processing in JavaScript:

```
// Example of asynchronous processing using async/await
async function fetchData(url) {
    try {
        let response = await fetch(url);
        let data = await response.json();
        return data;
    } catch (error) {
        console.error('Error fetching data:', error);
    }
}
```

- **Caching Strategies**: Implementing effective caching strategies can significantly enhance performance by reducing data retrieval times and offloading database queries. Caches can be placed at various levels, including client-side, server-side, and even at the network edge using Content Delivery Networks (CDNs).

Setting up a simple key-value caching mechanism using Redis for a Python application:

```
import redis

# Connect to the Redis server
r = redis.Redis(host='localhost', port=6379, db=0)

# Set a key-value pair
r.set('my_key', 'my_value')

# Retrieve the key-value pair
value = r.get('my_key')
print(value.decode('utf-8'))
```

- **Resource Management**: Effective management of resources provided by cloud platforms—such as compute instances, databases, and storage—ensures that applications are not overburdened or starved for resources. This includes configuring proper instance types and sizes, tuning database queries with indexes, and managing memory efficiently.

For SQL-based systems, optimizing queries and indexing tables can yield significant improvements in data retrieval performance.

For instance, adding appropriate indexes can drastically reduce search times:

```
CREATE INDEX idx_employee_lastname ON employees (last_name);
```

- **Service Mesh for Microservices**: In microservice architectures, using a service mesh (such as Istio or Linkerd) provides tools for managing service-to-service communication, which can help in optimizing performance. By automating network configurations and providing insights into traffic patterns, service meshes bolster application efficiency and resilience.

- **Auto-Scaling and Load Balancing**: Ensuring that workloads are evenly distributed across resources and dynamically scaling during load surges are critical to maintaining performance levels. Load balancers distribute incoming service requests, while Kubernetes' Horizontal Pod Autoscaler or AWS Auto Scaling adjusts the number of running instances based on actual load conditions.

```
{
    "loadBalancerArn": "arn:aws:elasticloadbalancing:...",
    "subnets": ["subnet-012345678"],
    "scheme": "internet-facing",
    "type": "application",
    "ipAddressType": "ipv4"
}
```

- **Reducing Latency through Network Optimization**: Optimizing network performance involves reducing latency and improving bandwidth utilization. Techniques such as minimizing the number of hops, optimizing data serialization, and employing techniques like HTTP/2 or WebSockets can aid in reducing latency.

- **Continual Performance Testing and Benchmarking**: Implementing automated performance testing as part of continuous integration pipelines ensures that performance regressions are detected early. Using tools like Apache JMeter or Locust allows testing different scenarios, ensuring that the application can cope with anticipated loads.

Performance benchmarking is also an integral part of the tuning process. By establishing baseline performance metrics, improvements can be quantitatively measured. Consider the following shell script, which uses Apache Bench to simulate 1000 requests to a web server with a concurrency of 100:

```
ab -n 1000 -c 100 http://example.com/
```

- **Using Serverless Architectures**: Serverless architectures aim to improve performance and cost-effectiveness by allowing developers to focus purely on code execution without worrying about infrastructure management. They provide auto-scaling, high availability, and reduced operational overhead.

- **Applying Machine Learning to Predict and Adjust Loads**: Emerging use of machine learning for predicting usage patterns and proactively adjusting resources is gaining traction. This involves gathering historical data, creating models to predict demand, and pre-scaling resources ahead of identified peaks.

Performance tuning in cloud applications is a continuous process that demands a comprehensive understanding of the application's architecture, the underlying infrastructure, and user behavior patterns. The full potential of cloud environments can only be harnessed when applications are tuned for maximum efficiency, enabling organizations to deliver performant, scalable, and cost-effective solutions. Through proactive tuning and regular benchmarking, performance levels can be maintained and improved, providing a superior user experience while leveraging the dynamic resources available in the cloud.

9.5 Cost Optimization in Cloud Environments

In today's competitive business landscape, managing and optimizing costs within cloud environments is an essential aspect of sustaining profitability while maintaining agility and scalability. Cloud platforms, such as Amazon Web Services (AWS), Microsoft Azure, and Google Cloud Platform (GCP), offer incredibly versatile functionality at a range of price points. As cloud services are predominantly driven by a pay-as-you-go model, understanding how to optimize these costs is vital for organizations.

Cost optimization in cloud environments involves several strategies that ensure efficient utilization of resources, avoidance of unnecessary expenditures, and leveraging of discounts and reserved resources. This section delves into various cost optimization techniques, detailing strategies, examples, and tools to help navigate this complex but rewarding task.

- **Resource Rightsizing**: One of the fundamental steps in cost optimization is rightsizing cloud resources. This involves matching resource allocations with actual demand to prevent over-provisioning and underutilization. Monitoring tools and reports provided by cloud providers can identify idle or underutilized resources.

    An example of identifying potential candidates for rightsizing can be seen using AWS Trusted Advisor checks which provide metrics and recommendations for optimizing resource usage.

    ```
    {
      "checkId": "eW7HH0l7J9",
      "timestamp": "2023-10-17T14:36:33Z",
      "resourcesSummary": {
        "resourcesFlagged": 3,
        "resourcesProcessed": 10,
        "resourcesSuppressed": 0,
        "resourcesIgnored": 0
      },
      "flaggedResources": [
        {
          "resourceId": "i-0abcd1234efgh5678",
          "isSuppressed": False,
          "metadata": [
            "t2.medium instance in us-west-2b",
            "Average utilization: 10%",
            "Utilization threshold: 20%"
          ]
        }
      ]
    }
    ```

- **Buying Reserved Instances and Savings Plans**: Reserved instances (RIs) and savings plans provide significant discounts compared to on-demand pricing by committing to a specific capacity for a one or three-year term. By analyzing past resource

9.5. COST OPTIMIZATION IN CLOUD ENVIRONMENTS

utilization trends, organizations can strategically commit to reserved resources where predictable workloads exist.

AWS Savings Plans provide a more flexible alternative to traditional RIs, offering compute capacity discounts for commitments to a particular spend over a duration, allowing for usage across a broader range of services and regions.

- **Leveraging Spot and Preemptible Instances**: Spot instances on AWS and preemptible VMs on GCP offer cost savings of up to 90% for workloads that are flexible and can accommodate interruptions. These instances are ideal for non-critical, fault-tolerant, or batch processing workloads.

Here's how you might configure an auto-scaling group to use spot instances on AWS:

```
{
    "AutoScalingGroupName": "batch-processing-asg",
    "MixedInstancesPolicy": {
        "LaunchTemplate": {
            "LaunchTemplateId": "lt-0abcd1234efgh5678",
            "Version": "1"
        },
        "InstancesDistribution": {
            "OnDemandAllocationStrategy": "prioritized",
            "SpotAllocationStrategy": "lowest-price",
            "SpotInstancePools": 2,
            "OnDemandBaseCapacity": 0,
            "OnDemandPercentageAboveBaseCapacity": 20
        }
    },
    "MinSize": 5,
    "MaxSize": 20
}
```

- **Optimizing Data Storage**: Efficient management of cloud storage contributes significantly to cost savings. This includes moving infrequently accessed data to cheaper storage classes (e.g., AWS S3 Glacier for archival), implementing lifecycle policies for automated data transitions, and ensuring redundant or stale data is deleted.

A sample AWS S3 lifecycle policy to transition objects to Glacier after 30 days:

```
{
    "Rules": [
        {
```

CHAPTER 9. SCALING AND OPTIMIZING CLOUD-NATIVE INFRASTRUCTURE

```
        "ID": "MoveToGlacierRule",
        "Status": "Enabled",
        "Filter": {},
        "Transitions": [
          {
            "Days": 30,
            "StorageClass": "GLACIER"
          }
        ]
      }
    ]
  }
```

- **Network Cost Optimization**: Data transfer can accrue significant costs, especially in architectures with high data ingress and egress. To minimize these expenses, it's crucial to optimize network configurations by placing resources within the same region where feasible and utilizing dedicated network paths for high-frequency data transfers.

  Employing content delivery networks (CDNs) like AWS CloudFront can also reduce costs by caching content closer to end-users, minimizing data transfer out from origin locations.

- **Automating Shutdown of Non-Essential Resources**: Non-production environments such as development or testing labs do not need to remain active 24/7. Automated scripts or functions (e.g., using AWS Lambda or Google Cloud Functions) that power down resources during off-hours can lead to considerable savings.

  Sample Python Lambda function for stopping EC2 instances outside working hours:

```python
import boto3
import datetime

def lambda_handler(event, context):
    ec2 = boto3.client('ec2', region_name='us-west-2')
    current_hour = datetime.datetime.now().hour

    # Define working hours: 8 AM - 6 PM
    if current_hour < 8 or current_hour > 18:
        response = ec2.describe_instances(
            Filters=[
                {
                    'Name': 'tag:Env',
                    'Values': ['development']
                },
                {
```

9.5. COST OPTIMIZATION IN CLOUD ENVIRONMENTS

```
                'Name': 'instance-state-name',
                'Values': ['running']
            }
        ]
    )
    for reservation in response['Reservations']:
        for instance in reservation['Instances']:
            ec2.stop_instances(InstanceIds=[instance['InstanceId']])
            print(f"Stopped instance: {instance['InstanceId']}")
```

- **Containerization and Microservices**: Shifting workloads to containerized environments can harness better resource allocation and scaling, thus optimizing costs, especially when using orchestration platforms like Kubernetes that provide granular control over resource scaling.

  Kubernetes' clusters can dynamically scale both applications and infrastructure, balancing loads during peak times and releasing resources during idle periods, thus managing cost efficiencies effectively.

- **Continuous Cost Monitoring and Analysis**: Automation of spend tracking and budget alerts helps organizations maintain control over their cloud expenses. Platforms like AWS Cost Explorer, Azure Cost Management, and GCP Billing Reports offer analytical insights into expenditure patterns and provide tools for forecasting and budgeting future expenses.

- **Optimizing Software Licensing**: Evaluating software licenses for applications running in cloud environments for cost-effectiveness and requirements ensure that you aren't overpaying for unused features. Transitioning to open-source software can also yield significant cost savings.

- **Adopting Serverless Architectures**: While not suitable for all workloads, serverless solutions (e.g., AWS Lambda, Azure Functions, GCP Cloud Functions) eliminate the need to manage any infrastructure and only charge for actual execution time, which can lead to cost reductions for event-driven applications.

- **Applying AI for Predictive Analysis**: Leveraging AI-driven analytics can provide enhanced predictive capabilities to anticipate and adjust cloud resources during anticipated peaks and troughs, optimizing costs in advance.

Cloud cost optimization is an ongoing process requiring continuous attention and regular reassessment to adapt to evolving workloads and business requirements. Through a combination of strategic and operational tactics encompassing rightsizing, instance reservations, storage management, and more, organizations can achieve significant financial efficiencies without compromising performance. By making cost optimization an integral part of cloud strategy, businesses can enhance their economic resilience while capitalizing on the scalability and flexibility that cloud computing offers.

9.6 Ensuring High Availability and Resilience

High availability and resilience are critical attributes of cloud-native applications. These principles ensure that applications remain operational and responsive despite failures or unexpected incidents in the infrastructure. Designing systems with high availability and resilience involves a combination of architectural best practices, redundancy, failover mechanisms, and continuous monitoring.

High availability (HA) aims to minimize downtime and maintain service continuity. It is quantified as a percentage indicating the operational status of the system over a defined timeframe. For example, 99.99% availability translates to approximately 52 minutes of downtime annually. Achieving these high levels of availability necessitates detailed planning, robust architecture, and precise execution.

Resilience emphasizes the ability of a system to recover quickly from disruptions, adapting to potential failures seamlessly. Combining both high availability and resilience results in a system that not only continues to function during failures but also restores itself swiftly afterwards.

Several strategies and techniques are employed to achieve high availability and resilience in cloud-native environments:

- **Redundant Architecture**: Building redundancy into the system's architecture is foundational to high availability. This involves deploying application components across multiple avail-

9.6. ENSURING HIGH AVAILABILITY AND RESILIENCE

ability zones or regions to ensure that failure in a single zone does not disrupt service continuity.

Consider the following example of a Kubernetes deployment leveraging multiple availability zones:

```yaml
apiVersion: apps/v1
kind: Deployment
metadata:
  name: web-deployment
spec:
  replicas: 3
  selector:
    matchLabels:
      app: web
  template:
    metadata:
      labels:
        app: web
    spec:
      containers:
      - name: nginx
        image: nginx:1.19
      affinity:
        podAntiAffinity:
          requiredDuringSchedulingIgnoredDuringExecution:
          - labelSelector:
              matchExpressions:
              - key: app
                operator: In
                values:
                - web
            topologyKey: "kubernetes.io/hostname"
```

This YAML defines a deployment with an anti-affinity rule, ensuring pods are distributed across nodes to prevent single-point failures.

- **Load Balancing**: Load balancers distribute incoming traffic across multiple servers or instances, preventing overload on any individual component. In multi-region deployments, global load balancers can route users to the nearest or healthiest endpoints.

AWS Elastic Load Balancing (ELB) configuration for an Application Load Balancer:

```
{
  "name": "my-app-load-balancer",
  "type": "application",
  "scheme": "internet-facing",
  "subnetMappings": [
    {
      "SubnetId": "subnet-012345678"
```

```
        }
    ],
    "securityGroups": [
        "sg-03034567"
    ],
    "ipAddressType": "ipv4"
}
```

- **Database Replication**: Implementing replication strategies, such as master-slave replication or multi-master setups, ensures data availability in the event of database server failures. Cross-regional data replication further secures data availability against regional outages.

  Example of MySQL master-slave configuration:

  Master database configuration:

  ```
  [mysqld]
  log-bin=mysql-bin
  server-id=1
  binlog-format=row
  ```

  Slave database configuration:

  ```
  [mysqld]
  server-id=2
  relay-log=slave-relay-bin
  ```

- **Automated Recovery and Failover**: Using automated recovery involves implementing scripts or using managed services that detect failures and automatically initiate failover to backup systems. Managed databases such as Amazon RDS provide automatic failover capabilities to standby instances.

- **Microservices Architecture**: Microservices architecture enhances availability and resilience by breaking the application into independent services. This design limits the blast radius in case of service failure, allowing unaffected components to continue functioning.

  Service Mesh frameworks like Istio enable fine-grained traffic management and circuit-breaking patterns, pivotal in ensuring system resilience.

- **Stateless Operations**: Designing applications to be stateless, where state information is stored externally (e.g., in distributed caches or databases), enhances resilience. Stateless services can easily be restarted or scaled without worrying about session persistence.

- **Backup and Disaster Recovery**: Regular backups and a solid disaster recovery plan are integral to resilience. Utilizing cloud-native backup solutions enables point-in-time recovery, data snapshots, and cross-region backups.

    For instance, AWS Backup automates the scheduling and retention of backups for EC2 instances, RDS databases, and more.

- **Continuous Monitoring and Alerting**: Proactively identifying potential issues before they escalate enables quick mitigation. Implement comprehensive monitoring and alerting using tools such as Prometheus, CloudWatch, or Azure Monitor. Set up dashboards and alerts for key metrics and thresholds.

    Prometheus alerting rule example for node downtime:

    ```
    groups:
    - name: node_alerts
      rules:
      - alert: NodeDown
        expr: up == 0
        for: 5m
        labels:
          severity: critical
        annotations:
          summary: "Node is down"
          description: "The node {{ $labels.node }} is not reachable for 5
              minutes."
    ```

- **Testing for Failure Scenarios**: Regularly testing the system for failure scenarios helps uncover weaknesses. Chaos engineering, a discipline of experimenting with software systems in production to build confidence in their resilience, is a practice gaining popularity. Tools like Chaos Monkey by Netflix can be employed to simulate outages and assess system behavior.

- **Security Considerations**: Ensuring robust security measures such as firewalls, encryption, and access control is vital to maintaining availability. DDoS protection services from your cloud provider can guard against attacks that threaten to overwhelm system capacity.

- **Service Level Agreements (SLAs) and Negotiation**: Understanding and negotiating SLAs with cloud providers is crucial. SLAs specify uptime guarantees and the recompense provided by the provider in case of failure, forming the baseline expectation for service delivery.

Ensuring high availability and resilience in cloud applications requires a holistic approach. Architecture must be underpinned by redundancy, automation should handle failures gracefully, and comprehensive monitoring and testing should guide continuous improvement. By integrating these principles and strategies, organizations can deliver robust, reliable services that meet both business requirements and user expectations, maintaining operational continuity even when faced with the inevitable challenges of complex cloud infrastructures.

9.7 Using Crossplane for Dynamic Scaling

Crossplane is an open-source control plane that extends Kubernetes, providing a platform to manage cloud infrastructure and services using Kubernetes-style APIs. It enables dynamic scaling and management of multi-cloud environments by treating infrastructure as code, leveraging customizable resource compositions to deliver complex applications via Kubernetes Custom Resources Definitions (CRDs). This capability is especially crucial in dynamic cloud environments where resource demands fluctuate rapidly.

Crossplane's architecture facilitates the deployment and management of diverse cloud resources using a unified API, consolidating them into a scalable infrastructure with Kubernetes-native constructs. This streamlines the administration and scaling mechanisms across different cloud services, enabling efficient management of resources such as databases, clusters, and network components.

Here's an overview of how Crossplane can be employed for dynamic scaling:

- **Cloud Provider Configuration**: Crossplane integrates with major cloud providers, including AWS, GCP, and Azure, via provider-specific packages. These packages include preconfigured CRDs and controllers that understand how to provision and manage specific cloud resources. The installation starts with configuring a Crossplane provider.

For instance, installing the AWS provider involves the following command:

```
kubectl crossplane install provider crossplane/provider-aws:v0.22.0
```

This command installs the AWS provider, enabling Crossplane to manage AWS resources such as EC2 instances, RDS databases, and S3 buckets.

- **Infrastructure as Code (IaC) with Custom Resources**: Crossplane treats infrastructure like Kubernetes resources using CRDs. Each CRD represents a manageable piece of infrastructure, such as a database or a cloud network. This approach allows dynamic reconfiguration and scaling without leaving the Kubernetes ecosystem.

An example for creating an AWS RDS instance using Crossplane might look like this:

```yaml
apiVersion: database.aws.crossplane.io/v1beta1
kind: RDSInstance
metadata:
  name: example-db
spec:
  forProvider:
    dbInstanceClass: db.t2.micro
    masterUsername: admin
    masterPasswordSecretRef:
      name: db-password
      key: password
    allocatedStorage: 20
  providerConfigRef:
    name: default
```

This YAML snippet describes an RDS instance configured for provisioning. The resource is defined with a specific class size and a reference to a secret containing the master password.

- **Composite Resource Definitions and Compositions**: By using Composite Resource Definitions (XRDs) and Configurations, Crossplane enables developers to compose complex infrastructure stacks that can dynamically scale individual components based on application needs. This aspect reinforces scalability by managing dependencies and orchestrating across multiple resources effortlessly.

Consider an advanced scenario where your application requires a scalable database and an isolated network; Crossplane aggregates these into a singular CompositeResourceDefinition, allowing for coordinated scaling of respective resources.

- **Dynamic Scaling Policies and Automation**: Crossplane integrates seamlessly with Kubernetes autoscaling policies, ensuring systems automatically scale in response to real-time changes in application demand or infrastructure state. Automation scripts or GitOps workflows can be established using existing CI/CD tools to handle infrastructure scaling without manual intervention.

A Kubernetes 'HorizontalPodAutoscaler' integrating with Crossplane-managed workloads can provide rules for scaling pods horizontally to accommodate request surge:

```
apiVersion: autoscaling/v2beta2
kind: HorizontalPodAutoscaler
metadata:
  name: web-scalable
spec:
  scaleTargetRef:
    apiVersion: apps/v1
    kind: Deployment
    name: web-app
  minReplicas: 2
  maxReplicas: 10
  metrics:
  - type: Resource
    resource:
      name: cpu
      target:
        type: Utilization
        averageUtilization: 75
```

- **Crossplane and GitOps**: Merging Crossplane with GitOps principles ensures that infrastructure changes follow source-controlled versions, guaranteeing consistency and auditability. With GitOps, infrastructure configurations are stored as code within a repository, enabling seamless continuous delivery pipelines that enforce updates and scaling directives.

Flux or Argo CD are examples of tools facilitating the GitOps workflow in alignment with Crossplane's dynamic modeling and state management.

- **Observability and Metrics Collection**: Observability tools are pivotal in tracking how effectively dynamic scaling strategies perform. Integrating Prometheus or Datadog with Crossplane's extended metrics enables stakeholders to visualize scaling operations' impact and efficiency, assisting in early detection of any resource constraints or deviations.

  Observability dashboards provide quick insights into CPU load benchmarking and scaling response times, ensuring the agile adaptation of infrastructure to align with strategic business objectives.

- **Resilience and Fault Recovery**: By aligning with Kubernetes' native resilience strategies via Crossplane, dynamic scaling can incorporate self-healing mechanisms. If a component encounters failures, Crossplane's consistency models and retry logic ensure resources re-scale or restart appropriately, minimizing intervention needed from system administrators.

- **Examples of Multi-Cloud Scaling**: A practical use case for Crossplane's dynamic scaling could involve deploying an application needing resources from multiple cloud vendors without intricately learning each provider's API landscape. Crossplane abstracts these details into coherent APIs, reducing complexity, and enabling centralized scaling policies managed through Kubernetes.

- **Securing Scaled Resources**: Security is an integral facet when managing dynamically scaling systems. Crossplane facilitates robust security practices by imposing policies via open-policy agents (OPA) or RBAC, ensuring that only authenticated and authorized requests initiate scaling actions. Policies efficiently guard against misconfigurations and unauthorized access.

- **Community and Ecosystem Support**: Crossplane exhibits a strong community contributing enhancements, plugins, and examples encompassing various cloud-native scaling strategies. The Crossplane Slack channel, GitHub repos, and community calls provide a collaborative space where ideas on optimizing scalability across diverse platforms are nurtured and shared.

Using Crossplane for dynamic scaling accentuates the inherent strengths of Kubernetes by transcending application lifecycle management with infrastructure management, fostering a unified operational model that is scalable, resilient, and cloud-agnostic. As cloud environments grow in complexity and scale, tools like Crossplane will inevitably become quintessential for effectively managing the breadth of resources today's digital enterprises command. By bridging workloads across private and public boundary lines while maintaining predictability, Crossplane positions itself as a key enabler for robust cloud-native operational paradigms.

Chapter 10

Case Studies and Best Practices

In examining case studies and best practices, we explore real-world implementations of cloud-native infrastructure management with Crossplane, illustrating successful strategies and lessons learned. These examples demonstrate effective multi-cloud deployments, security enhancements, and cost optimization techniques through the use of Crossplane. By analyzing diverse scenarios, we identify proven approaches to scaling, operational efficiency, and integrating DevOps methods. Highlighting these experiences provides practical insights into overcoming challenges and optimizing infrastructure, enabling organizations to apply similar strategies tailored to their specific environments and objectives.

10.1 Real-World Crossplane Implementation

Crossplane serves as a powerful tool in the cloud-native infrastructure management ecosystem, enabling a seamless integration of cloud services across various platforms. In understanding its real-world applications, it is imperative to delve into specific case studies where Crossplane has been successfully implemented. These implementations not only illustrate practical strategies for infrastructure management but also expose the challenges and innovative solutions that organizations have adopted.

The fundamental advantage of Crossplane lies in its ability to extend the Kubernetes API, facilitating the orchestration of diverse cloud resources. Organizations have leveraged this capability to achieve significant improvements in operational efficiency and cloud-native strategy execution. We explore several instances across different industries to highlight the versatility and effectiveness of Crossplane.

Consider a global e-commerce company leveraging Crossplane to manage their multi-cloud operations. This organization operates on both AWS and GCP, aiming to utilize best-of-breed services from each provider while maintaining a high level of operational efficiency. A critical challenge was the fragmented infrastructure management, which involved siloed teams with different cloud management expertise. Crossplane was adopted to create a unified control plane enabling centralized management across these cloud environments.

Initially, the adoption of Crossplane required the integration of custom resource definitions (CRDs) that reflect the necessary cloud resources. These CRDs act as the Kubernetes-native components that define the desired state and configuration of cloud resources. Here is a basic example of a CRD for an AWS S3 bucket:

```
apiVersion: storage.aws.crossplane.io/v1alpha1
kind: S3Bucket
metadata:
  name: my-app-bucket
spec:
  forProvider:
    locationConstraint: us-west-2
    acl: private
  providerConfigRef:
    name: aws-provider
```

With such configuration, developers can manage S3 buckets in AWS as native Kubernetes resources, dictated by the same principles of desired state configuration and reconciliation that govern Kubernetes itself. This eliminates the need for intricate AWS-specific scripts or interfaces, thereby streamlining operations.

The e-commerce company realized increased agility by empowering development teams to deploy and manage infrastructure resources independently while aligning with the broader organizational controls and policies. This setup also allowed them to dynamically scale resources in response to shifting demands. By employing Kubernetes' reconciliation loop, Crossplane continually ensures that the actual state of the cloud resources matches the intended specifications.

A second illustrative case study involves a healthcare provider aiming to achieve data sovereignty and compliance across multiple jurisdictions with differing regulations. They adopted a hybrid cloud strategy utilizing on-premise infrastructure complemented by public clouds, each hosting different segments of their services. The primary challenge was maintaining compliance with stringent data protection laws while ensuring clinical services' availability and failover capabilities.

Crossplane facilitated the seamless integration of their hybrid environments. By defining composite resources through Crossplane, they abstracted cloud-specific complexities and provided standardized application deployment blueprints that respected jurisdictional policies. For instance, patient data remained on-premise or within specific geographical locations dictated by the sensitive nature of healthcare data.

An example of a composite resource might look like this:

```
apiVersion: apiextensions.crossplane.io/v1
kind: Composition
metadata:
  name: datapipeline
spec:
  compositeTypeRef:
    apiVersion: database.example.org/v1alpha1
    kind: DataPipeline
  resources:
  - base:
      apiVersion: database.aws.crossplane.io/v1alpha1
      kind: RDSInstance
      spec:
        forProvider:
          region: eu-central-1
        writeConnectionsSecretToRef:
          namespace: crossplane-system
          name: rds-conn
    patches:
    - fromFieldPath: "spec.parameters.region"
      toFieldPath: "spec.forProvider.region"
```

By abstracting these services into composable infrastructures, they could manage and audit resource usage effectively. Crossplane's external resource observability also provided audit trails, crucial for regulatory compliance, ensuring that all resource adjustments were monitored and documented.

Another domain where Crossplane showcases its utility is the tech startup sector. Startups often grapple with limited resources and high growth volatility, requiring them to rapidly iterate and scale infrastructure to meet new demands swiftly. Startups can benefit from Crossplane's integration capabilities by leveraging its multi-tenancy features, allowing different product teams to manage and operate distinctly tailored infrastructure requirements independently.

Consider a startup developing a decentralized application using cloud-native services across Azure and GCP. They capitalize on Azure's strength in identity services while utilizing GCP's advanced machine learning capabilities. The startup faced the obstacle of coordinating these disparate services efficiently without overextending their limited DevOps resources.

Utilizing Crossplane's provider-agnostic framework, they defined common templates with reusable Crossplane compositions, significantly reducing the complexity in managing external services. This abstraction layer allowed the startup to focus on rapid feature development and deployment without delving into provider-specific APIs, which enables a more agile development lifecycle.

A practical example of a Crossplane configuration in such a startup might involve setting Kubernetes clusters:

```
apiVersion: containerservice.azure.crossplane.io/v1alpha3
kind: AKSCluster
metadata:
  name: my-aks-cluster
spec:
  forProvider:
    resourceGroupName: my-resource-group
    location: eastus
    kubernetesVersion: "1.19.7"
  providerConfigRef:
    name: azure-provider
```

Zulu Networks, a fictional tech company, exemplified these principles by shifting to Crossplane to gain efficiencies through better integration and automation. They stored configuration states within a GitOps framework, achieving a high level of automation and minimizing manual intervention, thus empowering them to scale their operations swiftly.

Crossplane's ability to integrate with existing CI/CD pipelines enhances automation, enabling continuous deployment and monitoring of cross-cloud resources. The integrations are seamless, providing an interface that ensures resources are provisioned following the most recent commit or approved change in version control, highlighting Crossplane's role in forward-looking, automated infrastructure management strategies.

Such illustrations underscore the transformative nature of Crossplane in real-world applications. As organizations continue to face dynamic operational landscapes and the need for dexterous infrastructural management, Crossplane remains a pivotal technology. Insights gained from these case studies exhibit the evolving cloud-native best practices that allow organizations to overcome complex infrastructure challenges with cohesive and flexible management solutions.

10.2 Multi-Cloud Deployment Scenarios

In today's cloud landscape, organizations increasingly adopt multi-cloud strategies to leverage the varied strengths of different cloud service providers. This paradigm enables businesses to avoid vendor lock-in, enhance fault tolerance, and utilize the best-in-class tools for distinct workloads. Crossplane emerges as a key player in this approach by providing a unified interface to manage resources across multiple clouds efficiently. This section delves into specific scenarios where multi-cloud deployments, orchestrated by Crossplane, have been instrumental in achieving operational excellence.

A quintessential multi-cloud scenario involves a technology company using Amazon Web Services (AWS) and Microsoft Azure to manage various parts of its application stack. Consider a software firm that relies on AWS for its computing and storage needs while using Azure's AI-powered analytics tools integrated into their data processing pipeline. The complexity in such setups arises from the disparate management

CHAPTER 10. CASE STUDIES AND BEST PRACTICES

interfaces and operational paradigms, often leading to fragmented and inefficient resource management practices.

Crossplane mitigates these challenges by offering a homogeneous layer over the heterogeneous cloud environments, allowing developers and DevOps teams to take advantage of Kubernetes' declarative configuration management for external cloud resources. By using Crossplane, this software firm can translate their multi-cloud strategy into a seamless continuous delivery pipeline. This begins with configuring providers:

```
apiVersion: v1
kind: Secret
metadata:
  name: aws-provider-secret
type: Opaque
data:
  credentials: BASE64ENCODED_AWSCREDENTIALS

apiVersion: v1
kind: Secret
metadata:
  name: azure-provider-secret
type: Opaque
data:
  credentials: BASE64ENCODED_AZURECREDENTIALS
```

Providers in Crossplane abstract cloud API interactions, necessitating their configuration before provisioning resources. The above Kubernetes Secrets store credentials for AWS and Azure, allowing Crossplane to authenticate with these services securely and interact as needed.

With provider credentials configured, developers can define a multi-cloud infrastructure using Crossplane by creating Composite Resource Definitions (XRDs) and their Compositions. This approach permits the abstract division of application structures across cloud providers. For example, deploying a web application might involve hosting the frontend and API gateway in AWS while utilizing Azure for database services.

The definition of an application's composite resource might resemble:

```
apiVersion: apiextensions.crossplane.io/v1
kind: CompositeResourceDefinition
metadata:
  name: webappresources.example.org
spec:
  group: example.org
  names:
```

10.2. MULTI-CLOUD DEPLOYMENT SCENARIOS

```
      plural: webappresources
      singular: webappresource
      kind: WebAppResource
    scope: Namespaced
    versions:
    - name: v1alpha1
      served: true
      referenceable: true
      schema:
        openAPIV3Schema:
          type: object
          properties:
            spec:
              type: object
              properties:
                frontendBucketName:
                  type: string
                databaseSKU:
                  type: string
```

Building upon these specifications, compositions can define the specific cloud resources and their configurations for AWS and Azure, respectively.

```
apiVersion: apiextensions.crossplane.io/v1
kind: Composition
metadata:
  name: webapp-aws
spec:
  compositeTypeRef:
    apiVersion: example.org/v1alpha1
    kind: WebAppResource
  resources:
  - base:
      apiVersion: storage.aws.crossplane.io/v1alpha1
      kind: S3Bucket
      spec:
        forProvider:
          acl: private
    patches:
    - fromFieldPath: "spec.frontendBucketName"
      toFieldPath: "metadata.name"
```

```
apiVersion: apiextensions.crossplane.io/v1
kind: Composition
metadata:
  name: webapp-azure
spec:
  compositeTypeRef:
    apiVersion: example.org/v1alpha1
    kind: WebAppResource
  resources:
  - base:
      apiVersion: database.azure.crossplane.io/v1beta1
      kind: MySQLServer
```

293

```
spec:
  forProvider:
    sku:
      name: ""
patches:
- fromFieldPath: "spec.databaseSKU"
  toFieldPath: "spec.forProvider.sku.name"
```

In the multi-cloud architecture deployed via Crossplane, the application frontend, served from an AWS S3 bucket, automatically scales with user demand due to AWS's global infrastructure. Simultaneously, Azure's managed MySQL service provides database capabilities customized to the application's load, defined by the particular SKU selected. This configuration exemplifies the hosted cloud resources' integration and can be transparently managed through Kubernetes CRDs.

Further building on these examples, a financial services corporation may need a disaster recovery (DR) strategy leveraging Crossplane's multi-cloud capabilities. Such a setup can achieve maximum uptime by replicating vital services across major cloud regions and providers. In the event of a failure in one region, the application can seamlessly transition to a secondary site in another provider's region without any noticeable service disruption to end-users.

Through Crossplane, consistent management of such a DR infrastructure becomes feasible with Kubernetes Custom Resources ensuring that service replicas across AWS, GCP, and Azure are orchestrated for failover. Crossplane's reliance on Kubernetes' extensibility means that existing DevOps skill sets are applicable, drastically reducing the learning curve and enhancing cross-functional team collaboration.

The practical importance of multi-cloud configurations is evident as organizations grapple with complex compliance requirements that dictate geographical or jurisdictional service provisioning. Crossplane gives operators the tools to implement prescriptive compliance strategies by masking extensive cloud APIs behind reusable community or custom-developed resource registries and controllers.

Consider an organization that exploits GCP's machine learning offerings in combination with AWS's API gateway for their application services. Such an arrangement requires periodic retraining of models based on user data, demanding synchronous cloud resource manipulation and high-speed data processing. Here, Crossplane's dynamic provisioning extends the capabilities of Kubernetes custom controllers, with resource configuration managed as code—enabling reproducibility and automation in development and production environments alike.

Crossplane remarkably reduces manual configuration errors and environmental discrepancies that plague multi-cloud deployments by encapsulating configurations as CRDs and utilizing GitOps frameworks for reconciliation. GitOps integrates configuration management directly with version control systems, allowing every infrastructure update to be versioned and automatically applied.

By leaning on Crossplane for multi-cloud deployments, organizations leverage advanced Kubernetes-native policies to achieve holistic cloud infrastructure management, unlocking innovative business solutions. Through Crossplane, businesses applying multi-cloud strategies realize resource efficiencies, resilience, and improved compliance adherence, setting a dynamic path for future automation and scalability ventures.

These deep insights into Crossplane's real-world multi-cloud deployment scenarios underline its capability to transform how organizations build, deploy, and manage cloud-native applications. These practices pave the way for robust and efficient infrastructure strategies in the cloud computing domain, advocating for proactive cloud management methodologies.

10.3 Scaling Cloud Resources with Crossplane

The dynamic nature of cloud-native applications necessitates robust mechanisms for scaling resources in response to fluctuating workloads. Crossplane, as a Kubernetes-based framework, provides a comprehensive suite of tools aimed at scaling cloud resources efficiently and consistently across multiple cloud providers. It leverages the declarative nature of Kubernetes, enabling enterprises to scalably and predictably manage infrastructure as code across diverse environments.

Scaling strategies using Crossplane involve not only increasing or decreasing the computational resources but also managing the complexity of dependencies between services and systems in a distributed architecture. To facilitate scaling, Crossplane abstracts cloud-specific resources through Kubernetes Custom Resource Definitions (CRDs), enabling seamless updates and modifications to cloud resources using standard Kubernetes tools and practices.

Consider a web application that experiences variable demand across geographical locations. Ensuring optimal performance and availability during peak loads involves scaling both horizontally, by adding more instances or services, and vertically, by upgrading the resource capacity of existing instances. Crossplane supports both scaling mechanisms by integrating with a variety of cloud providers, abstracting their scaling APIs into Kubernetes configurations.

An example of horizontal scaling can be driven by defining a Crossplane composite resource that represents an application layer responsible for handling web traffic. Utilizing a Kubernetes Horizontal Pod Autoscaler (HPA), the application dynamically adjusts to load by scaling pods that interface with Crossplane-managed resources like load balancers and virtual machine instances.

A Crossplane configuration to manage a scalable load balancer in AWS might look like this:

```
apiVersion: network.aws.crossplane.io/v1alpha3
kind: LoadBalancer
metadata:
  name: web-lb
spec:
  forProvider:
    region: us-east-1
    type: application
    scheme: internet-facing
    securityGroups:
    - default
  providerConfigRef:
    name: aws-provider
```

By leveraging Kubernetes' native support for scale-driven events, Crossplane interacts with cloud resources to fulfill scaling requests. On AWS, for instance, we can configure autoscaling groups dynamically to add or remove EC2 instances based on web traffic metrics, such as CPU utilization or incoming request count. Crossplane oversees this process, ensuring that changes in demand are met with appropriate

10.3. SCALING CLOUD RESOURCES WITH CROSSPLANE

resource allocation.

In scenarios where vertical scaling is preferred, Crossplane can adjust the specified characteristics of cloud resources to increase their performance capacity. An example is changing the instance type of an AWS EC2 or a GCP Compute Engine, managed directly through updates in the CRDs, which Crossplane reconciles with the actual state in the cloud provider.

The following YAML manifest vertically scales an AWS RDS instance:

```
apiVersion: database.aws.crossplane.io/v1beta1
kind: RDSInstance
metadata:
  name: scalable-database
spec:
  forProvider:
    region: us-west-2
    dbInstanceClass: db.m5.large
    masterUsername: admin
    allocatedStorage: 100
  providerConfigRef:
    name: aws-provider
```

By increasing the dbInstanceClass, Crossplane updates the database instance to a more powerful configuration, enhancing throughput and processing capabilities. The reconciliation loop ensures that the state defined in Crossplane is maintained, automatically applying any necessary changes to the cloud environment.

A practical instance of Crossplane's scaling capabilities is observed in a technology company implementing high-performance data analytics pipelines utilizing both on-premise and cloud resources. The pipeline includes machine learning tasks that significantly benefit from hardware accelerators like GPUs. By defining distinct classes of compute resources tailored for different stages of the pipeline, Crossplane facilitates optimal resource allocation and de-allocation according to task demands, thus managing both cost and performance effectively.

Moreover, in multi-tenant environments where cloud resources need efficient distribution among varying workloads, Crossplane manages dedicated resource quotas and policies to ensure fair resource allocation. Through Kubernetes ResourceQuota and LimitRange, Crossplane helps enforce limits, ensuring that no single application overwhelms shared cloud infrastructure.

By implementing these Kubernetes constructs, organizations can establish scaling strategies tailored to specific workloads. This involves declarative resource management, adding or removing nodes, adjusting resource sizes dynamically, or deploying more instances of services when needed.

In complex systems composed of interdependent services, ensuring that scaling efforts do not introduce bottlenecks requires a keen focus on observability and metrics-driven scaling approaches. Crossplane integrates with Kubernetes-native monitoring tools to offer metrics and logging for tracking the performance and scaling efficacy.

Consider an enterprise aiming to adopt a hybrid cloud strategy by extending its Kubernetes environment into additional capacity pools across Google Cloud Platform (GCP) and Azure for non-critical workloads. The company's IT operations are required to ensure that any failure of cloud resources triggers an automated response to provision equivalent resources in the secondary cloud environment.

Crossplane's integration facilitates this with GCP and Azure through Kubernetes Events and Alerts. The Crossplane logic in the operator monitors these events to automatically trigger provisioning as dictated by pre-defined policies, ensuring consistency and reliability of the service offering.

Thus, Crossplane serves as a pivotal technology, ensuring that the scaling of cloud resources is not only effective but aligned with the strategic objectives and constraints within the enterprise. It delivers a unified and consistent scaling framework that transcends individual cloud services, offering strategized scaling that caters to demand, performance, and enterprise objectives.

Through content analysis of robust scaling mechanisms, Crossplane accentuates its significance via successful adoption in diverse environments for resource scaling. Organizations enhance their capabilities to manage growing demands dynamically, leveraging Crossplane to deliver a cohesive and integrated approach to scaling in a cloud-native paradigm. This seamless resource scaling transcends traditional boundaries, marking a significant milestone in cloud-native infrastructure management.

10.4 Security and Compliance Best Practices

In the era of cloud-native applications, ensuring security and compliance is paramount, especially in environments where organizations leverage multiple cloud service providers to host their services. Crossplane, as an abstraction layer managing diverse cloud resources through Kubernetes, offers unique opportunities to instill robust security and compliance practices. By leveraging Kubernetes-native mechanisms, Crossplane allows organizations to enhance their security posture while maintaining compliance with regulatory frameworks across jurisdictions.

A foundational element of security in Crossplane-managed environments is the principle of least privilege. Crossplane utilizes Kubernetes Role-Based Access Control (RBAC) to strictly define and enforce what users and services can do within the Kubernetes cluster, ensuring that entities have only the permissions they need. This reduces the risk of malicious or inadvertent actions that could compromise security. Configuring RBAC for Crossplane might involve setting roles for accessing specific cloud resources:

```
kind: Role
apiVersion: rbac.authorization.k8s.io/v1
metadata:
  namespace: crossplane-system
  name: crossplane-viewer
rules:
- apiGroups: ["*"]
  resources: ["*"]
  verbs: ["get", "list", "watch"]
```

This role permits read-only access to Crossplane resources, aligning with the principle of providing the minimal necessary permissions to users or services operating within the Kubernetes environment.

Compliance frameworks, such as GDPR, HIPAA, and PCI DSS, impose strict requirements on how data is stored, processed, and transmitted. Crossplane's cloud resource management benefits from Kubernetes' intrinsic tools for ensuring compliance, such as namespaces and network policies, which segment resources and define rules for data access and transfer.

Namespaces in Kubernetes partition resources within a cluster to isolate environments, users, and applications, allowing organizations to implement multi-tenant strategies effectively. For example, creating dedicated namespaces for each team or department can enforce resource limits and network boundaries, enhancing security posture:

```
apiVersion: v1
kind: Namespace
metadata:
  name: finance-department
---
apiVersion: networking.k8s.io/v1
kind: NetworkPolicy
metadata:
  name: finance-access-policy
  namespace: finance-department
spec:
  podSelector:
    matchLabels: {}
  policyTypes:
  - Ingress
  - Egress
  ingress:
  - from:
    - namespaceSelector:
        matchLabels:
          user: finance
```

By implementing namespaces alongside network policies, organizations can control access to critical workloads, ensuring that data remains secure and compliant with regulations by limiting intra-cluster communication to only necessary and authorized paths.

Moreover, Crossplane's ability to leverage Kubernetes Secrets to store sensitive data like cloud provider credentials ensures that encryption and secure access management practices are at the forefront. Crossplane recommends storing sensitive keys and configuration data using Kubernetes secrets encrypted at rest, with restricted access via RBAC:

```
apiVersion: v1
kind: Secret
metadata:
  name: azure-provider-credentials
  namespace: crossplane-system
type: Opaque
data:
  credentials: BASE64ENCODED_CREDENTIALS
```

By embedding secrets within Kubernetes, Crossplane not only simplifies the management of sensitive information but also aligns resource

10.4. SECURITY AND COMPLIANCE BEST PRACTICES

configurations with compliance requirements for data protection and encryption practices.

Crossplane's reconciliation process plays a vital role in compliance by constantly ensuring that the deployed state of resources conforms to defined specifications. This mechanism acts as an enforcement tool, automatically rectifying deviations due to unauthorized changes. Integrating continuous compliance checks within the CI/CD pipeline becomes feasible with this reconciliation approach, providing auditable trails of configurations and any anomalies via centralized logging and monitoring.

Additionally, infrastructure as code (IaC) paradigms enabled by Crossplane ensure reproducibility and auditability, crucial for compliance audits. Every configuration change in a Crossplane-managed setup can be reflected in version control, establishing a comprehensive, verifiable history of alterations and configurations. Organizations can meet stringent compliance audits by demonstrating the efficacy and consistency of infrastructure management practices over time.

Further, employing Crossplane with Policy-as-Code tools such as Open Policy Agent (OPA) bolsters compliance and security measures. OPA enables policy checks at various operational stages, particularly during planning or execution of deployments, ensuring adherence to organizational and regulatory policies. Crossplane configurations can be validated against compliance rules defined as code, facilitating automated checks that deter policy deviations before they impact production.

Policies governing sensitive records, data residency, or even the use of specific cloud services can be encoded into policy files, hardly leaving room for misconfigurations that conflict with compliance mandates. These proactive measures serve as preventive controls, enhancing the overarching security and compliance framework.

Moreover, the collaborative nature of a Crossplane-managed cloud infrastructure permits effortless adoption of emerging security practices and integration into preexisting workflows. DevSecOps teams can easily build upon a Kubernetes foundation, crafting continuous security models without rewriting existing cloud governance frameworks. Crossplane thus supports a mature security posture that scales with evolving enterprise needs while maintaining a robust compliance orientation.

The architecture of Crossplane-aware applications and cloud resources ensures that designated security layers like virtual private clouds, security groups, and application firewalls are fully integrated into the deployment model. As resources scale dynamically, Crossplane ensures that the associated configurations keep security provisions intact, preventing exposure caused by inconsistencies in resource replicas or dynamically allocated instances.

The synergy between Crossplane and Kubernetes delivers a formidable platform for marrying security best practices with dependable compliance strategies. Crossplane's architecture provides the necessary abstractions and controls to enforce security measures consistently across cloud-resource interfaces, offering a comprehensive solution to cloud security challenges. By marrying these strategies with Kubernetes' powerful and flexible control systems, organizations can trust Crossplane to uphold their security and compliance requirements while leveraging the full potential of multi-cloud infrastructures.

10.5 Optimizing Costs Across Cloud Providers

Cost optimization remains a crucial consideration for organizations deploying and managing cloud-native applications. The complexity of multi-cloud deployments often results in challenges associated with varying billing models, unanticipated expenses, and resource inefficiencies across cloud providers. Crossplane, by offering an abstraction layer over various cloud services, provides significant opportunities for organizations to implement cost optimization strategies grounded in automation, observability, and efficient resource utilization.

Cost optimization with Crossplane begins with the adoption of a declarative model of resource management. This model offers organizations the ability to define and manage their cloud resources as code, promoting repeatability, consistency, and traceability, which are essential for achieving cost efficiency. Crossplane's integration with version control systems ensures that changes to infrastructure configurations are auditable and can be reversed if necessary, thereby reducing errors due to manual intervention.

10.5. OPTIMIZING COSTS ACROSS CLOUD PROVIDERS

One area where Crossplane significantly aids in cost optimization is through its support for the automatic scaling of cloud resources. As organizations face fluctuating demand, adjusting resource allocation dynamically prevents over-provisioning, a common cause of excess costs in cloud spending. Crossplane's composition resources for Kubernetes enable fine-grained scaling strategies that align closely with actual usage patterns. For instance, utilizing AWS's Spot instances can dramatically lower computing costs when workloads are flexible in terms of specific compute times:

```
apiVersion: compute.aws.crossplane.io/v1alpha1
kind: EKSCluster
metadata:
  name: web-cluster
spec:
  forProvider:
    region: us-west-2
    version: 1.21
    workerNodes:
    - instanceType: m5.large
      maxCount: 20
      minCount: 2
      spotPrice: "0.02"
  providerConfigRef:
    name: aws-provider
```

In this configuration, setting the spot price for worker nodes allows the organization to take advantage of AWS EC2 Spot pricing, optimizing compute costs by utilizing spare capacity at discounted rates while still maintaining a base level of guaranteed capacity for critical workloads.

Crossplane also permits organizations to implement cross-cloud scaling strategies. By distributing workloads across multiple providers, organizations can leverage the competitive pricing of different services. For example, while using Google's compute resources, an organization might choose Azure's advanced data services. This requires a flexible and quick resource provisioning system not bound by the constraints of a single provider's API, all of which Crossplane provides through its pluggable provider architecture:

```
apiVersion: cache.azure.crossplane.io/v1alpha1
kind: Redis
metadata:
  name: caching-layer
spec:
  forProvider:
    location: centralus
    properties:
```

```
  sku:
    name: Basic
    family: C
    capacity: 1
  providerConfigRef:
    name: azure-provider
```

Adjusting cloud service pricing tiers dynamically according to workload needs, or simply turning off non-critical resources during off-peak hours, can yield significant savings. Role-based policies or scheduled tasks facilitate such dynamic adjustments, ensuring that compute and storage resources—often the largest contributors to cloud bills—are truncated to reflect real-time demand profiles.

Additionally, cloud providers often offer varied cost models including on-demand, committed-use, and reserved instances. Crossplane users can better align their workloads with these pricing models, choosing for instance to run baseline workloads on reserved instances with aggressive cost savings, while utilizing on-demand instances only for handling unexpected peaks.

Crossplane's integration with monitoring and observability tools enhances cost optimization by providing actionable insights into resource utilization patterns. Metrics from Prometheus or Grafana, when coupled with Crossplane's cost data collected from cloud billing reports, allow for the fine-tuning of configurations to eliminate wasteful expenditure:

```
apiVersion: monitoring.grafana.crossplane.io/v1alpha1
kind: AlertManager
metadata:
  name: cost-alerts
spec:
  rules:
  - alert: HighCloudCosts
    expr: sum(rate(cloud_provider_costs{}[1h])) > 1000
    annotations:
      description: "Cloud cost has exceeded \$1000 in the past hour"
      summary: High Cloud Costs Alert
```

Using predefined thresholds, alerts can be triggered when costs breach acceptable limits, enabling quick intervention or recalibration of resource usage policies.

Beyond resource scaling, effective cost optimization involves evaluating long-term financial commitments to cloud providers. Organiza-

10.5. OPTIMIZING COSTS ACROSS CLOUD PROVIDERS

tions may use Crossplane to facilitate strategic cost allocation and accountability measures, aligning departmental cost centers with specific cloud resources through metadata and labeling:

```
apiVersion: networking.aws.crossplane.io/v1alpha3
kind: VPC
metadata:
  name: department-vpc
  labels:
    department: finance
    environment: production
spec:
  forProvider:
    cidrBlock: 10.0.0.0/16
  providerConfigRef:
    name: aws-provider
```

These labels ensure that accurate cost monitoring and chargeback processes can be facilitated, establishing a culture of accountability and transparency that encourages efficient resource utilization.

Crossplane also aids in automating cost control through lifecycle management policies. Cloud resources can be provisioned with auto-expiration dates or set to scale down post-peak activity periods. Organizations can leverage Crossplane to implement policies that automatically archive or delete inactive resources, culminating in efficient storage practices and reduced long-term expenses.

Comprehensively, Crossplane equips organizations with the capabilities to automate, observe, and optimize their cloud infrastructure in seeking out cost efficiencies. It achieves this not only through the automation of routine management tasks but also by integrating cost-saving best practices into a framework that is scalable, dynamic, and responsive to business needs.

By maintaining an overarching view across multiple cloud environments, Crossplane users can capitalize on the best pricing structures, intelligently allocating resources to reflect real-time business requirements. Thus, the extensive capabilities offered by Crossplane position it as an instrumental technology for organizations aiming to achieve disruptive cost optimization in a competitive cloud-services ecosystem.

10.6 DevOps Integration Success Stories

In the constantly evolving landscape of cloud-native applications, organizations strive to deliver software faster and more reliably. The integration of Crossplane into DevOps pipelines has led to significant successes, providing teams with the necessary tools to unite infrastructure management with continuous integration/continuous delivery (CI/CD) processes. Crossplane facilitates the combination of development and operations by making the process of provisioning and managing cloud resources more automated, repeatable, and efficient. This section explores compelling success stories showcasing the synergy between Crossplane and DevOps methodologies.

One impactful integration of Crossplane can be seen in a leading SaaS provider that sought to enhance its deployment strategy by reducing infrastructure provisioning times while maintaining high operational reliability. Before Crossplane, the company had a fragmented provisioning process across multiple public clouds, leading to inconsistent environments and a slower pace of deployments. By adopting Crossplane, the organization was able to codify its entire infrastructure provisioning process, shifting to a more streamlined, GitOps-driven approach.

GitOps configures applications and infrastructure declaratively and uses version control systems as the single source of truth. By implementing Crossplane within their CI/CD pipelines, the SaaS provider could address cross-cloud deployments consistently, utilizing GitHub Actions to trigger resource changes based on Git events:

```
name: Deploy Infrastructure
on:
  push:
    branches:
      - main
jobs:
  deploy:
    runs-on: ubuntu-latest
    steps:
      - name: Checkout source
        uses: actions/checkout@v2

      - name: Setup Crossplane CLI
        run: |
          curl -sL https://raw.githubusercontent.com/crossplane/crossplane/release-1.6/install.sh | sh
```

10.6. DEVOPS INTEGRATION SUCCESS STORIES

```
- name: Deploy resources
  run: |
    kubectl apply -f infrastructure.yaml
```

Integrating GitHub Actions provided automation, enabling seamless application delivery and infrastructure synchronization while embedding continuous feedback loops within the software development lifecycle. Such automation reduced lead time for changes, demonstrating substantial improvements in overall velocity and responsiveness to market demands.

Another success story involves a FinTech company that adopted Crossplane as a central part of redefining its legacy operations approach. Prior to implementation, the organization faced lengthy lead times in provisioning resources needed for new service launches, compounded with compliance constraints particular to financial services. The company leveraged Crossplane to unify its infrastructure management, integrating it within a Jenkins-based CI/CD system for tailored workflows that adhered to compliance frameworks.

Key to achieving this integration was the use of Crossplane's provider configurations that supported secure authentication and authorization aligned with regulatory standards. Jenkins, acting as the orchestrator, facilitated scheduled and on-demand cloud resource provisions, enabling the team to concentrate on financial product innovation rather than backend complexity.

```
pipeline {
    agent any
    stages {
        stage('Checkout') {
            steps {
                checkout scm
            }
        }
        stage('Setup Crossplane') {
            steps {
                sh '''
                    curl -sL https://raw.githubusercontent.com/crossplane/crossplane/
                        release-1.6/install.sh | sh
                '''
            }
        }
        stage('Provision Cloud Resources') {
            steps {
                sh 'kubectl apply -f cloud_resources.yaml'
            }
```

```
      }
    }
}
```

Adopting this integration enabled significant advantages, including rapid scalability of test environments, reduced infrastructure overhead, and the ability to replicate environments on demand—leading to higher resource utilization and satisfying stringent compliance requirements.

A third organization, a media production company undergoing digital transformation, leveraged Crossplane to improve its content delivery networks and media processing pipelines. The company needed a solution that supported its transition to distributed cloud architecture, fostering innovation through repeatable DevOps processes and infrastructure agility.

Implementing Crossplane, they automated the end-to-end deployment of complex pipelines involving multiple cloud services for video encoding, distribution, and analytics. By encompassing Kubernetes custom resources in conjunction with Crossplane, the organization achieved efficient rollout and rollback scenarios using GitLab CI/CD, reducing downtime and operational risks:

```
stages:
  - deploy

deploy-job:
  stage: deploy
  script:
    - apk add --no-cache curl
    - curl -sL https://raw.githubusercontent.com/crossplane/crossplane/release-1.6/install.sh | sh
    - kubectl apply -f media_pipeline.yaml
  only:
    - master
```

The integration of Crossplane here led to a greater focus on innovative media solutions, with teams able to deploy and test changes rapidly without infrastructure concerns. By abstracting cloud complexity, Crossplane empowered the DevOps team to harmonize its rapidly growing cloud services, which led to a more responsive and cost-efficient media delivery network.

Crossplane's contributions towards enhancing collaboration between developers and IT operations teams is evident across various industries. As organizations integrate Crossplane into their DevOps toolchain, they experience transformative improvements in deployment speed, risk reduction, and resource efficiency, underpinning successful digital transformation efforts.

In summary, these DevOps integration success stories illustrate the potential of Crossplane as a pivotal enabler of agile, scalable, and responsive infrastructure management. By adopting Crossplane, organizations can leverage a Kubernetes-native architecture to comprehensively integrate infrastructure provisioning into CI/CD workflows, ultimately driving peak performance and value from their cloud and development operations.

10.7 Lessons Learned and Future Trends

The evolving landscape of cloud-native infrastructure management presents numerous opportunities and challenges, shaping the way organizations utilize technologies like Crossplane for resource orchestration. An analysis of lessons learned from deploying Crossplane across various environments reveals crucial insights that guide best practices and future trends in cloud infrastructure management.

One of the primary lessons learned is the importance of embracing a unified infrastructure management model that blends both internal and external cloud resources. Crossplane excels by enabling this integration through its Kubernetes-native platform, facilitating an organization-wide consistency in how cloud resources are defined and managed. Organizations report that by abstracting cloud provider APIs into Kubernetes Custom Resource Definitions (CRDs), operational complexity decreases, allowing developers to focus more on application logic and less on infrastructure specifics.

This shift fosters improved collaboration between teams, with developers and operations aligning their efforts under a common interface. The adoption of Crossplane, however, requires upskilling teams in both Kubernetes and cloud infrastructure theory, highlighting the importance of continuous education to ensure effective implementation. Organizations prioritize training and knowledge sharing as part of their cloud-native transformation journeys, emphasizing the acquisition of skills pertinent to managing declarative configurations and understanding the nuanced behaviors of each cloud provider.

Another salient lesson is the critical role of observability in maintaining operational efficiency. Given Crossplane's reliance on maintaining the desired state of resources, monitoring systems must be robust to track the real-time health and performance of cloud infrastructure. By integrating Crossplane with monitoring tools like Prometheus and Grafana, organizations have successfully implemented proactive monitoring strategies, triggering alerts for deviations from expected states and optimizing resource allocation dynamically.

```
apiVersion: monitoring.coreos.com/v1
kind: PrometheusRule
metadata:
  name: crossplane-monitoring
  namespace: monitoring
spec:
  groups:
  - name: crossplane.rules
    rules:
    - alert: ResourceStateMismatch
      expr: kube_statefulset_status_replicas !=
          kube_statefulset_status_replicas_ready
      for: 10m
      labels:
        severity: warning
      annotations:
        summary: "StatefulSet Replica Discrepancy"
        description: "The number of replicas ready does not match the desired number
          of replicas for more than 10 minutes."
```

A frequent obstacle encountered involves managing state drift within cloud environments when resources are modified outside Crossplane's purview. Such drift can lead to misalignments in resource management, emphasizing the necessity for a comprehensive GitOps strategy where infrastructure changes are version-controlled, and changes happen only through predefined pipelines. This enhances traceability and auditability, fulfilling compliance requirements and ensuring consistency.

A pertinent aspect of deploying Crossplane concerns the integration of security best practices. Lessons indicate that organizations successfully leveraging Crossplane prioritize stringent Role-Based Access Control (RBAC) policies and Secret Management practices. Storing sensitive credentials exclusively in Kubernetes Secrets encrypted at rest—integrated with external vaults when necessary—ensures that security remains a top priority across the management of multi-cloud environments.

As cloud technologies advance, several trends are expected to shape the future trajectory of Crossplane and cloud-native infrastructure management:

- **Convergence of Kubernetes and Cloud Services:** Kubernetes is cementing its status as the universal API for the cloud, poised to gain even deeper integration with native cloud services. Crossplane will likely expand its provider offerings, fostering a more seamless experience in provisioning and managing cross-cloud capabilities under Kubernetes. This trend towards a more unified cloud management framework could streamline multi-cloud operations for enterprises, potentially reducing vendor lock-in and facilitating strategic cross-cloud service compositions.

- **Increased Emphasis on Automation and Intelligence:** Automation remains a cornerstone of modern cloud operations, and Crossplane's role is set to grow with innovations in machine learning and AI-enabled infrastructure management. Predictive scaling, automated failover, cost optimization, and self-healing systems represent potential areas where Crossplane could advance. Leveraging data analytics to inform infrastructure decisions dynamically could revolutionize an organization's approach to resource allocation, improving efficiency and resilience.

- **eBPF and System Observability Enhancements:** As extended Berkeley Packet Filter (eBPF) technology evolves, offering granular observation and manipulation of system-level behaviors with minimal overhead, it is likely to enhance the observability tools associated with Crossplane. By integrating eBPF with monitoring solutions, organizations can achieve insights into not only Crossplane's cloud resources but also into the intricate performance metrics of workloads, networks, and storage systems, delivering a comprehensive picture of operational health and efficiency.

- **Expansion of DevSecOps Practices:** Security is set to become a more embedded aspect of the CI/CD pipelines leveraging Crossplane. This integration would ensure that security policies form an integral part of resource management right from development through deployment. Embracing DevSecOps principles will enable automated security validations at every step, perhaps utilizing tools like Open Policy Agent (OPA) to ensure that deployments comply with organizational security policies and guidelines automatically.

```
apiVersion: security.openpolicyagent.org/v1
kind: Constraint
metadata:
  name: deployments-must-have-requests
spec:
  match:
    kinds:
      - apiGroups: [""]
        kinds: ["Pod"]
  constraints:
    - {key: "resources.requests.cpu", operator: "Exists"}
    - {key: "resources.requests.memory", operator: "Exists"}
```

The trajectory of Crossplane also aligns with broader industry movements towards decoupling applications from specific cloud environments, fostering a cloud-agnostic strategy. Organizations are likely to leverage Crossplane's abstractions for innovative applications like edge computing, where resources are distributed across geographically dispersed nodes, demanding a flexible and uniform management interface.

In summary, while Crossplane's capabilities open pathways to managed resources efficiently across clouds, important lessons emphasize the necessity for robust training, infrastructure observability, version control, and security practices. Equally, future trends indicate exciting developments where Crossplane can leverage emerging technologies and practices to redefine cloud-native infrastructure management, enabling organizations to maximize agility, scalability, and reliability in their operations.

10.7. LESSONS LEARNED AND FUTURE TRENDS

www.ingramcontent.com/pod-product-compliance
Lightning Source LLC
Chambersburg PA
CBHW052141220526
45471CB00004B/1474